# DISCOVERING DENALI

# Discovering Denali

## A Complete Reference Guide to Denali National Park and Mount McKinley, Alaska

*Dow Scoggins*

iUniverse Star
New York Lincoln Shanghai

Discovering Denali
A Complete Reference Guide to Denali National Park and
Mount McKinley, Alaska

iUniverse Star
an iUniverse, Inc. imprint

For information address:
iUniverse, Inc.
2021 Pine Lake Road, Suite 100
Lincoln, NE 68512
www.iuniverse.com

ISBN: 0-595-29737-4

# Contents

# *Foreword*

The first time I explored Denali National Park was in 1985 with two of my best friends, Rick Roberts and Tom Coughlin. We spent four weeks backpacking, fishing, and rafting in and around Denali. This trip took almost a year of planning since we were on a budget, and we wanted to make this trip a once in a lifetime adventure. In years to come, I would explore different areas of Alaska with my wife, Deedie, but Denali was always something special. Then a couple of years ago, my next door neighbor, Lucy Parker Steudel, asked me if I would take her 18 year old son, Drew Parker to Denali for his high school graduation present. She wanted to give her son a trip of a lifetime, and after hearing all my Alaska stories, she thought Denali would be the perfect place. When I started planning for this trip, I found the same half-dozen books and information I used previously 15 years earlier. I could not find any new information about Denali. As my wife would say, the opportunity was too much for me. I wrote this book, hoping to make it easier for others to explore this splendid wilderness.

Compiling it had its own reward, especially working with all the people who contributed. People like Dennis Garrett, the owner of the Blue Ribbon Mine in Petersville. Dennis wrote the section about the Petersville State Recreational Area, and he introduced me to the artwork of Alaskan Sidney Lawrence. And, internationally acclaimed artist and mountaineer Dee Molenaar, Dee donated his sketches of the climbing routes of Denali. Since I have only visited Alaska in the spring and summer, I am truly thankful to Sam McConkey, who contributed the section on the Northern Lights, which are best viewed in the late winter. Some of the other Alaskans who helped include: Geri Denkewalter from the Talkeetna-Denali Visitor Center, who helped me with the all of the activities and businesses surrounding the tri-river area of Talkeetna and the town of Trapper Creek; Jeannine Lowe of the Denali Outdoor

Center who provided information on activities and businesses surrounding the entrance of Denali National Park and the town of Healy; and the rangers at Denali National Park.

A special thanks goes to wildlife and nature artist and friend, Jack Chilton. Jack furnished several illustrations for this book. He charged a pizza or a beer for each illustration. This book would have never been completed if it were not for the proof reading of my friend, Robert "Lopaka" Tink and the editing efforts of my wife, Deedie.

This book is dedicated to Clark D. Scoggins, my father, who used to recite the Spell of the Yukon, The Cremation of Sam McGee and The Shooting of Dan McGrew by Yukon poet Robert W. Service when I was a boy. Most importantly, he instilled a spirit in me to always live your dreams and always reach for the stars.

This book is also dedicated to my oldest son, Dustin, 6, who dreams of Alaska himself, even more than Disney World; and to the Alaskan bear that chased Rick Roberts and me across a river and through some woods, but then went his on his merry way, allowing me to compile this book instead of being a filling meal.

Enjoy Denali! There's no place like it in the world.

# Preface
## Denali or McKinley?

In 1917, Woodrow Wilson signed legislation protecting two millions acres as Mount McKinley National Park. But the parks founder, Charles Sheldon wanted it to be called Denali National Park and to have Mt. McKinley's name changed back to the Athabascan name of Denali, "the high one." Finally, in 1980, congress changed the park's name to Denali, but refused to rename the mountain.

Recently, the State of Alaska Board of Geographic Names has officially changed the mountain's name back to Denali. Negotiations continue today with the United Sates National Geographic Office to officially return the original native name to this magnificent mountain. This book will only refer to this mountain as Denali.

# Chapter 1

## History of Denali National Park

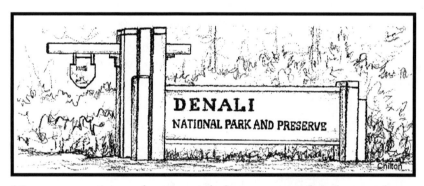

Many generations of native Athabascans wandered over the areas surrounding Denali long before Caucasians began to discover and explore it. These nomadic natives called the mountain, "The High One", or Denali, and hunted the lowland hills of Denali's northern reaches spring through fall for caribou, sheep, and moose. They preserved berries, netted fish, and gathered edible plants for winter. When snows began to fall, they migrated to lower elevations, closer to the river valley's better protection from severe winter weather.

### First Caucasian Sightings of the Mountain

In 1792, George Vancouver spotted the great mountain while surveying the Alaska coast. He described it as the great Snow Mountain, but did not name it.

In the 1800's, Russian fur traders hunted and trapped in the Alaska fron-tiers. These traders called the mountain Bulshaia Gora, "big mountain."

## Mining Era

Nearly everyone has heard of the Bonanza Strike near Dawson City in the Yukon, and the rush of miners to make a fortune. However, most people are unaware of the booms and busts that occurred within the current boundaries of Denali National Park and Preserve, in a place now known simply as Kantishna. (In fact, in 1889, one of the earliest prospectors, Frank Densmore, wrote such an enthusiastic description of Denali the Yukon prospectors named the mountain after him. For years, Denali was known to Caucasians as Densmore Mountain).

In the summer of 1903, the main brunt of the gold rush in the Yukon was over and hundreds of prospectors were out of work. Coincidentally, Yukon District Judge James Wickersham and four others took the sum-mer as an opportunity to explore the region around the great moun-tain, with the intention of being the first to summit. Unsuccessful in that realm, they were successful in discovering gold just north of base of Denali. Their claims captured the attention of the unemployed prospectors in Fairbanks, and the rush to Denali and the Kantishna Hills began.

Two men who figured prominently in the Kantishna Hills mining history were Joseph Dalton and Joseph Quigley. In 1904, Dalton's party successfully prospected the Toklat River Basin. A year later, Joe Quigley and his partner, Jack Horn, found gold in paying quantities in Glacier Creek. After staking the creeks, they carried the news back to Fairbanks. Within weeks, thousands of gold seekers found their way up the Tanana, Kantishna and Bearpaw Rivers; mining towns sprang up overnight. Eureka, a summer mining camp centrally located near active pay streaks, was one. These areas and towns are located within 30 miles of the base of Denali.

Within six months the 'easy pickings' were gone and the rush was over. Miners left in droves, leaving behind less than 50 inhabitants. Some ventured into hard-rock mining: silver, lead, zinc and antimony. However, transportation problems plagued the success of this mining district; there were no roads to get equipment in and out of the mines.

Three events lead to re-opening the mines 30 years later: President Franklin Roosevelt raised the price of gold to $15/ounce, the park road was completed and the post-depression era produced cheap labor. Central to this second boom was the development of the Banjo Mine on Quigley Ridge, which was the first commercial-scale lode gold milling operation that eventually become the fourth largest lode mine in the Yukon Basin. This golden era came to an end with the coming of World War II.

Mining activity increased again in the 1970s; there was no longer a gold standard and prices soared. By the mid-1980s, the Kantishna gold mining district ranked 27th in the state for overall production of gold; nearly 100,000 ounces had been extracted from these hills.

Today, very little remains at the sites of the old towns that flourished nearly 100 years ago. Today, activity in the Kantishna Mining District has shifted to different gold mine: tourism. Only the town of Eureka, now called Kantishna, is left to remind us of those golden years not so long ago.

## The Park's Creation

The park was originally established to protect its large mammals. Charles Sheldon conceived the plan to conserve the region as a national park because hunters were killing the caribou and Dall sheep in the area to feed the miners in the Kantishna Hills Mining Area. Naturalist, hunter, and conservationist, Sheldon first traveled here in 1906 and again in 1907 with a packer and guide named Harry Karstens. (Karstens later made the first ascent of Denali's south peak and served as the park's first superintendent.) Sheldon devoted much of his 1907 travels to studying boundaries for the proposed national park, which would include territories suitable for a game refuge. When Sheldon returned to the East in 1908, the Game Committee of the Boone and Crockett Club, which he chaired, launched the campaign to establish a national park. Largely due to these efforts, Mount McKinley National Park was established in 1917. Its populations of Dall sheep, caribou and other wildlife were now legislatively protected. However, Mount McKinley itself was not wholly included within the boundaries. Sheldon wanted to call the park Denali, but his suggestion would not be followed until 1980. That year the boundary was expanded to include the Denali caribou herds wintering and calving grounds and the entire Mount McKinley massif. More than tripled in size, the park became Denali National Park and Preserve.

## The Mountain's Name

Denali (The High One) is the Native American word for North America's highest peak. Denali rises 20,320 feet (6,194m) in the mountain chain called the Alaska Range. Denali was renamed Mount McKinley for William McKinley, a nominee for president, by the Princeton graduate and gold prospector, William Dickey. Dickey was one of the hundreds of prospectors seeking gold in the 1896 Cook Inlet stampede. He wrote an article for the New York Sun where he described the mountain as the highest in North America at over 20,000 feet.

Since the turn of the 19th century, the official name of this great mountain has not rested in peace. In 1914, following his historic first ascent of the mountain in 1913, Hudson Stuck wrote in the preface of his book *The Ascent of Denali*: "Forefront in this book, because forefront in the author's heart and desire, must stand a plea for the restoration to the greatest mountain in North America of its immemorial native name."

The State of Alaska Board of Geographic Names has also officially changed the mountain's name back to Denali, but the United States National Geographical Society still recognizes the mountain's name as Mount McKinley(Author's note: I agree with Hudson Stuck, and have reserved the right to call the mountain Denali, after its true heritage, in this book).

## What Is Denali's True Height

On June 21, 1989, a team of researchers and support climbers reached the summit of Denali. They carried a Global Positioning System receiver that when used in conjunction with a Global Positioning Satellite, measures geographical heights. Preliminary indications show the elevation of Denali to be 14' lower than the height previously measured by more traditional survey methods. The newly computed height of 20,306' remains the official height of Denali. According to one of the park's rangers, the National Geographic Society still prints 20,230 feet because it would be too much trouble changing all its maps.

Regardless, it's one big mountain.

# Chapter 2

# Driving and Transportation to the Park

When Denali National Park was created in 1917, only a few visitors came to see it. Most of the people in the park were rangers or miners on their way to the Kantishna Mining Area. Since no roads or railways had been built to the park entrance, a visitor almost had to blaze his own trail to get in. But in 1924, the Alaska Railway completed its run from Anchorage to Denali to Fairbanks, and a total of 62 visitors came to the park that year. In 1970, the George Parks Highway was completed to parallel the railroad, allowing visitors to drive directly to Denali instead of going around the Alaska Range. In the early years, the railroad was the easiest way to the park. Today, you can reach the park by car, shuttle bus, airplane, even bicycle. Over 300,000 visitors come during the summer months, while another 100,000 visit the rest of the year.

**Driving:**

Driving to the park from Anchorage can take hours, days, or even weeks, depending on your preference. This 240-mile drive has numerous state parks to explore, recreational areas to discover, streams and rivers to fish, mountains to hike and towns to visit. If you want to drive, renting a car is easy. Most major car rental agencies are in the Anchorage International Airport. Several RV or motor home rentals are also available. However, some rented cars and RVs are not allowed to go off the major roads, plan your trip accordingly.

**Adventurous Route:**

Adventurers can drive to Denali from the lower 48 via Seattle or via the Yukon Territory. If you drive to Seattle or Vancouver, you can catch an Alaska Marine Highway Ferry, which will transport your car or RV to Anchorage. Or you can take the long way via the Alaska Highway, and drive through Canada's British Columbia and Yukon Territory. Once you enter Alaska via the Yukon Territory, you will take the Denali Highway directly into the park. Buying a publication called *The Milepost* is highly recommended for exploring Alaska and the Yukon in a car or RV.

**Fastest Route:**

The quickest way to Denali National Park from Anchorage is to hire a small plane and land right at the entrance of the park. The term "small plane" usually means a single prop plane, which may hold one to six people depending on the amount of luggage.

**Relaxing and Historic Route:**

The most relaxing and historic way to get to Denali National Park from Anchorage or Fairbanks is by the Alaska Railroad, named the best railroad trip in the United States by America's Best Online.

## Alaska Railroad Map

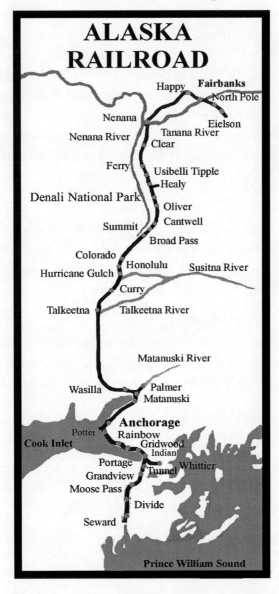

# Alaska Railroad

In 1914, Congress allocated monies to build a railway from Anchorage to Fairbanks, three years before Denali National Park existed. Eight long years later, President Warren G. Harding visited the town of Nenana to drive a golden spike in the railway, signifying the completion of the Alaska Railroad. In 1924, the railroad's first full year of service, the railroad brought a total of 62 passengers to see the grandeur of Denali National Park. Today, the Alaska Railroad brings hundreds of thousands passengers to see Denali every year.

## The Anchorage-Denali-Fairbanks Train

The Anchorage-Denali-Fairbanks train has passenger cars, a vista-domed coach and a dining car. During the ride to Denali, conductors and guides share the history of the area and provide tourist information. The train operates daily during the summer months and less frequently during the off-season.

Daily passenger service operates between Anchorage, Denali and Fairbanks from mid-May through mid-September. The remainder of the year, weekend service operates between Anchorage and Fairbanks

Alaska Railroad's express trains depart Anchorage for Fairbanks (or Fairbanks for Anchorage) each morning, arriving at Denali National Park in the early afternoon and reaching their final destination in the evening. These Express Trains operate with stops (only for reserved passengers) at Wasilla and Talkeetna before arriving at Denali National Park. Reservations are required for the Express Trains.

Alaska Railroad's local trains depart Anchorage for Hurricane Gulch and return three times weekly, making all station and flag stops at intermediate points. These local trains are ideal for fishermen, campers, and hikers, as they will stop anywhere along the route, giving passengers more travel flexibility. Reservations are also required for the trains (See Instructions for Flagging a Train for more details).

## Prices

Pricing is based on "Peak" and "Value" seasons. Peak season is June 5 to September 4; Value season is May 16 to June 4 and September 5 to 19.

Fairbanks to Anchorage via Denali departs Fairbanks 8:15 AM and arrives Denali National Park 12 noon. Fare $224 peak season $177 value season (per person, double occupancy) at the time of this printing.

Fairbanks to Denali and Return departs Fairbanks 8:15 AM and arrives Denali National Park 12 noon. Fare $181 peak season $139 value season per person/double occupancy at the time of this printing.

There is no extra charge for stopovers in Denali, however there is a charge for stopovers at other stations on the Express Train.

Baggage: Each adult is allowed two pieces of baggage with a combined total up to 150 lbs. Children are allowed 75 lbs. of baggage. Excess baggage may be checked with payment of excess baggage rates. Bicycles are transported via the EXPRESS trains under Excess Baggage Rules at $20 each per station.

For information concerning schedules and fares, write: The Alaska Railroad, Passenger Services Dept. ATG, P.O. Box 107500, Anchorage, AK 99510, or call 907-265-2494. For reservations, you may write the above address or telephone 800-544-0552. Phones are answered only during regular office hours, 8 AM to 5 PM, Monday to Friday.

## Dining Car

The railway's diner cars have a casual, relaxed atmosphere. No reservations are required and all food is prepared onboard. A wide selection of beverages and desserts is available.

Entree Samples:

*McKinley Breakfast*-Scrambled eggs, Canadian bacon or reindeer sausage with country style potatoes and toast.

*Bird Creek Chicken Sandwich*-Grilled marinated chicken breast topped with cheddar cheese, greens, Roma tomatoes and honey Dijon dressing on a French baguette with chips.

*Polychrome Pass*-A rainbow of fresh fruit served with yogurt and pastry or roll of your choice.

*Indian River Sandwich*-Reindeer sausage with grilled onion and bell pepper, topped with Swiss cheese on a French baguette with chips.

*Bristol Bay Grill*-Pan seared salmon fillet with roasted red pepper aioli, accompanied with rice pilaf and fresh vegetable sauté.

## Private Rail Cars

If you want to add a little luxury to your trip, two of Alaska's premier tour companies have private rail cars that operate between Anchorage and Fairbanks. These cars are towed by the Alaska Railroad but offer a unique kind of rail experience.

*Princess' Midnight Sun Express* ULTRA DOME rail packages depart from Anchorage or Fairbanks and include overnight accommodations at the new Mt. McKinley Princess Lodge, Denali Princess Lodge, or both. You travel to Princess' riverside retreats aboard the private, fully domed Midnight Sun Express railcars featuring the largest domed ceilings on any railcars in Alaska; fine dining is available with meals prepared to order by our on-board chefs and large outdoor viewing platforms. A variety of tours are offered featuring Princess' unique riverside lodges and exclusive ULTRA DOME railcars. Call 800-835-8907 for reservations.

*The McKinley Explorer* has private domed railcars and operates daily. Luxury seating is available upstairs with private bar and elegant dining room downstairs. Service from mid-May through mid-September. For reservations call 1-800-544-2206 or write: Gray Line of Alaska, 300 Elliott Avenue West, Seattle, WA 98119.

## Instructions for flagging a train

Flagging allows the backpacker, hunters, and fisherman to hike the backcountry of Alaska and board the train anywhere along the route. You must make special arrangements to flag a train if you want it to actually stop.

## Instructions

Stand 25 feet outside the nearest rail with your gear. Wave a large piece of white cloth over your head until the Engineer acknowledges you by sounding the train whistle. Remain 25 feet away from the track until the conductor opens the door and motions you to board. Restrain your pets on a leash while the train is approaching or passing. Please use extreme caution at all times. (Flag Stop Service available on Anchorage-Fairbanks and Anchorage-Hurricane route only!)

# Summer Railroad Schedule
## Anchorage~Denali ~Fairbanks
## (Fares Subject to Change)

| City | Northbound | Southbound |
|---|---|---|
| Fairbanks | 8:15 PM | 8:15 am |
| Denali Nat. Park | 3:45 PM | 12:00 PM |
| Talkeetna | 11:25 am | 4:40 PM |
| Wasilla | 9:45 AM | 6:20 PM |
| Anchorage | 8:15 AM | 8:15 PM |

## One-way Rail Fare, per person
Peak Season June 3~September 4, 2000
Value Season May 13~June 2 & September 5~23, 2000

| Route | Peak | Value |
|---|---|---|
| Anchorage to Talkeetna | $70 | $56 |
| Anchorage to Denali | $120 | $96 |
| Anchorage to Fairbanks | $160 | $128 |
| Talkeetna to Denali | $50 | $40 |
| Talkeetna to Fairbanks | $90 | $73 |
| Denali to Fairbanks | $48 | $38 |

Child (age 2-11) fares are 50% of adult rates.
Full service dining car and gift shop onboard.
Baggage Service available

ANCHORAGE ~ SEWARD
Daily Service May 13-Sept. 10, 2000

| City | Southbound | Northbound |
|---|---|---|
| Anchorage | 6:45 AM | 10:25 PM |
| Seward | 11:05 AM | 6:00 PM |

Anchorage to Seward round-trip-$86, one way $50
Children's fares are 50% of adult rates.

| City | Southbound | Northbound |
|------|-----------|-----------|
| Anchorage | 10:00 AM | 9:45 PM |
| Whittier | 12:30 PM | 6:45 PM |

Rail Fare, per person
Anchorage to Whittier round-trip-$52
Anchorage to Whittier one-way-$26. Hand carry baggage only.

## Winter Train Schedule
Runs Every Saturday Except 12/25 and 1/1

| From: | S=Station Stop F=Flag Stop | Time | Return Same Day |
|-------|------|------|------|
| Anchorage | S | 8:30 AM | 8:30 AM |
| Birchwood | F | 9:15 AM | 9:15 AM |
| Eklutna | F | 9:27 AM | 9:27 AM |
| Matanuska | F | 9:45 AM | 9:45 AM |
| Wasilla | F | 10:05 AM | 10:05 AM |
| Houston | F | 10:25 AM | 10:25 AM |
| White's Crossing | F | 10:39 AM | 10:39 AM |
| Willow | F | 10:45 AM | 10:45 AM |
| Kashwitna | F | 10:55 AM | 10:55 AM |
| Caswell | F | 11:04 AM | 11:04 AM |
| Montana | F | 11:13 AM | 11:13 AM |
| Sunshine | F | 11:22 AM | 11:22 AM |
| Talkeetna | S | 11:35 AM | 11:35 AM |
| Chase | F | 11:46 AM | 11:46 AM |
| Curry | F | 12:10 PM | 12:10 PM |
| Sherman | F | 12:27 PM | 12:27 PM |

| Gold Creek | F | 12:39 PM | 12:39 PM |
|---|---|---|---|
| Canyon | F | 12:50 PM | 12:50 PM |
| Chulitna | F | 1:02 PM | 1:02 PM |
| Hurricane | F | 1:20 PM | 1:20 PM |
| Hurricane Gulch | F | 1:25 PM | 1:25 PM |
| Honolulu | F | 1:42 PM | 1:42 PM |
| Colorado | F | 2:05 PM | 2:05 PM |
| Broad Pass | F | 2:17 PM | 2:17 PM |
| Summit | F | 2:30 PM | 2:30 PM |
| Cantwell | F | 2:40 PM | 2:40 PM |
| Windy | F | 2:55 PM | 2:55 PM |
| Carlo | F | 3:12 PM | 3:12 PM |
| Oliver | F | 3:30 PM | 3:30 PM |
| Denali Park | F | 3:46 PM | 3:46 PM |
| Garner | F | 4:16 PM | 4:16 PM |
| Healy | F | 4:30 PM | 4:30 PM |

# The George Parks Highway
### Anchorage to Fairbanks - 356 miles

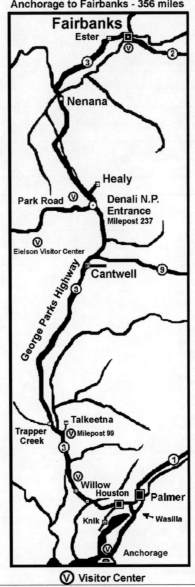

# George Parks Highway

Depending on how much of Alaska you want to explore along the way, driving to Denali from Anchorage could take hours, days or even weeks on this 358 mile Highway. From hiking the wilderness trails, mountaineering the Chugach Mountains, fishing for King Salmon, or rafting some class four rivers, adventurers can get easily sidetracked easily an this 237 mile road to Denali. Just make sure you fill up in Anchorage before hitting the road, and be prepared to pay quite a bit for gas.

A half-hour into the trip, make sure you stop at the Matanuska-Susitna visitor center at milepost 35. The folks here can give information on all the activities and festivals in the area. For information about Denali State Park and Denali National Park visit the Talkeetna Denali Visitors Center located at Milepost 99.

Below is a listing of what you can expect at various mileposts along the George Parks Highway. The George Parks Highway also known as the Parks Highway or Highway 3 should not be confused with the Park Road which runs through Denali National Park, and should not be confused with the Denali Highway which runs from Paxson to Cantwell.

| | |
|---|---|
| Mile 4 | Anchorage Borough Camper Park. |
| Mile 12 | Hiland Road exits to Eagle River Campground and Picnic Area. Access via short side road. 50 campsites, 12 picnic sites and shelters, toilets, water. |
| Mile 17 | Fire Lake Fish Hatchery. |
| Mile 23 | Mirror Lake. Picnic wayside for northbound traffic only. Swimming, boating. |
| Mile 25 | Thunderbird Falls is about one mile from the highway. The trail to the falls goes through private property down to a picnic area. Elevation gain: 100 ft (30 m) Difficulty: Easy. Rolling terrain with boardwalk and |

viewing areas. Special features: Birch forest on steep hillside overhanging Eklutna Canyon.

Mile 26    **Eklutna Campground**, 50 campsites, picnic shelters, toilets, water, and hiking trails. Fee area. Eklutna Lake is the largest lake in Chugach State Park with good fishing for Dolly varden and rainbow trout. Short hike to Eklutna glacier. Side road (opposite Eklutna Recreation road) leads to old Eklutna Village with historic Russian Orthodox Church and Indian Cemetery.

Mile 35    **Mat-Su Visitors Center.**

Mile 37    **Suburban Propane**, RV gas, appliance repairs, motor fuels, bottle filling.

Mile 39    Seward Meridian Road and Green Ridge Camper Park.

Mile 40    **Mountain Village Plaza**, Northern Recreation, RV parts and service. El Toro restaurant, Windbreak Hotel and Cafe.

Mile 41    **Cottonwood Creek Mall.** Safeway, Pay Less Drug Store and Lamont's.

Mile 42    George Parks Monument.

Mile 42    **Wasilla.** Access to Hatcher Pass via Main Street. (See Wasilla).

Mile 47    **Museum of Alaska Transportation.** (907-376-1211).

Mile 49    Seven/Eleven, **Mile 49 Café.**

Mile 52    **Big Lake recreational areas.** Turn West at Mile 52 on the Parks Highway, and drive 3.8 Miles to Fishers Y. Keep to the left and you will come to East Lake Mall. Groceries, liquor store. From Fishers Y, paved and unpaved roads lead to Big Lake, Beaver Lake, Rocky Lake, Horseshoe Lake, and numerous campgrounds. The lakes are connected by dredged waterways. Fishing is good for rainbow, lake trout, Dolly varden, burbot, and landlocked salmon.

| | |
|---|---|
| Mile 57 | **Houston Public Campground.** Maintained by community of Houston on Little Susitna River. Water, toilets. |
| Mile 57 | Houston has all visitor facilities, groceries, restaurant, post office, campground, and lodging by the Little Susitna. Excellent fishing and riverboat services available. Gas also available. |
| Mile 64 | **Nancy Lake Marina.** Camping space with restrooms, showers, groceries, boat rentals. Cabins, fishing, gas. |
| Mile 66 | **Nancy Lake State Recreation Area.** Campground with 30 campsites and 30 picnic sites & shelters, water, toilets, boat ramp. Fee area. The 700-acre lake has fishing for rainbow and Dolly varden, with occasional catches of silver salmon, whitefish, and burbot. Early spring and late fall are best times for fishing. This campground is heavily used on weekends. |
| Mile 67 | **Nancy Lake State Recreation Area.** This 22,000-acre area contains miles of scenic roadway ending at the South Rolly Lake Campground, 98 campsites, picnic shelters, water, toilets, hiking trails, fishing, canoeing. Fee is $10 or the state park annual camping pass. A well-developed canoe trail system provides access to many lakes inaccessible by road. In winter, the area is popular for snowmobiling. |
| Mile 68 | **Hilltop Tesoro**, Museum of Hatcher Pass. |
| Mile 69 | **Willow** visitor facilities located along the Parks highway. |
| Mile 69 | **Ruth's Rustic Lodge** 907-495-9000. |
| Mile 70 | Willow Airport. |
| Mile 71 | **Willow Creek State Recreation Area** has 145 campsites, water, toilets, hiking trails. Fee area. Fishing access to Willow Creek and its confluence with the Susitna River. Excellent salmon fishing. |

Mile 71 | Hatcher Pass Road leads into the hard rock mining district in the Talkeetna Mountains. A 60-Mile loop can be made over this pioneer road which climbs over Hatcher Pass (3,886 ft.) and exits at either Wasilla or Palmer. The old **Lucky Shot and Independence mineshaft areas** offer good rock hounding, fishing, berry picking, and photography possibilities. Parts of this road may be unsafe for large motorhomes or vehicles towing trailers. **Hatcher Pass Lodge** has meals and accommodations, but no gas. Fishing possibilities along the first few miles of the Hatcher Pass road are: Deception Creek (two miles east of Willow, July-August for rainbow, dolly varden, silver salmon), Upper Willow Creek (six-seven miles east of Willow above canyon rapids, small Dolly varden abundant), Upper Little Susitna River (15 Mile east of Willow, cloudy water but good summer-fall fishing for dolly varden).

Mile 71 | Lower Willow Creek. Rainbow trout, dolly varden, grayling, silver salmon. This creek is the only navigable creek to the Big Susitna River.

Mile 72 | **Willow Island Resort.** Visitor facilities, RV Park, Cabins, Camping, Fishing Guides. 907-495-6343.

Mile 80 | **Lucky Husky, Dogsled rides.** 907-495-6470.

Mile 88 | **Cline's Caswell Lake Bed & Breakfast.** Two guestrooms with shared bath, private unit with kitchen and bath. Outdoor wood sauna, Great breakfast. A lakeside cabin in deep woods, lots of birds and wildlife. Nature hikes and mountain biking. 907-495-1014.

Mile 88 | **Sheep Creek Lodge.** Tesoro Gas & Oil. Beautiful rustic log lodge with cabins, restaurant, bar and liquor. Free camper parking. 907-495-6227.

Mile 90 | **Mat-Su RV Park and Campground.** 907-495-6300.

| | |
|---|---|
| Mile 91 | **Susitna Dog Tour & Bed and Breakfast.** Dogsleds, cross-country skiing, skijoring. 907-495-6324. |
| Mile 96 | **Montana Creek State Recreation Site.** 60 campsites, picnic shelters, water, toilets and hiking trails. |
| Mile 99 | **Talkeetna Denali Visitor Center.** Paved road leads 14 Miles/22.5 km to Talkeetna. Sunshine Gas-Tesoro gas and oil products. 800-660-2688. |
| Mile 99 | Talkeetna Spur Road. |
| Mile 99 | **H&H Lakeview Restaurant & Lodge**, RV parking and camping, gas, showers 907-733-2415. |
| Mile 115 | **Trapper Creek.** |
| Mile 115 | **Trapper Creek Inn & General Store**, Gas, Laundromat, showers, RV Park 907-733-2302. |
| Mile 115 | Trapper Creek's Old Historic Post Office. |
| Mile 121 | Rest Area. Tables, firepits, water, toilets . |
| Mile 132 | Border of Denali State Park. |
| Mile 134 | **Mary's McKinley View Lodge.** Great View of Denali. 907-733-1555. |
| Mile 135 | Denali Viewpoint. |
| Mile 137 | **Lower Troublesome Creek State Recreation Site.** 10 Camp Sites. Water and toilets available. Access to Lower Troublesome Creek Trailhead north to Byers Lake. |
| Mile 147 | **Byers Lake State Park Campground.** 66 Camp sites. Toilets, water, picnic tables, fishing. There is a hiking trail to Curry Ridge and south to Troublesome Creek. |
| Mile 162 | **Denali View North Campground.** 20 sites. |
| Mile 164 | **Little Coal Creek trailhead** and parking. Toilets and hiking trail. This is a 27 mile trail to Byers via the Kesugi Ridge. The trail offers relatively easy access, incredible views and offers an excellent alternative to Denali National Park. |
| Mile 169 | Denali State Park Northern Boundary. |

| | |
|---|---|
| Mile 170 | Scenic viewpoint, parking. |
| Mile 173 | Parking, viewpoint. |
| Mile 174 | Hurricane Gulch Bridge Rest Area. |
| Mile 185 | East Fork rest area. Picnic tables, shelter, water, firewood, barbecue pits, and dump station. |
| Mile 189 | **Igloo Service** Gas, food plus an extremely large igloo. An Alaskan landmark. |
| Mile 193 | **Sourdough Paul's Bed and Breakfast.** Handbuilt. Five star rated outhouse. 907-892-6000. |
| Mile 196 | Good views of Denali and Broad Pass, parking. |
| Mile 209 | **Reindeer Mountain Lodge.** Open year round. Fishing, hunting, snowmobiling. 907-768-2420. |
| Mile 210 | **City of Cantwell.** |
| Mile 210 | Original Denali Highway heads east for 133 Miles to Paxson, Mile 185.5 on the Richardson Highway. (Authors note: This highway is a true wilderness highway and sometimes it can be rough.... and rewarding). |
| Mile 210 | **Cantwell Food Mart.** Gas, restrooms, ATM. |
| Mile 210 | **Cotter's Service.** Gas, Groceries, General Store. |
| Mile 224 | **The Perch.** Great restaurant. Cabins. 907-683-2523. |
| Mile 224 | **McKinley Creekside Cabins.** Café and bakery. 907-683-2277. |
| Mile 224 | **Carlo Heights Bed and Breakfast and Rick Swenson's Denali Sled Dog School.** Rick Swenson is a four-time Iditarod Winner. 907-683-2576. |
| Mile 229 | **Denali Cabins and Gift Shop** 907-683-2643. The cozy fully furnished cabins are an excellent place to stay while enjoying Denali National Park. |
| Mile 231 | **Denali Grizzly Bear Cabins and Campgrounds.** Groceries, showers, liquor store. 907-683-2696. |
| Mile 231 | Crabbie's Crossing, second bridge northbound over the Nenana River. Denali National Park Boundary. |

Mile 234.      Parking, scenic view.

Mile 237       **Entrance to Denali National Park and Preserve.**

Mile 238       **Denali Raft Adventures.** Paddle the Nenana River. 888-683-2234.

Mile 238       **Denali Bluffs Hotel.** 112 rooms. Closest hotel to Denali NP. 907-683-7000.

Mile 238       **Denali River View Inn.** Phone: 907-683-2663.

Mile 238       **Denali Princess Lodge.** Riverside lodging. Associated with Princess Cruise Lines. 800-426-0500.

Mile 239       **Denali Windsong Lodge.** Courtesy transportation to/from railroad depot & visitors center. 907-245-0200.

Mile 239       **Denali Sourdough Cabins.** Walking distance to most services and a courtesy shuttle. 1-800-354-6020.

Mile 239       **Denali Outdoor Center.** Rafting tours and bike rentals. Only bike rentals near the park entrance. Whitewater Kayak School. 1-888-303-1925.

Mile 239       **Northern Lights Theatre and Gift Shop.** A 45-minute multi-media panorama on 34-foot wide-screen shows nature's wildest light show. 907-683-4000.

Mile 239       **McKinley Chalet Resort.** 235 room resort. Also, has the Alaska Cabin Nite Dinner Theatre. 1-800-276-7234. Also, check Alaska Raft Adventures at the resort.

Mile 240       Iceworm Gulch.

Mile 245       **Denali RV Park & Motel.** 90 full and partial RV hookups. 800-478-1501.

Mile 247       Road that leads to Otto Lake.

Mile 247       **Black Diamond Golf Course.** Midnight Sun Golfing. 907-683-4653.

Mile 248       **McKinley Campground.** Free showers. 89 sites. Nightly movie. 907-683-2379.

Mile 248       **Healy.** Access via paved, 2-1/2-Mile side road. Healy is a quaint, historical mining and railroad town. Drab railroad buildings, and wooden plank platforms which front the tracks resemble a movie set. Across the river are the coal mining settlements of Suntrana and Usibelli. (For lodging information in Healy, check out the Healy Section).

Mile 249   **Denali North Star Inn**, P.O. Box 240, Healy, AK 99743, 1-800-684-1560. Comfortable, reasonably priced rooms Local shuttle service, authentic Alaskan gifts, and barber shop/beauty salon. Recreation and exercise facilities, saunas, laundry, tanning beds.

Mile 249   **Stampede Lodge and Bushmaster Grill.** Historic Alaskan lodge and restaurant. Good deals on rooms. 800-478-2370.

Mile 249   **Larry's Healy Service Tesoro** gas and oil products.

Mile 249   **Dry Creek Bed & Breakfast.** 907-683-2386.

Mile 251   **EarthSong Lodge.** Denali's naturalist retreat. Owner wrote one of the best books on hiking in Denali National Park called the *Backcountry Companion.* 907-683-2863.

Mile 259   **Rex Dome** is to the northeast, Walker and Jumbo Domes to the east. Liberty Bell mining area lies between the peaks and highway.

Mile 269   Rest Area. Sheltered picnic table, firepits, toilets. Steep road leads to June Creek and lower parking area. There is limited turnaround space for large RVs.

Mile 276   **Tatlanika Trading Company.** Tents sites and RV camping. Showers. Native Artist Gallery. Museum.

Mile 280   **Clear Sky Lodge.** Cocktail Lounge. Restaurant. Airport. Liquor Store. 907-582-2251.

Mile 283   Access road on left northbound to Clear and Anderson.

Mile 304   **Tripod Motel,** 907-832-5590. Rooms start at $39.95 all with private baths and TV, kitchenettes available.

Mile 304   **Nenana Tesoro** 907-832-5419. Gas and oil products.

| | |
|---|---|
| Mile 304 | **Nenana.** Population 500. |
| Mile 309 | **Monderosa Restaurant.** Claims to have the states biggest and best hamburgers. |
| Mile 319 | Parking with view of Denali on clear day. |
| Mile 328 | **Skinny Dick's Halfway Inn.** Rooms, camping, free parking. No hookups, but no charge. |
| Mile 344 | Monument in honor of George Alexander Parks, former governor of Alaska. Also here is a Blue Star Memorial plaque honoring the armed forces. |
| Mile 351 | Turn-off for Ester (pop. about 200), a former gold mining camp. Drive .4 Miles, turn right on road marked Ester, and drive .2 Miles to an intersection. Turn left for Ester post office and **Ester Gold Camp** (hotel with dining and old-time Saloon). The **Malemute Saloon** at Ester has been one of Fairbanks' leading visitor attractions for the last 28 years. |
| Mile 353 | **Gold Hill Country Store.** Package liquor, groceries and convenience items, gas, oil and ice. |
| Mile 356 | Turn-off to **University of Alaska,** Geist Road, Chena Ridge Loop and Chena Pump Road, where the old Chena Pump House National Historical Site is located. The Chena Pump house is one of Fairbanks' finest restaurants. |
| Mile 358 | Exit to **Fairbanks International Airport.** |

## The Original Denali Highway
## From Paxon to Cantwell–133 miles

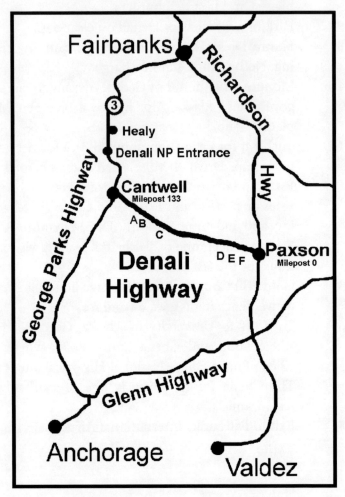

A–Brushkana Creek Campground

B–Adventures Unlimited Lodge

C–Gracious House and Campground

D–Tangle Lakes Lodge

E–Tangle River Inn

F–Denali Highland Adventures

# The Original Denali Highway

Prior to the 1950s, the only way to get to Denali National Park was to take the Alaska Railroad or hire a bush pilot. In the 1950s, the Denali Highway was built to allow drive-in visitors; it was unpaved and went from Paxson to Cantwell. It was the only road into Denali National Park and Preserve until 1972, when the George Parks Highway was completed.

The 135-mile unpaved Denali Highway was all but forgotten by tourists once the shorter and safer Parks Highway opened. Only the locals and true outdoorsmen took the Denali Highway. But, the ones who took it were rewarded by magnificent views, wildlife, great fishing, and the frozen beauty of glaciers overlooking a sculpted plain.

The Alaska Range can be seen on most of the route. The towering triad of Mount Hayes, Hess Mountain and Mount Deborah, three Alaska range peaks all over 11,000 feet, are captivating. Weather permitting, even the "Great One"—Denali—can be seen.

There are dozens of campsites and turnouts on the highway, and lake trout and grayling thrive in many lakes and streams, reached by hiking or driving designated off-road vehicle trails. Mountain biking is also popular on the highway.

Three roadhouses provide lodging, dining and gas between Paxson and Cantwell. Gas is available in both towns and at inns along the highway: the Tangle River Inn at Mile 20, the Maclaren River Lodge at Mile 42 and Gracious House Lodge at Mile 135. Mile markers start in Paxson.

From Paxson (located at mile 185.5 on the Richardson Highway), the Denali Highway is paved for the first 21 miles. The junction at Cantwell is at mile 210 on the Parks Highway.

## Mileposts for the Denali Highway (Hwy 8)

Mile 0          Paxson Junction. The Paxson Lodge has rooms, restaurant and service station.

| | |
|---|---|
| Mile 7 | Parking with view. Access to Sevenmile Lake. Good lake trout fishing in summer. |
| Mile 10 | Short hike to Ten Mile Lake. Fishing for lake trout, grayling and burbot in summer. |
| Mile 14 | Parking with view. View of over 35 lakes and potholes. Also view of Mount Stanford, Mount Drum, and Mount Wrangell. |
| Mile 17 | Two-mile trail to Little Swede Lake, and three-mile trail to Swede Lake. Excellent fishing area. |
| Mile 18 | **Denali Highland Adventures.** Fishing, boating, canoeing, and four-wheelers. |
| Mile 20 | **Tangle River Inn,** visitor facilities. Restaurant, liquor store, canoe rental. 907-822-8703. |
| Mile 21 | **Tangle Lakes Wayside.** North side of road. Twelve units on Tangle Lake (one of seven large, connecting lakes with grayling, trout). Boat launch allows access to Tangle Lakes system. Moose, caribou plentiful. Many hunters use the area as a base camp during fall hunting season. |
| Mile 21 | Tangle River Boat Launch. South side of road. Access to Tangle River, Tangle Lakes, and upper Tangle Lakes Canoe Trail. Seven campsites and picnic area. |
| Mile 22 | **Tangle Lakes Lodge** visitor facilities. Restaurant. Fishing, birding. Canoe rental. 907-688-9173. |
| Mile 25 | **Landmark Gap Lake Trail.** This trail extends approximately four miles to the southern end of Landmark Gap Lake. One marshy spot will be encountered but this trail is still suitable for mountainbikes and for hiking. The lake is known for its excellent fishing for grayling and lake trout. |
| Mile 30 | **Glacier Lake Trail.** This trail extends approximately three miles to Glacier Lake. Tracked vehicles are advisable as the trail is extremely wet and crosses a large |

boggy area and two small creeks. During wet seasons, it may be possible to reach the lakes by floating canoes down the creeks. This trail is not recommended for mountain biking; hikers should be prepared for extremely wet conditions.

Mile 35     MacLaren Summit. 4,086 ft. Highest highway pass in Alaska.

Mile 37     **Osar Lake Trail.** Approximately eight miles in length, the trail provides access to Osar Lake. It crosses glacial eskers, is fairly dry, and is recommended for mountain bikes and hiking.

Mile 37     **Maclaren Summit Trail.** This short trail provides access across the tundra at the Maclaren Summit. It is passable for mountain bikes and recommended for hiking. Since it is within Alaska State Department of Fish and Game's Controlled Use Area, hunting with motorized vehicles is not allowed.

Mile 40     **Seven Mile Lake Trail.** This trail parallels Boulder Creek for much of its 6.5 mile length. It ends at Sevenmile Lake. The trail has one peaty area at the beginning for approximately 1.5 miles; beyond this it is suitable for hiking and mountain bikes.

Mile 44     **Maclaren River Road.** This established road on the west side of the Maclaren River is 12 miles long and ends at the Maclaren Glacier. After four miles, one must ford the West Fork of the Maclaren River, a glacial stream that runs high after heavy rains. This is followed by five miles of good trail, then half mile of willow thicket, then three miles of good trail to the glacier.

Mile 48     Informal campsite by a small lake.

Mile 56     Rest area with restroom and informal camping.

Mile 68     Hatchet Lake Road. four-wheel drive only.

| | |
|---|---|
| Mile 77 | Airstrip. |
| Mile 79 | Valdez Creek Road leads to abandoned mining camp of Denali. |
| Mile 81 | Snodgrass Lake Trail. 4.2 miles. |
| Mile 82 | **Gracious House and campground**. Bar and café. 907-333-3148. |
| Mile 87-104 | The Alaska Range is visible north of the highway. Good views of Mt. Hayes, Hess, and Deborah. |
| Mile 99 | **Adventures Unlimited Lodge**.Café, Fishing and boating. 907-561-0132. |
| Mile 104 | **Brushkana Creek Campground**. Camping units, tables and firepits. Fishing for grayling and dolly varden. |
| Mile128 | Good view of Denali. |
| Mile 133 | Cantwell Junction. Junction of George Parks and Denali Highways. |

## Car and RV Rentals

If you are considering renting a car or RV in Alaska, ask: 1) Does the vehicle have unlimited mileage? Alaska is a big state and more than likely you will want to see a lot of it. 2) Where can you take the vehicle? Some rental places only allow their vehicles to be driven on major or paved roads. So, scenic areas like Petersville Road and Petersville State Recreation Area would be off limits. Check before you rent.

Sweet Retreat Motorhome Rentals
6820 Arctic Boulevard, Anchorage, Alaska 99518
800-759-4861 Anchorage Area: 907-344-9155
Website: *www.alaskan.com/sweetretreat*

Great Alaskan Holidays, Inc.
3901 West International Airport Road
Anchorage, Alaska 99502

Phone: 888-2-ALASKA, 888-225-2752, 907-248-7777
Email: *reservations@greatalaskanholidays.com*
Website: *www.greatalaskanholidays.com*
Rates for RV range from $85-$215(unlimited miles)/day

Alaska Panorama RV Rentals
712 W. Potter Drive
Anchorage, Alaska 99518
Phone: 907-562-140, 800-478-1401
Website: *www.alaskan.com/alaskapanorama*

ABC Motorhome Car Rentals
3853 W. International Airport Rd
Anchorage, AK 99502
Phone: 907-279-2000
Rates for RV from $100-$190(unlimited miles)/day

## Car Rentals

### Car Rental at the Anchorage Airport

| | |
|---|---|
| ALAMO | 1-800-327-9633 |
| AVIS | 1-800-831-2847 |
| BUDGET | 1-800-527-0700 |
| DOLLAR | 1-800-800-4000 |
| HERTZ | 1-800-654-3131 |
| NATIONAL | 1-800-227-7368 |
| PAYLESS | 1-800-PAYLESS |
| THRIFTY | 1-800-367-2277 |

### Car Rental at the Fairbanks Airport

| | |
|---|---|
| AVIS | 1-800-831-2847 |

BUDGET                 1-800-527-0700
DOLLAR                1-800-800-4000
NATIONAL             1-800-227-7368
PAYLESS               1-800-PAYLESS
THRIFTY               1-800-367-2277

## Car Rentals in Healy, AK

Teresa's Alaskan Car Rental              907-683-1377

## Shuttle Bus Service

**Denali Overland Transportation Co.**-Passengers are mainly groups of mountain climbers-many arriving from foreign countries, with limited time to accomplish something that may have taken years to plan. Can pickup at Airport.
P.O.Box 330, Talkeetna, AK 99676
Phone: 907-733-2385
Email: *denaliak@alaska.net*

**Talkeetna Shuttle Service**-15 passenger vans with roof racks. Service available between Anchorage and Talkeetna.
Phone: 907-733-2222
Email: *tshuttle@alaska.net*

**Alaska Backpacker Shuttle**-Scheduled runs from Anchorage to Talkeetna mid April through mid June, other dates and times by reservation. Airport pick up and drop off available.
Phone: 800-COM-TOAK
Email: *backpack@alaska.net*

**Park Connection Coach Service:** The Park Connection motorcoach runs daily between Denali, Talkeetna and Anchorage.
Phone: 800-208-0200
Website: *www.alaska-tour.com/AlaskaMotorcoach.html*

**Parks Highway Express Inc.** Leaves Anchorage and the Anchorage Youth Hostel at 8:00 every morning in the summer. $70 round trip to Denali. Also Provides service to Fairbanks, Valdez and Dawson City. Bikes $5 extra.
P.O. Box 84278
Fairbanks, AK 99708
Phone: 888-600-6001
Website: *www.alaskashuttle.com*

Airservice from Merrill Airfield (located next to
**Anchorage International Airport) to Denali**

Merrill Airfield in Anchorage is one of the busiest small aircraft airfields in the world. Almost one out of every 10 Alaskans has a pilot license and most areas in Alaska are only accessible by plane. Since the Denali National Park and Healy have small landing strips, only a handful of air shuttle services are available from Anchorage to Denali.

**Alaska Wilderness Flightseeing**
Phone: 907-274-2550
Website: *www.flyak.com*

**Bush Airventures**
Offer tours to Denali, Prince William Sound, Iditarod Trail, and more.
Phone: 907-279-9600
Email-*flybai@alaska.net*
Website: *www.alaska.net/~flybai/*

**Passage Air Service**
Passage Air Service offers flightseeing, glacier and wildlife viewing, daytrip, charter, and multi-day air tour vacations across Southcentral Alaska. Popular destinations include: Denali National Park's Mount

McKinley, the tallest mountain on the continent, and the nearby communities of Talkeetna and Healy.
Phone: 907-688-9464
Website: *www.passageair.com*

**Sound Aviation**
Phone: 907-277-6863
Website: *www.thehangar.net/sound_aviation.htm*

**Vernair**
Offers a free Ground Shuttle in Anchorage for our Customers and free On-Site Parking for Your Car, Motor home, or Tour Bus. Also offer an assortment of tours to Denali and other Alaska landmarks.
Phone: 907-258-7822
Website: *www.alaska.net/~vernair/*

# Chapter 3

## *Transportation Within the Park*

### Shuttle Bus System

Shuttle buses are the main way to see Denali National Park since no cars are allowed after the 15-mile mark is via shuttle buses. These buses, which are similar to school buses, allow visitors to get off and on as often as they like. The drivers usually have many years' experience and can point out the flora and fauna of the park. But all riders are expected to help spot wildlife along the way. The drivers will stop for all wildlife (except ground squirrels!).

Hikers and visitors wishing to day hike, camp, backpack, or picnic in the park can get off one bus at almost any spot in the park and then be picked up by another at no charge. Shuttle buses allow passengers to get off and on different shuttles or camper buses on a space available basis. These buses provide no food or beverages, so bring your own and make sure they fit underneath the seat or overhead rack. Remember, a shuttle trip can last as short as two and a half-hours for a one way trip to Polychrome Pass, or as long a 13 hours round trip to Kantishna, so bring appropriate supplies. Also, the shuttle buses will stop approximately every two hours so you can stretch your legs and use the facilities.

Advanced reservations are available by calling 800-622-7275. Visitors can call starting in late February for that year's reservations. From outside the U.S. dial 907-272-7275. Reservation requests can also be faxed or mailed starting in December for the following year's reservations. The fax number is 907-264-4684, and the mailing address is:

VTS 241 Ship Creek Avenue,
Anchorage, AK 99501

Sixty-five per cent of the shuttle bus seats and 100 percent of campground permits are available with advance reservations. When the advance bus seats are sold out, the remainder of seats is available only at the Visitor Center.

## Shuttle Fees and Stops

### Shuttle Bus Fees-All Distances and Times are One-way

| Type of Pass | Toklat | Eielson | Wonder Lake | Kantishna |
|---|---|---|---|---|
| Milepost | Mile 53 | Mile 66 | Mile 85 | Mile 89 |
| Time | 2H 50m | 3H 45m | 5H 25m | 6 hrs |
| Adult Single | $17.00 | $23.00 | $30.00 | $33.00 |
| Young Adult Ages 15-17 | $8.50 | $10.50 | $15.00 | $16.50 |
| Youth Single Child | Free | Free | Free | Free |
| Teklanika Pass Adult | $22.00 | $22.00 | $22.00 | $22.00 |
| Teklanika Pass Ages 15-17 | $11.50 | $11.50 | $11.50 | $11.50 |
| Teklanika Pass Child | Free | Free | Free | Free |
| Camper Pass Adult | $18.50 | $18.50 | $18.50 | $18.50 |
| Camper Pass Ages 15-17 | $9.25 | $9.25 | $9.25 | $9.25 |
| Camper Pass child | Free | Free | Free | Free |

# Shuttle Bus Departure Times

### June 10 to June 28:

| | | | | |
|---|---|---|---|---|
| Toklat: | 6:30am | 9:30am | | |
| Eielson: | 6:00am | 7:30am | 8:30am | 9:30am |
| | 10:30am | 11:30am | 1:00PM | |
| Wonder Lake: | 7:00am | 8:00am | 9:00am | 10:00am |
| Camper Bus: | 6:30am | 2:30PM | | |

### June 29 to August 11

| | | | | |
|---|---|---|---|---|
| Toklat: | 6:30am | 9:30am | | |
| Eielson: | 5:30am | 6:30am | 7:30am | 8:30am |
| | 9:30am | 10:30am | 11:30am | 1:00PM |
| Wonder Lake: | 7:00am | 8:00am | 10:00am | |
| Camper Bus: | 6:30am | 8:30am | 2:30PM | |

### August 26 to September 2

| | | | | |
|---|---|---|---|---|
| Toklat: | 6:30am | 9:30am | | |
| Eielson: | 7:30am | 8:30am | 10:00am | 11:00am |
| | 1:00PM | | | |
| Wonder Lake: | 7:00am | 8:00am | 9:00am | 10:00am |
| Camper Bus: | 6:30am | 8:30am | 2:30PM | |

### August 12 to August 25

| | | | |
|---|---|---|---|
| Toklat: | 9:30am | | |
| Eielson: | 7:30am | 8:30am | 10:00am |
| | 11:00am | 1:00PM | |
| Wonder Lake: | 7:00am | 8:00am | 9:00am |
| Camper Bus: | 6:30am | 8: 30am | 1:30PM |

# Bicycling in the Park

Denali ranks among the most bike-friendly of national parks. Bikes are allowed over the entire length of the 90-mile Park Road. Bikers can also take bicycles on the camper shuttle bus(not regular shuttle bus).

## Bicycle Rules of the Park Road.

1. Bicycles are restricted to the Park Road. They may not be used on trails, the roadside path, or in the backcountry.
2. Bicyclists must comply with all traffic and wildlife regulations. Ride single file. Remember that buses have priority on the gravel portions of the road. Vehicles will slow down to avoid "dusting" you. However, you should pull over and slow down or stop when buses are passing or approaching you due to the narrow road.
3. Wildlife roam the roads, too. Take care when rounding blind corners and brushy areas. Just like hiking in the backcountry, make noise when you are in areas of low visibility. Do not get to close to animals.
4. During the spring and fall when road closures occur, bicyclists are permitted to ride beyond closed gates.
5. Bicycle Camping: Register for a campsite in advance or at the Visitor Center. If you prefer to backpack, make sure you have a backcountry permit and leave your bike locked at a campground bike rack. Any excess food or gear must be stored in campground food lockers. Bikes may not be left along the road.

## Mountain Bike Rentals

Denali Outdoor Center
Phone: 888-303-1925, 907-683-1925
P.O. Box 170 Mile 238.9 Parks Hwy.
Denali National Park, Alaska 99755
DOC offers front suspension bikes by Trek and Schwinn with grip-shift, bar ends, toe clips, rear rack, pump and repair kit. All of our rental rates include a helmet and water bottle. Half-day rates are based on six-hour

checkouts. Full day rates are based on 24-hours. Multi-Day rates require a two-day minimum.

**Mountain Bike Rental Rates:**

| | |
|---|---|
| Half-Day | $25.00/day |
| Full-Day | $40.00/day |
| Multi-Day | $37.00/day |
| 5 or more Days | $35.00/day |

### Bicycling Outside the Park

Denali Outdoor Center recommends adventurers bike the "stampede trail," a dirt road approximately 12 miles north of the park entrance. This is where John Krakauer's book *Into the Wild* was based. Good views of the Healy Mountain Area.

Other good rides include the road to Petersville State Recreational Area and the original Denali Highway.

### Bike Rentals Outside the Park

## Palmer
Lifetime Adventures
P.O. Box 1205-MS Palmer, AK 99645
Phone: 800-9KATMAI
Email: *adventures@matnet.com*
Website: *www.matnet.com/adventures*
Located at Eklutna Lake and Katmai National Park. On-site kayak and bike rentals, lessons, guided trips. Equipment available for infants to adults. Backcountry expeditions, all skill levels.

## Wasilla
Wasilla Backpackers Hostel
3950 Carefree Drive Wasilla, AK 99654
Phone: 907-357-3699
Website: *www.wasillabackpackers.com*

## Driving in the Park

Anyway you get there, the drive to Denali is spectacular. The Denali Highway and the George Parks Highway, (HWY 3) are both superb. However, the majority of the park is closed to private vehicles. The grand exception comes each year during the second week of September, when 1,600 vehicles are allowed to drive the 90-mile length of the Denali Park Road. How do they get to do it?

The annual lottery for driving the park road happens each fall. For four days, 400 cars are allowed to drive the length of the park road. To apply for a road travel permit, you need to call the office and find out the days that will apply. Then send your choice of dates in preferential order and include a self-addressed, stamped envelope. Mail this between July 1 and 31. Only one entry per person will be accepted. Send it to:

"Road Lottery"
c/o the Denali National Park Office
Denali National Park, AK 99755

Following the lottery, on or about September 16, you may be able to drive to mile 30, the Teklanika rest area, until the road closes for the winter. Then cross-country skis, snowshoes or dog sleds are the only modes of access to the interior wilderness portion of the park from park headquarters. The park's equipment operators begin to plow the park road and chop at the overflow ice in mid-March. By April, you can drive to mile 15. Road clearing continues; by early May, you can drive to mile 30, Teklanika until Memorial Day weekend.

There are other exceptions to Denali's ban on private autos. For instance, permission is granted to visitors who are too disabled to ride the shuttle, or who are professional photographers and artists who must transport heavy equipment

# Chapter 4

## *Visitor and Information Centers*

## Entrance to Denali National Park and Other Area Visitor and Information Centers

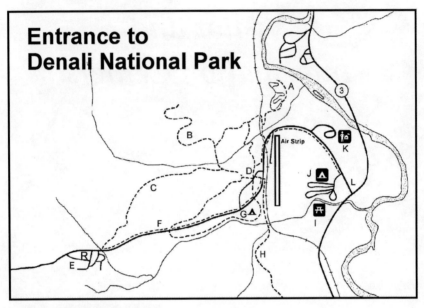

A. Horseshoe Lake Trail
B. Mount Healy Trail
C. Rock Creek Trail
D. Hotel & Post Office
E. Kennel & Dog Sled
F. Roadside Trail
G. Morino Campground
H. Triple Lakes Trail
I. Picnic Area
J. Riley Creek Campground
K. Denali National Park Main Visitor Center
L. Convenience Store & Shower
R. Ranger Station

## Denali Visitor Center at the Main Entrance

At the Denali Visitor Center you will find the information you need to plan a visit to the park. The book and gift store in the visitor's center has a great collection of maps and books about hiking, topography and the flora and fauna of Denali National Park. If you have not already reserved a camping site and or shuttle ticket, a display will list the availability of all camp sites and shuttle services. Also, you will need to pay your entrance fees here.

### Park Entrance Fees

|  | *Fees* | *Length of Time* |
|---|---|---|
| Individual | $5 | 7 days |
| Family | $10 | 7 |
| Annual pass | $20 | 1year |
| Golden pass | $50 | 1 year |
| Golden age | $10 | life |
| Golden access (Disability) | free | |

At the Denali Visitor Center you can also:
• Get information about shuttle bus tours along the Denali Park Road. All shuttle bus tours depart from the Visitor Center. (See shuttle schedule)
• Find out about Ranger-Naturalist programs.
• Get a backcountry permit. It is required for overnight hiking trips.
• Reserve a site at one of Denali's campgrounds. All campground sites are assigned at the Visitor Center or by advanced reservation.
• Find out about great places to day hike.
• Visit the Alaska Natural History Association bookstore. You will find the best selection of maps, books, posters, and other Denali material.

## Eielson Visitor Center
## (Park Road, milepost 66)

Open daily from 9:00 AM–7:00 PM from June 1 (road conditions permitting) through September 20. Rangers provide information, assistance and a daily guided walk at 1:30 PM. The bookstore has books, maps, postcards, and other educational materials for purchase. Running water and flush toilets available. There is no food service (but, if you get caught in a rainstorm and its freezing weather, one of the rangers may offer you cup of hot tea). This center is only accessible via shuttle bus, bicycle or foot.

This center has a seismonitor to measure earthquakes in the area. The last time I was camping at Wonder Lake, I slept through a 4.0 earthquake.

The center is named after Carl Ben Eielson, known as the "Father of Aviation" in Alaska. He piloted the first airmail route in 1924. He and Captain George Wilkins earned international acclaim for their non-stop, 2,200-mile flight over the North Pole on April 15, 1928. Wilkins and Eielson also completed a 1,200-mile flight in the Antarctic, where they discovered six new islands. Unfortunately, in 1929, Eielson was killed while attempting to rescue passengers and cargo from an ice-bound ship in the Bering Strait.

## Talkeetna-Denali Visitor's Center
## (Located at Parks Hwy Mile 99 at the Talkeetna Spur Road)

Alaska's Talkeetna Denali Visitors Center is a full-service booking agency for statewide activities, accommodations and travel needs. Local Alaskan experts help you design your trip. They can reserve everything from scenic flights to McKinley to one night's lodging or full package tours.

Talkeetna Denali Visitors Center can provide you with road maps as well as detailed maps of local biking, hiking trails, and cross-country skiing trails. Also, visitors should grab a free copy of the local newspaper, The Talkeetna Good Times to read about local culture and what is happening around Talkeetna and Denali National Park.

### Talkeetna Denali Visitor Center
Hours : Open 8-6 April-Labor day, Monday–Friday 8-4:30 rest of year
P.O. Box 688, Talkeetna, AK 99676
Phone: 907-733-2688
Website: *www.alaskan.com/talkeetnadenali*

## Denali Mountaineering Ranger Station
## (located in Downtown Talkeetna)

In 1977, the National Park Service established a ranger station specifically for mountaineers in the small community of Talkeetna. Since 1984, the station has been staffed year-round to provide information and assistance to mountaineers before, during and after their climbs. The mountaineering rangers have extensive experience in the Alaska Range and can provide invaluable information.

A collection of over 150 high quality photographs of the Central Alaska Range by Bradford Washburn is available for viewing at the ranger station. The station maintains a reference library including a complete set of American Alpine Journals, a map collection, and specific route information for numerous other peaks, including Ruth, Kitchatnas and Little Switzerland. Please feel free to use all of these resources while in Talkeetna to better prepare for your climb.

For more information about climbing Denali, visit or write to:
Talkeetna Ranger Station
Denali National Park and Preserve
P.O. Box 588
Talkeetna, Alaska 99676 USA
Phone: 907-733-2231

## Mat-Su Valley Visitors Center
## (Located at Parks Highway Milepost 35)

This visitor center is located at the junction of Parks Highway and Glenn Hwy/Tok Cutoff just outside Palmer. The Matanuska-Susitna Valleys are rich in history and agricultural production. Lakes and rivers dot the valleys.

Mountains in the Alaska Range, plus the Talkeetna, Chugach and Wrangell Mountains surround the valleys. The area is home to the Alaska State and County Fairs, Iditarod Trail Sled Dog Race, Hatcher Pass Independence Mine State Historical Park gold mines, and the Knik and Matanuska Glaciers.

There are farms in the area that raise musk ox, reindeer, wolves and giant vegetables. Other attractions are Denali flightseeing, hiking and golfing.

Mat-Su Convention & Visitors Bureau
Hours: 8:30 AM to 6:30 PM, seven days a week.
HC01 Box 6166 J21 ~ Palmer, AK 99645 USA
Phone: 907-746-5000
E-mail: *info@alaskavisit.com*
Website: *www.alaskavisit.com*

## Alaska Public Lands Information Centers

The Alaska Public Lands Information Centers are interagency visitor centers authorized by the Alaska National Interest Lands Conservation Act. The centers serve the public on behalf of eight federal and state agencies which manage public lands in Alaska. The agencies are the National Park Service, Fish and Wildlife Service, Bureau of Land Management, Geological Survey, Forest Service, the Alaska Department of Fish and Game, Division of Tourism and the Department of Natural

Resources. Alaska's state and federal public lands are rich and varied. The centers provide one-stop access to visitor information on Alaska's public lands including Denali and Denali National Park.

Whether you hike, camp, photograph, hunt, fish, or take a scenic drive, your first step should be into the Alaska Public Lands Information Centers. Find them conveniently located in downtown Anchorage, Fairbanks, Ketchikan, and also in Tok along the Alaska Highway.

At the centers, you'll find natural and cultural resource exhibits, fish and wildlife information, trip-planning, films and videos, book and map sales, recreation and visitor information, and interpretive programs.

In Anchorage, the Center is located next door to the Anchorage Convention & Visitors Center, which is housed in a log cabin.

Alaska Public Lands Information Center
605 West 4th Ave, Suite. #105 Anchorage, AK 99501
Phone: 907-271-2737
Website: *www.nps.gov/aplic/center/index.html*

# Chapter 5

## *Weather–Be Prepared!*

I once asked a park ranger in Denali National Park what the forecast was that day. He said, "Chance of sunshine, partly cloudy, rain, snow, and possibly an earthquake." That's the best way to say, be prepared for anything. Within a 24 hour period, summer weather can change from 70 degrees and sunny to 30 degrees and snowing..

Rain falls about half the days each summer and accounts for most of the 15 inches of average annual precipitation recorded at park headquarters. In winter, up to three feet of snows may blanket the park's lowlands. Winters have the most constant weather patterns: clear and cold. Ice usually caps rivers from late October to late April. Winter temperatures may drop to 40 degrees below and stay constant for days, although January temperatures also can reach 40 degrees above zero.

Denali is most easily observed in winter. During summer, there's a 35 percent chance of seeing the summit from Eielson Visitor Center. The clouds may suddenly part for an instant, reveal the peak, then close again without opening for several more days. The best chance in the summer to see the mountain is from about 10 PM to 6 AM.

| Month | Temperatures(F) | | Precipitation (inches) | |
|---|---|---|---|---|
| | Max | Min | Rain | Snow |
| January | 10 | -8 | 0.8 | 11 |
| February | 17 | -4 | 0.6 | 10 |
| March | 25 | 1 | 0.5 | 9 |
| April | 39 | 15 | 0.5 | 6 |
| May | 54 | 29 | 0.9 | Trace |
| June | 65 | 39 | 2.3 | Trace |
| July | 66 | 42 | 2.8 | Trace |

| Month | Temperatures(F) | | Precipitation (inches) | |
|---|---|---|---|---|
| | Max | Min | Rain | Snow |
| August | 63 | 39 | 2.5 | Trace |
| September | 52 | 30 | 1.6 | 4 |
| October | 33 | 14 | 1.0 | 13 |
| November | 18 | 1 | 0.8 | 15 |
| December | 08 | -8 | *0.7* | *12* |
| Total | 15.0 | | 18.0 | |

## Daylight

| Month | Hours |
|---|---|
| January | 5-7 |
| February | 7-10 |
| March | 10-13 |
| April | 13-16 |
| May | 16-19 |
| June | 19-21 |
| July | 18-20 |
| August | 15-18 |
| September | 12-15 |
| October | 8-12 |
| November | 6-8 |
| December | 4-6 |

High-June 21–20 hours 49 minutes   Low–December 21–4 hours, 21 minutes

Summers are generally cool and a little damp with an average high in the mid-60s. Layered clothing, including good rain gear and hiking boots, is recommended for summer.

For current weather information at Denali National Park:
call 1-800-472-0391 or check
www.americasbestonline.com/discover.htm

# Chapter 6

## *The Wildlife and the Land*

There's a land where the mountains are nameless,
And the rivers all run God knows where;
There are lives that are erring and aimless,
And deaths that just hang by a hair;
There are hardships that nobody reckons;
There are valleys unpeopled and still;
There's a land—oh, it beckons and beckons,
And I want to go back—and I will.

*Robert Service*

# Denali's Wildlife

People expect to see extensive wildlife in Denali National Park, forgetting that it is a massive wildlife sanctuary. Always consider yourself lucky when you spot wildlife, and consider yourself extremely fortunate if you see the Denali "Grand Slam": Dall sheep, caribou, moose and—from a distance-a grizzly bear (seeing one up close might not be so lucky). All together, Denali National Park contains 37 species of mammals, 157 species of birds, and one type of frog.

If you spot these animals while hiking or biking, try to keep the following distances between you and the animals:

| Animal | Distance |
| --- | --- |
| Grizzly Bear | ¼ mile |
| Wolf | 75 feet |
| Caribou | 75 feet |
| Moose | 75 feet |
| Dall Sheep | 75 feet |
| Raptor nests (Eagle, falcon, etc.) | 300 yards |
| Fox, lynx dens | 100 yards |
| Coyote dens | 100 yards |
| Wolf dens | 1 mile |

Spring, summer, and fall provide a brief respite from the subarctic's long season of deep cold. For most animals, it is a busy time during which they must gatherr most of their annual food supplies. And for people, it's the best time for watching them.

The following are brief descriptions of common wildlife in the area and their habits, as well as tips on when and where to photograph them.

## Arctic Ground Squirrel

One animal that visitors are guaranteed to see is the arctic ground squirrel. These animals number in the thousands, if not millions, in the park. These little guys can be spotted playing in the tundra, attacking tents, being carried by a golden eagle or being eaten by a grizzly bear-their high populations offer a dependable food source. The squirrels provide 90% of the diet for golden eagles and 50% for red foxes. The park's lynx, wolf and wolverine populations also eat ground squirrels.

## Beaver

Beaver in Denali National Park are numerous around the tundra ponds in the western part of the park and many can be found within walking distance of Wonder Lake.

Beaver in the wild live about 10 to 12 years. They have been known to live as long as 19 years in captivity. They continue to grow throughout their lives and may reach three to four feet in length. Although most adult beavers weigh 40 to 70 pounds, very old, fat beavers can weigh as much as 100 pounds. The beaver's heavy chestnut brown coat over a warm soft underfur keeps the animal comfortable in all temperatures. They have large, webbed feet and a broad, black tail that can be used as a 'rudder' when swimming. When slapped against the water, it serves as a sign of warning, but it can signal other emotions as well.

The beaver is designed to swim and work under water. Its nose and ear valves close when under water. A beaver can cut and chew submerged wood without getting water in its mouth by drawing its loose lips tightly behind the protruding front teeth.

## Dall sheep

Dall sheep, relatives of bighorn sheep, graze the alpine tundra. Ewes and rams live apart in summer, when lambs are born. In early summer sheep are at lower elevations, but they follow the snowmelt higher and higher as summer progresses. Over 2,000 Dall sheep call Denali home. The Rams weigh up to 160 pounds and the ewes up to 110 pounds. You may have to do some hiking to get a good look at these mountain animals, but the effort is well worth it. The Igloo area is an excellent viewing site for ewes with lambs. Rams can often be found along Primrose Ridge between the Savage and Sanctuary Rivers.

## Caribou

Caribou, like the sheep, travel in groups. Both male and female caribou sport antlers, the only deer species to do so. Caribou migrate great distances from their calving grounds south of the Alaska Range and northwest of Denali to their winter range in the northern reaches of the park and preserve. The Denali herd has fluctuated greatly over the last 30 years. Today groups of 20 or more may be seen from the park road, greatly reduced from the thousands seen many years ago. The caribou's movement patterns change from year to year and season to season. They are most often seen in the open areas beyond the Savage River. In the summer, the caribou can be seen resting in snow banks in order to escape mosquitoes. Caribou will lose a quart of blood a day to mosquitoes during the summer months.

## Marmots

The marmots are large relatives of the squirrel. The two types of marmots that live in Denali are the hoary marmot and the Alaska marmot. Closely related, they weigh 10 pounds or more and may exceed 24 inches in total length. The animals attain their maximum weight in late summer, when they accumulate thick layers of fat that will sustain them through winter hibernation. Body shape is similar in both species: head short and broad, legs short, ears small, body thickset, tail densely furred, and front paws clawed for digging burrows. Hoary and Alaska marmots are predominantly gray with a darker lower back and face and a dark, reddish tail. The hoary marmot has a white patch above its nose and usually has dark brown feet, giving it the Latin name caligata, meaning "booted." The Alaska marmot does not have a white face patch, its feet may be light or dark, and its fur is much softer than the stiff fur of the hoary marmot.

## Moose

Moose, the deer family's largest members, are not herd animals. Bulls may group in threes or fours or wander alone until they pursue several cow moose during the rut, or mating season. The calves are born in May and will stay with the cow one or two years. In spring, the cow and calf feed on willows and other new green vegetation. Be cautious about traveling in or near willow thickets in spring, as cow moose can be very dangerous while protecting her calf from a perceived threat. The forested area along the park's east boundary is excellent for cows and calves. The bulls can frequently be photographed in the Igloo area or feeding in the tundra ponds near Wonder Lake.

## Wolves

Wolves are rarely seen, but they play an important role. In winter, wolves generally hunt in packs, although a lone wolf can be sighted as well. Pack organization is strongest during the whelping (pupping) season in spring. The presence of wolves in Denali is an indication of the quality of this wilderness. Wolves reappeared in Denali in the early 1980's after a long absence.

## Denali Grizzlies

The Denali Grizzly is commonly known as the Toklat grizzly. Due to the lack of fish in the park (because almost all streams are silty glacial streams), their color is a light brown to blonde. Almost 1/3 of the size of an Alaska Brown/Grizzly Bear, they survive on a diet of various roots, berries, ground squirrel and young moose. Grizzly bears play an important role as predators in the park, culling old, newborn, and sick animals from the caribou, moose, and sheep populations. The park's current grizzly population is approximately 300. The largest concentration of bears is located around the Sable Pass area between mile marker 38-43 on the park road. In 1959, the park service closed this area to hikers and asked visitors not to enter.

## Avoiding Bears

Denali National Park and Preserve is home to both black and Grizzly bears. Black bears inhabit the forested areas of the park, while grizzly bears mainly live on the open tundra. Most bears seen by visitors along the park road are grizzlies.

The bears of Denali are wild creatures, free to behave as they wish. If annoyed, these solitary animals can be very dangerous to intruders. For your own protection, as well as to keep the Denali bears healthy and wild, please carefully read and abide by the following rules:

Be alert at all times, in all places. Bears are active both day and night and can be found anywhere. Watch for their tracks.

Avoid surprising bears. They may perceive you as a threat if you startle them.

Sing, shout, or make other loud noises as you walk to warn bears of your presence. Be especially careful in dense brush, where visibility is low, and along rivers, where bears cannot hear you over the noise of the water.

Never intentionally approach a bear. Bears should live as free from human interference as possible. Give them space. It is illegal to approach within ¼ mile of a bear.

## If you encounter a bear

Do not run! Running may cause a chase response from an otherwise non-aggressive bear. Bears can run faster then 30 miles per hour. You cannot outrun them. If the bear is unaware of you, detour quickly and quietly away. Give the bear plenty of room, allowing it to continue its activities undisturbed.

Back away slowly if the bear is aware of you but has not acted aggressively. Speak in a low, calm voice while waving your arms slowly above your head. Bears that stand up on their hind legs are not threatening you, but merely trying to identify you.

Should a bear approach or charge you, do not run–do not drop your backpack (it can serve as protection). Bears sometimes charge, coming within 10 feet of a person before stopping or veering off. Dropping a pack may encourage the bear to approach for food. Stand still until the bear moves away, then slowly back off.

If a grizzly makes contact with you, play dead. Curl up into a ball with your knees tucked into your stomach, and your hands laced around the back of your neck. Leave your pack on to protect your back. If the attack is prolonged, fight back vigorously.

## Campground Rules to Avoid Attracting Bears

1) All food, food containers, coolers and dirty cooking utensils must be stored in a closed, hard-sided vehicle or in campground food storage lockers whenever they are not in use. This includes freeze-dried and canned foods, as well as beverages and odorous items, such as soap and sunscreen.
2) Keep a clean camp. Trash and garbage must be stored in the same manner as food, or else deposited in a bear-resistant garbage can located in the campground. Scrape unwanted food from pots and plates into a bear-resistant garbage can.
3) Never leave food, containers, or garbage unattended even for just a few minutes.

(Authors note: A friend of mine used his tent as a napkin and wiped his hands on it. Bad idea! A bear decided to eat his tent.)

## Backcountry Camping and Bears

In most of Denali's backcountry units, all food and garbage must be stored in special Bear Resistant Food Containers (BRFCs). Issued at the Backcountry Desk with your backcountry permit. These containers are lightweight, cylindrical canisters specifically designed to keep bears from obtaining food and garbage from people in the backcountry. Since the introduction of mandatory BRFC use in 1984, there has been a 95% reduction in bears obtaining backpackers' food and an 88% decrease in property damage.

1) All food, including freeze-dried and canned foods, beverages, and odorous items, such as soap and sunscreen, must be kept in the BRFC when not in use.

2) Cook and store food at least 100 yards downwind from your tent in an area with good visibility in all directions. Keep an eye out for approaching bears. While eating, be prepared to put all food away in a hurry.

3) Keep a clean camp. Pack out all garbage, do not bury it.

**Please report all bear incidents and encounters to a park ranger. Park rangers and biologists need this information to document bear behavior for research and management purposes.**

## Mammal Check List

__Arctic Shrew

__Masked Shrew

__Dusky Shrew

__Pygmy Shrew

__Bat

__Black Bear

__Grizzly Bear

__Marten

__Short-tailed Weasel

__Least Weasel

__Mink

__Wolverine

__River Otter

__Red Fox

__Coyote

__Red Squirrel

__Northern Flying Squirrel

__Beaver

__Bog Lemming

__Brown Lemming

__Northern Red-backed mouse

__Meadow Vole

__Singing Vole

__Tundra Vole

__Chestnut-cheeked Vole

__Muskrat

__Porcupine

__Collared Pika

__Snowshoe Rabbit

__Moose

| | |
|---|---|
| __Wolf | __Caribou |
| __Lynx | __Mountain goat |
| __Hoary Marmot | __Dall Sheep |
| __Arctic Ground Squirrel | __Park Ranger |

## Birdlife

Denali birdlife is varied and interesting. Most birds migrate long distances between their nesting grounds in the park and their wintering areas. Wheatears winter in Africa; Arctic Terns in Antarctica and southern South America, Jaegers take to life at sea in the southern oceans. On the open tundra, you may easily see Ptarmigan, Lapland longspurs, and various shorebirds. Short-eared owls and northern harriers can be seen soaring low in search of rodents.

**Golden eagles** are named for the golden buff-colored feathers on the crown and nape of the neck. The adult body color is usually dark brown, and the dark-tipped tail is either darkly barred or spotted. Adult plumage is acquired over a three to four year period and involves a gradual reduction in the amount of white coloration. Immature Golden Eagles have white wing patches and white at the base of the tail. This bird has a wing span from six to seven feet and weighs eight to twelve pounds. It may carry a weight up to seven pounds.

**Arctic Tern**-The arctic tern, though small, is able to accomplish the remarkable feat of migrating over 22,000 miles each year, the longest of any bird. It does migrate in a straight line, but takes a lot of excursions, So, the actual distance even is greater. In fact, the arctic tern almost never lands. It is 12-15 inches in length, weighs less than two pounds, and is usually white with a black head and a bright orange beak.

# Bird Species around Denali National Park

c-common || cm- common migrant || fcm- fairly common migrant
||u–uncommon || um-uncommon migrant || rm- rare migrant || res-resident

___Rusty Blackbird um,
___Bufflehead fcm,
___Snow Bunting fcm,
___Canvasback rm
___Blacked-capped Chickadee c res
___Boreal Chickadee c res
___Sandhill Crane rm
___White-winged Crossbill uc res
___American Dipper uc res
___Short-billed Dowitcher um,
___Harlequin Duck um,br
___Red-necked Duck um
___Bald Eagle-rm
___Golden Eagle u res
___Gyr Falcon u res
___Northern Flicker cm
___Alder Flycatcher um
___Olive-sided Flycatcher um
___Common Golden eye um
___Barrow's Golden eye cm, br
___Canada Goose um
___Pine Grosbeak uc res
___Horned Grebe um
___Red-necked Grebe um
___Spruce Grouse um
___Bonaparte's Gull cm
___Mew Gull cm
___Northern Harrier cm

___Short-eared Owl um
___Western wood-Pewee rm
___Northern Pintail cm
___American Pipit cm
___Red-necked Phalarope cm
___Say's Phoebe um
___American Golden Plover cm
___Semipalmated Plover cm
___Willow Ptarmigan c res
___Rock Ptarmigan fc res
___White-tailed Ptarmigan uc,res
___Common Raven c res
___Common Redpoll c res
___American Robin cm
___Baird's Sandpiper um
___Least Sandpiper cm
___Solitary Sandpiper um
___Spotted Sandpiper cm
___Black Scoter um
___Surf Scoter um
___White-winged Scoter um
___Greater Scaup cm
___Lesser Scaup cm
___Northern Shoveler um
___Northern Shrike u res
___Common Snipe cm
___Townsends Solitaire um
___Oldsquaw cm

___Sharp-shinned Hawk rm
___Northern Goshawk rm
___Red-tailed Hawk um
___Rough-legged Hawk rm
___Long-tailed Jaeger cm
___Gray Jay c res
___Dark-eyed Junco cm
___American Kestral um
___Belted Kingfisher um
___Ruby-crowned Kinglet cm
___Horned Lark cm
___Lapland Longspur cm
___Smith's Longspur um
___Common Loon um
___Red-throated Loon um
___Pacific Loon rm
___Blacked-billed Magpie fc res
___Mallard fcm
___Common Merganser rm
___Red-breasted Merganser fcm
___Merlin um
___Boreal Owl u res
___Great Horned Owl u res
___Northern Hawk Owl u res
___Great Grey Owl u res
___Northern Waterthrush cm
___American Widgeon cm
___Whimbrel cm
___Hairy Woodpecker rm
___Lesser Yellowlegs cm

___American Tree Sparrow cm
___Savannah Sparrow cm
___Fox Sparrow cm
___Linclon's Sparrow cm
___White-crowned Sparrow cm
___Bank Swallow cm
___Cliff Swallow cm
___Tree Swallow um
___Violet-green Swallow cm
___Tundra Swan um
___Trumpeter Swan um
___Wandering Tattler um
___Green-winged Teal cm
___Blue-winged Teal um
___Arctic Tern cm
___Gray-cheeked Thrush um
___Swainson's Thrush fcm,
___Hermit Thrush um
___Varied Thrush um
___Arctic Warbler cm
___Orange-crowned Warbler cm
___Yellow Warbler cm
___Yellow-rumped Warbler cm
___Blackpoll Warbler cm
___Wilson's Warbler cm
___Bohemian Waxwing rm
___Northern Wheatear um
___Downy Woodpecker um
___Three-toed Woodpecker rm

## Amphibian-Wood Frog

Wood frogs, which take on the temperature of their environment, survive as far north as the Brooks Range because their bodies are able to freeze and thaw without bursting. As a wood frog's body freezes, its liver converts glycogen to sugary glucose. All its vital systems are flooded with the sweet liquid, which helps cells resist drying. Though its cells are protected, a hibernating wood frog resembles a frozen, small, green ice sculpture.

But wood frogs do have a limit as to how cold they can get, so they seek a snug winter nest when temperatures drop in the fall.

Only a few of these amphibians are spotted in Denali National Park, usually around the Wonder Lake area.

## Wildlife in the winter

Winter challenges wildlife with frigid temperatures and the cessation of plant growth. Food is scarce. Grizzlies fatten up in summer and remain in torpor or deep sleep most of the winter. Ground squirrels and marmots hibernate, their body functions virtually halted. Beavers and red squirrels hole up and subsist on food caches. Weasels, snowshoe hares, and ptarmigan, however, turn white and continue the struggle to survive above ground against extreme conditions

## Vegetation

More than 430 species of flowering plants as well as many species of mosses, lichens, fungi and algae grace the slopes and valleys of Denali. Only plants adapted to long, bitterly cold winters can survive in this subarctic wilderness. Deep beds of intermittent permafrost—ground frozen for thousands of years—underlie portions of the park and preserve. Only a thin layer of topsoil thaws each summer to support life. After the continental glaciers retreated 10,000 to 14,000 years ago, hundreds of years were required to begin building new soils, and to begin the slow process of revegetation. Denali's lowlands and slopes consist of two major plant associations, taiga and tundra.

*Taiga* (pronounced ti-ga), a Russian term meaning, "land of little sticks," aptly suggests the scant tree growth near the Arctic Circle. Much of the park and preserve's taiga lies in valleys along the rivers. White and black spruce, the most common trees, are interspersed with quaking aspen, paper birch alder, and balsam poplar. Stands of deciduous trees occur along streamside gravel bars or where fire or other action has disturbed soils. Woods are frequently carpeted with mosses and lichens. Many open areas are filled with shrubs such as dwarf birch, blueberry, and a variety of willow species. The limit of tree growth occurs at about 2,700 feet in the park and preserve.

*Tundra* is a fascinating world of dwarfed shrubs and miniature wildflowers adapted to a short growing season. There are two types, moist tundra and dry tundra, with myriad gradations in between. Moist tundra varies in composition: some areas contain tussocks of sedges and cottongrass; others contain dwarfed shrubs, particularly willows and birches. Plants of the dry tundra live scattered among barren rocks at higher elevations. Tiny highland plants grow closely matted to the ground, creating their own livable microclimate. Flowered dryas, dwarf tireweed, moss campion, dwarf rhododendron, and forget-me-not (Alaska's state flower) dot the rocky landscape, offering stunning summer displays of delicate blossoms. Although small in stature, they loom large in importance because their nutrients provide food that sustains even the largest species of park wildlife.

## Drunken Forests

Permafrost is a solid matrix of ice, soil, and rock, which can begin only inches below the surface and measure thousands of feet deep. It is continuous in the arctic. However, in the subarctic of Denali National Park patches of permafrost are intermingled with ground, which thaws in the summer. Variations in the winter and summer climate cause the extent of permafrost to vary from year to year so, in some places, ground which has been frozen for many years may thaw. As the ice turns to water, the soil is freed and sinks into spaces left by the retreating liquid. Thus, the ground often slumps beneath the trees, causing them to lean drunkenly.

## Alaska Range

The lofty peaks and rugged terrain of the Alaska Range offer great challenges to mountain climbers. Tourists are attracted to its enormous glaciers and Arctic scenery. The mountains stretch from the Aleutian Range in south central Alaska to the Yukon boundary in southern Alaska. They are a northwestward continuation of the Coast Mountains and Rocky Mountains of Canada. Four great mountain masses dominate the range. Several low passes and river valleys, some of which provide travel routes across the mountains, divide these mountains. The Alaska Range separates the interior tundra prairie of Alaska from the Pacific coastal region of the state.

The mountains form an enormous arc for about 600 miles, and vary in width from 120 miles at some points to 30 miles near the Canadian border. Denali, near the center of the Alaska Range, reaches 20,320 feet, which is the highest point in North America. Some other peaks in the Alaska Range, including Mount Hunter, Mount Hayes, and Mount Foraker, exceed 13,000 feet. The Alaska Range is crossed at Isabel Pass by the Trans-Alaska pipeline en route to its southern terminal at Valdez.

# Chapter 7

## *Camping in Denali National Park*

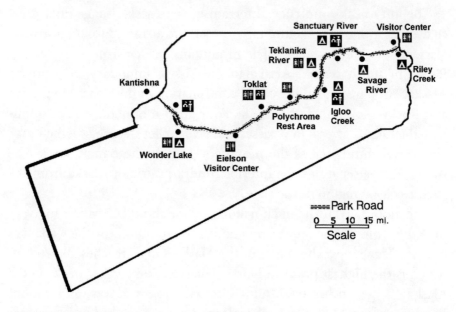

**Camping Reservations:**

Phone reservations for camping inside Denali beginning in late February for the following season. Campsites at Riley Creek, Savage, Teklanika and Wonder Lake may be reserved in advance by phone and fax through mid-September: Call 1-800-622-7275 from United States, or 272-7275 locally, in Anchorage, or 1-907-272-7275 outside the United States. Campers can fax at 907-264-4684, or mail reservations beginning in December for the next year. You can find Denali Campground Reservation forms at: *www.nps.gov/dena/campgrnd.htm.*

Campground sites often sell out. When sites available for advanced reservation are sold out, sites may still be available by walk-in at the Park EntranceVisitor Center up to two days in advance. Sanctuary and Igloo Campground sites are available only at the Visitor Center and not via phone, fax or mail-in. In addition to camping and entrance fees, there is a one-time $4.00 service fee for both phone and in-person reservations.

*Outside the Park:* If you don't have advance reservations, be prepared to camp outside the park when you first arrive; there may be a two night wait for park campsites.

*Reservation Refund Policy:* There is a $6.00 cancellation fee for each bus seat and/or campground site. This fee also applies to any changes made to existing reservations, but not to cancellations of reservations for children 12 and under.

*No electricity or water:* There are no water or electrical hook-ups at any campground in Denali National Park.

## Morino Campground

The Morino backpacker campground is available for campers without a vehicle. This 60-site campground is located one-quarter mile west of the Alaska Railroad Depot

Warning: Trains come by at 2:00AM and 4:00AM.

## Riley Creek Campground

Riley Creek Campground is located near the Visitor's Center at the entrance of Denali National Park. It is accessible by car and offers 100 sites, some of which can accommodate motorhomes, as well as three handicap accessible sites. There is a maximum of eight people, two vehicles (passenger cars, not motorhomes, space available) or two tents per site. There are flush toilets, and water is available, but no showers. Fires are permitted in fire grates only and ranger programs are conducted nightly at the campfire circle. Site assignment is on a first-come, first-served basis upon arrival at the campground. You will, however, need to check in at the visitor center prior to selecting your site.

## Savage River Campground

Savage River Campground is located 13 miles inside Denali National Park and is accessible by camper bus or by car. Savage River Campground has a total of 34 sites, some of which can accommodate motorhomes. There is also one handicap-accessible site. Site assignment is first-come, however you must check-in at the Visitor's Center. There is a maximum of eight people, one vehicle and two tents per site. There are water and flush toilets, but no showers.

## Teklanika River Campground

Teklanika River Campground is located 29 miles inside Denali National Park, beyond the point where private vehicles are allowed to drive. *However, if you remain at Teklanika Campground for a minimum of three consecutive nights you may drive your vehicle.* Once you arrive, you may not move your vehicle for any reason until the completion of your stay. If you anticipate health problems, please do not consider this site. You will be issued a permit for specific travel dates when you check-in at the Visitor's Center. *Early checkout for campers with private vehicles is not an option.* Please remember to use a dump station outside the park prior to driving out to Teklanika with your motorhome, and make sure you have enough provisions to last your entire stay. Do not schedule activities 'outside' the park during your Teklanika stay, as you will not have any transportation. Only one vehicle is allowed per site. You may tow your travel trailer for camping use only; all other towed items must be left at the Riley Creek overflow parking lot. There is a maximum of eight campers and two tents per site. Teklanika has one handicap accessible site.

Campers at Teklanika Campground who have driven are encouraged to purchase a "Teklanika Pass," which allows you go one specific shuttle bus destination further into Denali National Park from the Teklanika bus stop. This pass is valid for the duration of your Teklanika stay on a space-available access on any shuttle bus. You cannot, however, use the pass to exit the Park. If you go beyond the Savage River checkpoint at mile 14, not only will you need to purchase another pass to re-enter, but you won't not be able to return to Teklanika Campground on the same day due to shuttle schedule conflicts.

If you reserve Teklanika for less than three nights, your only transportation option is via camper bus, which you reserve at the same time you reserve your stay. Campers who use a regular camper bus to get to Teklanika Campground can ride on any park bus on a space-available basis during their stay, but also fall under the same restrictions as the Teklanika pass for exiting the park. Please discuss with fellow travelers how transportation limitations will affect your stay at Teklanika Campground.

## Wonder Lake Campground

Wonder Lake Campground is located 86 miles into Denali National Park and is accessible by camper bus only. It has 26 sites, of which two are handicap accessible. There are flush toilets and water at Wonder Lake, but not showers. A maximum of four people per site and two small two-person tents per site. For aesthetic reasons, no large tents, please. Site assignment is first-come, first-served. Wonder Lake Campground is small and in high demand. Please have alternative campground choices to this popular campground, as it sells out very quickly.

## Camper Buses

Camper Buses are made available for people traveling to campsites within Denali National Park. These school buses have been modified to carry large gear such as backpacks and tents, and carry a limited amount of people, so they are not designed for the casual day-trip passenger. This is the only type of bus that accommodates bikes, with a maximum of two bikes per bus. All camper bus tickets may be used, space available, to travel between miles 20 and 90 in the park. Please remember that once you have exited the park beyond the Savage River checkpoint (mile 14) your camper bus ticket is no longer valid and you won't be able to return to your campsite unless you buy another ticket. If you have questions or were planning on obtaining a camper bus for transportation with a backcountry permit; please call the National Park Service directly at 907-683-2294.

## Rules and Regulations for All Campgrounds

Quiet hours are from 10:00pm to 6:00am. Generator use is restricted to 8:00am to 10:00am and 4:00pm to 8:00am.

Individual campsites can be used by a party of no more than eight people, except Wonder Lake Campground, where occupancy is limited to a maximum of four people.

No more than one large tent or two small tents are allowed at any campsite. No large tents at Wonder Lake, please.

Food, coolers and cooking utensils (including stoves) must be properly secured in a hard-sided vehicle or food locker if not in use. Garbage must be properly disposed of. Substantial fines are levied for breaking this rules.

Check-in and check-out is 11:00AM. Daily.

Fires are permitted at Riley Creek, Savage and Teklanika Campgrounds, in established grates only. No fires at Morino, Sanctuary, Igloo and Wonder Lake Campgrounds.

Campers planning on having open fires should bring wood. Firewood is available at the Mercantile (Mile 1.5, across from the Railroad Depot).

No gas is available in the park. There are gas stations outside the park boundary.

Food and water are available at the Mercantile. Food is not available beyond the Mercantile.

Water and a trailer dump station are located at Riley Creek Campground.

Pets must remain on a leash and can be walked on roadways only. Do not leave pets unattended at any time. Pet food must be stored with all food in a hard-sided vehicle or food locker. Please deposit all pet waste in a trash can.

Overnight camping in parking lots or pullouts is prohibited.

### Recommended Backpacker Equipment List

- A good tent (no $19.99 Kmart specials).
- A large sponge to soak up moisture or water.
- Extra line. Great for hanging wet socks.
- Sleeping bag: Down or synthetic.
- Air Mattress or pad.
- Backpack.
- Small brightly colored daypack.
- Plastic bags to keep clothing dry.
- Toilet kit: small and light.
- Sunburn lotion and sunglasses. 20+ hours of bright sunshine can result in a burn.

- High-quality raingear (jacket/parka) and pants/chaps) and pon-chos to cover backpacks during day hikes or while sleeping.
- Jacket (wool, pile or other synthetic).
- Cool-weather hat.
- Mittens or heavy gloves.
- Set of long underwear (synthetic or wool, no cotton).
- Wool pants.
- Spare clothes (shirt, etc).
- Plenty of socks (wool or synthetic, warm-weather).
- Gaiters.
- River-crossing footwear.
- Hiking boots (make sure they are waterproof).
- Dress in layers and avoid cotton and down, as these fibers lose insu-lating efficiency when wet. Casual synthetics should not be con-fused with synthetics designed specifically for outdoor use.
- Sleeping gear.
- Cooking gear and food.

*Miscellaneous:* (According to Peggy Weyburn from *Adventuring in Alaska*)
- Knife: Swiss Army knife with scissors or hunting knife.
- Space Blanket: use for wind, rain and cold.
- First aid kit: if nothing else, carry Band-Aids and a small piece of soap to clean a wound.
- Bandana: wonderful multipurpose item. Use for bandage, sweat-band, towel, hot pad napkin, scarf, head net, and so on.
- Safety pins: pin a couple into your hatband or along an inner seam of your parka.
- Sierra Club cup or one similar to hang on your belt: this multi-pur-pose item is useful for noisemaking to keep bears away and for washing small wounds, heating water for tea or bouillon and, inci-dentally, for drinking.

- Extra candy bars, nuts, tea bags or two bouillon cubes: survival fare.
- Extra Clothes: wear a T-shirt and shorts, if you must, but always have long pants, warm shirt, parka, and warm headgear in your pack-survival items.
- Waterproof matches: dip big kitchen matches in melted wax.
- Old candle stub: fire starter.
- Flashlight: check batteries before starting; also carry a flare, or try a small solar or lithium powered flashlight.
- Compass: know how to use it in the higher latitudes. The further north you travel, the more the needle on your compass will point upward. In Denali, the compass will be about 16-18 degrees from vertical. The magnetic force centered in the North Pole will also skew your needle to east of north. Thus, in southeast Alaska, your compass needle will point to between 28 and 31 degrees east of true north. And in Fairbanks, the needle will be only 11 degrees from vertical.
- Toilet paper: please cover it with rocks or bury it; think how you would feel when you find someone else's.
- Bug repellent, an insect repellent stick has the advantage of not leaking.
- Head net: a small, priceless item, especially near lakes or ponds in the summer where mosquitoes can number in the millions.
- Duct tape: roll up a foot or two to carry for emergency repairs. Can also be used for blisters.
- Waterproof watch or cheap pocket watch: Although you may want to get away from it all, knowing the time can be extremely helpful, especially in the land of the midnight sun. People tend to lose track of days and time.

**Optional items:**

| | |
|---|---|
| Shorts | Swimsuit |
| T-shirt | Wetsuit (for glacial stream crossing) |
| Hat | Waterproof notebook |

Waterproof pen      Binoculars
Jeans                   Magnifying glass.

## List of Camping Stores in Alaska

**Anchorage**
**Alaska Mountaineering & Hiking**
2633 Spenard Rd
Anchorage, AK 99503-2308
Website: *www.alaskan.com/amh/*

**REI–Anchorage**
1200 W. Northern Lights Blvd.
Anchorage, AK 99503
907-272-4565
Website: *www.rei.com*

**Play It Again Sports**
2636 Spenard Road
Anchorage, AK 99503
907-278-7529

**Sports Authority**
8931 Old Seward Highway
Anchorage, AK 99515
907-349-6881

**Fairbanks**
**Beaver Sports**
3480 College Rd
Fairbanks, AK
907-479-2494

**Sport King**
1323 Kalakaket St
Fairbanks, AK
907-479-2820

**Healy**
**Speer Sporting Goods**
Sulfide Dr
Healy, AK 907-683-2472

**Talkeetna**
**Talkeetna Outdoor Center**
Talkeetna, AK 99676
Phone: 800-349-0064, 907-733-8352
Email: *journeys@alaska.net*
Website: *www.alaskajourneys.com*
A great resource for mountaineers on Denali, this center stocks over-
boots, ice saws, down mitts, noseguards, water bottle insulators and
much more.

# Minimum Impact Camping

To protect this beautiful area, minimum impact camping is appreci-
ated, especially in non-campground areas.

### Minimum Impact Camping Techniques

*Souvenirs*-Consider what it is that has brought you to Denali, then
remember that other people are attracted to the same things. Avoid
removing items of interest, such as rocks, flowers, or antlers. Leave these
things in their natural state for others to see and enjoy.

*Hiking*-Stay on the designated path when hiking existing trails. Look
for Dall Sheep trails in the higher elevations. Shortcutting a switchback
or avoiding a muddy trail by walking alongside the trail causes erosion
and unsightly multiple paths. Heavy, lug-soled boots have an adverse
affect upon fragile terrain. In the spring travel across snow and rocks as
much as possible; high mountain plants and soil are especially
susceptible to damage during thaws. In areas where the trail is difficult
to discern, a group should spread out rather than walk one behind the
other. This is especially true in wet meadows or on high tundra areas.

Groups of hikers larger than four to six people should break up into
smaller hiking parties. On rest breaks, select hardened areas to absorb
your impact. Consider wearing well-cushioned running shoes whenever it is safe and where conditions permit. It is strongly advised that
you carry a light pair of boots for safety reasons. Always use light
footwear in camp.

*Camping*-Select a level campsite with adequate water runoff, and use
plastic under your tent to stay dry without ditching. Be sure to locate
your site at least 100 feet away from natural water sources. Position your
tent, when possible, so that it blends into the surrounding environment
and is not in sight of the road.

*Garbage*-Be sure to carry out all of your food and packaging waste.

*Sanitation*–Since restrooms and latrines are far and few use the "cat-holer" technique. Proceed with trowel in hand to an area at least 200 feet away from water sources, trails and campsites. After carefully removing surface duff, dig a hole several inches into the soil, direct human waste and a minimum of toilet paper into the hole, then replace the soil and duff on top.

*Cleanliness*-Even when biodegradable, soap stresses natural organisms in the environment, so do as much of your cleanup as possible with soapless hot water. When using soap or toothpaste to wash yourself or your dishes, use it well away from natural water sources; pour the waste into highly absorbent soil.

*Water*-The increasing occurrence of backcountry dysentery caused by *giardia* clearly demonstrates the impact water pollution has on the wilds. *Giardia* thrives in water that has been contaminated with animal or human waste. Consider most backcountry water to be potentially contaminated even though it appears clean and may be running rapidly. To ensure its safety, boil water or use a chemical water purification agent. Clean water is vital to human and animal health; do everything you can to lessen your impact on water sources. Fresh water is generally available at the visitor centers and campsites.

# Chapter 8

## *Hiking in Denali National Park*

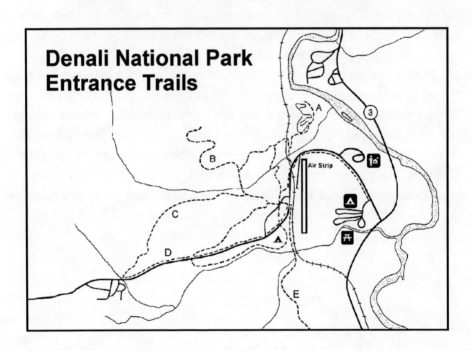

**Denali National Park
Entrance Trails**

A

B

C

D

E

3

Air Strip

When hiking in Denali National Park, trails are few and far in between. Since park rangers ask you to "make your own trail" or follow animal trails, and since most of Denali has no trails, a topographic map of the park is necessary. Near the park entrance, there are some easy trails with spectacular scenery:

A) **Horseshoe Lake Trail**–1.5 miles
Trail begins on the Park Road near the railroad tracks. Easy to moderate.
B) **Mount Healy Overlook**-2.5 miles
Trail head 100 yards behind the park hotel. Easy to moderate hike after the first third. Elevation gain of 1,700 feet. The trail passes through boreal forest to alpine tundra. Splendid view of the Alaska Range and Denali on a clear day.
C) **Rock Creek Trail**–2.3 miles one way.
Connects Denali National Park Hotel and post office with park headquarters and kennel. Time: Two hours one way, uphill.
D) **Roadside Trail**–1.8 miles
Connects the Denali National Park Hotel and Post Office to Park Headquarters and Kennel. This trail also extends to the Visitor Center.
E) **Triple Lakes**-4.0 miles
Trailhead begins close to the railroad station. Easy to moderate hike with climbs and descents. Excellent view along the ridge of the Nenana River and the triple lakes. Nice overnight camping, good fishing for grayling. Possible sightings of moose, beavers and numerous duck species.

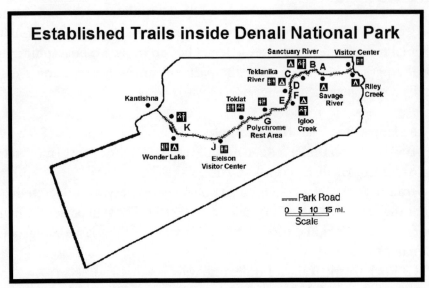

Established Trails inside Denali National Park

Sanctuary River    Visitor Center

B A

Teklanika
River    C

D

Riley
Creek

Kantishna

Toklat    E    F

Savage
River

G

Igloo
Creek

Polychrome    I
Rest Area

K

J

Wonder Lake    Eielson
Visitor Center

Park Road

0  5  10  15 mi.
Scale

Considering the size of Denali National Park, there are very few established trails. When asking the park rangers about established trails and the best areas to see in the park, they may not answer. They don't want one section or trail to be overused which would lead to permanent scarring of the land. The following are park trails; the sections referenced are described in the next chapter of this book.

A) **Primrose Ridge**-4.1 miles (Section 26)
Trail head close to the Savage River campground at mile 17. Easy hike, best trail of the park for wildflowers through grassy alpine tundra. Lots of birds to observe and often sight of Dall sheep.

B) **Mount Margaret**-2.3 miles (Section 26)
Same trail head as Primrose Ridge, intersection of trail after 1.8 miles of easy hiking. Moderate hike on rock. 5,059 feet. The flat top is covered by the oldest rock in the park. Excellent panoramic view of the park. Dall sheep, birds and lots of wild flowers can be seen on lower part of trail.

C) **Igloo Mountain**-1.0 mile (Section 29)

Trail head at mile 34, south of Igloo Campground. Moderate to strenuous hike. Very short but steep hike to 4,751 feet on unstable volcanic rock; can be done in less than half a day. Panoramic view of the Alaska Range. Good place to see Dall sheep.

D) **Cathedral Mountain**-2.9 miles (Section 6)

Trail head at mile 34, south of Igloo Campground. Easy hike to 0.8 mile.

The next mile is a moderate to a strenuous climb until you reach the summit at 4,905 feet. Good place to view Dall sheep with panoramic view of the Alaska Range.

E) **Sable Mountain:** (Section 29)

This trail features the best panoramic view of Denali National Park because of its central location. Trailhead is 3.3 miles past Igloo Campground, just after the road crosses Tattler Creek. Hike to the summit: 2.6 miles strenuous hike to 5,923 feet, but good trail makes it accessible in half a day. Take water with you, no creek water is available during the climb. Hike on the southern flanks: 5.0 miles of moderate hiking with excellent opportunity of seeing bears, caribou, moose, sheep, wolves and variety of birds.

F) **Upper Teklanika-Sanctuary Rivers**-35.0 miles (Sections 4 and 5)–**Experience hikers only.**

The trailhead is at mile 37, then drop down and cross Igloo Creek and hike east, keeping close to the southern flanks of Cathedral Mountain. You must improvise and follow GAME TRAIL. Bears are very common; excellent, strenuous hike to view Dall sheep rams. Spectacular glacier-carved scenery along the crest. Wildflowers and birds are numerous, with possible sighting of caribou in the valley.

G) **East Branch of the Toklat**-9.0 miles (Section 9)

Trail head at mile 51 past the Polychrome Overlook rest and bus stop. Easy hike. Excellent overnight camping. Frequent bear sighting. Good chance of seeing Dall sheep, caribou, moose, foxes and maybe a rare wolf all along the trail.

H) **Stony Creek Base Camp**-Various distances (Section 33)

Several easy hikes can be done along Stony Creek and its numerous small tributaries. One of the best places in the park to view bears, caribou and golden eagles. Extensive wildflowers. Excellent view of Denali on a clear day.

I) **Toklat River-Sunrise Glacier**-20.0 miles (Sections 10,12,& 13)

Begin the hike 1/4-mile past Toklat Ranger Station when road runs near the river flat. Long, strenuous hike. Easy hike for the first 3 miles then strenuous with stream crossings, so watch for bears in the lower part of the valley. Close view of Sunrise Glacier and beautiful scenery all along the way. Recommended for experienced backpackers in good physical condition.

J) **Mount Eielson**- 14.0 miles (Section 13)

Trail head on the right of Eielson Visitor Center at mile 65. Easy to strenuous hike up to the summit of Mount Eielson (5,802 feet). Good place to see bear, sheep and caribou.

K) **Moose Creek Station**-3.5 miles (Section 35)

Trail head at mile 74. Easy to moderate hike to the Moose Creek Ranger Station (station not for public use). Good grayling fishing in the creek.

# Chapter 9

## *Denali National Park by Section*

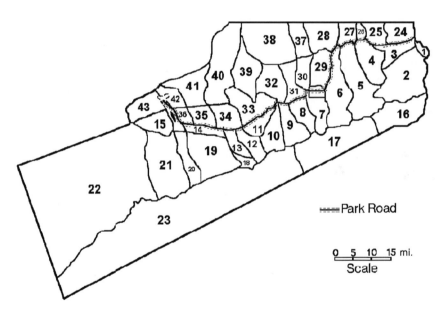

**Author's Note:** Broad descriptions of the sections are featured in this chapter, including the total number of backcountry overnight campers permitted in each, and a number of the established trails(if any). Registration at the Park's Entrance Visitor Center is required for overnight camping. Note that "scree" slopes, which are extensive in Denali, refer to slopes covered by loose rock and broken shale, so caution is advised when climbing there.

## Denali National Park Western Sections

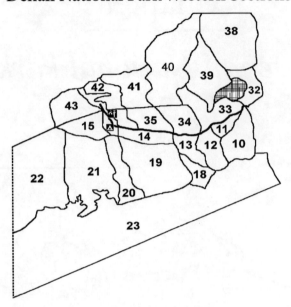

## Alaska Range

- Upper Tolkat River Valleys–10
- Highway and Thorofare Pass–11
- Mount Eielson & Upper Thorofare River–12
- Upper McKinley Bar & Pirate Creek Drainage 13,14,18,19
- McGonagall Pass–20
- Muddy River Drainage–21
- The West End–22

## The Outer Range

- Mount Sheldon Area–39
- Upper Stone Creek–east 33
- Mount Galen Area–west 33
- Lower Toklat and East
- Fork Rivers–38

## The Kantishna Hills

- Moose Creek Area-34,35,36
- McKinley Bar Area–15
- Kantishna Hills–41,42,43

## Denali National Park Eastern Sections

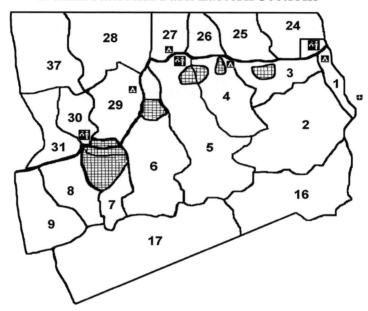

## Alaska Range

• Riley Creek, Jenny Creek & Triple Lakes–1, 2, 3, 16
• Upper Savage River Drainage–4
• Upper Savage River & Double Mountain–5
• Upper Teklanida River Drainage–6
Upper East Fork River & Polychrome Glaciers-7, 8
Upper Toklat River Valleys–9, 10
South Side-16-17

## Outer Range

• Mount Healy–24, 25
• Primrose Ridge & Mt. Wright–26
• Sushana River Drainage–27
• Sable Mountain Area–28, 29
• Polychrome Mountains & The Wyoming Hills 30,31,32

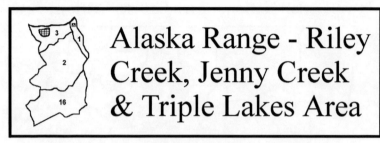

## Alaska Range - Riley Creek, Jenny Creek & Triple Lakes Area

**Mile 0-12. Topography Maps Healy C-4 and Healy C-5**

In section one, Riley Creek flows east and north from the eastern slopes of Fang Mountain, past the entrance of the park road to the Nenana River. Along the way, many side streams enter Riley Creek. Between the Riley Creek drainage and the eastern park boundary is a small valley where the Triple Lakes are found. The Triple Lakes area is one of the few accessible fishing areas in the park.

In section three, Jenny creek begins in the hills to the north of Riley Creek and flows in a western direction, meeting the Savage River near the Savage River Campground. Between these drainages rise gentle hills and ridges reaching the 5,000 feet mark.

Sections 2 and 16 are not directly accessible by the park road, but can be directly accessed from the George Parks Highway. Sections 1,2,3 & 16 consist of some dry tundra found in the higher elevation to thick taiga spruce forests.

**Hiking:** All four sections are challenging due to the low brush cover. Well-hiked areas are near Triple Lakes. Some easy hiking can be found along the gravel bars where Riley Creek flows.

**Established Trails:** The Triple Creek trail starts near the road in section 1 and goes down the middle of this section.

**Mountains:** Fang Mountain (6,726') is located where sections 2,4,5 all come together. It's a difficult climb due to loose rocks.

**Animals:** Moose can be spotted in the lower elevations with an occasional grizzly or black bear.

**Fishing:** You can try your luck fishing for grayling in Triple Lakes in section one.

**Total Overnight Campers allowed:** section 1–12, section 2–12, section 3–4, section 16–8.

Notes:

_____

_____

_____

_____

_____

_____

_____

_____

_____

_____

_____

_____

_____

_____

_____

_____

_____

_____

_____

_____

_____

_____

_____

_____

_____

# Alaska Range - Upper Savage River Drainage

**Mile 12-15. Topography Maps Healy C-5**

In section four, the Savage River flows northwest from the hills around Fang Mountain, past the Savage River Campground. Hikers should be able to cross the river since the water levels run from ankle to knee high. Water may be higher in the spring due to winter melt. For its first four miles, the Savage River flows mostly over a small gravel bar in a valley with 5,000' hills on either side. For the four miles to Jenny Creek and the three miles to the road, the river is in the open tundra flats, usually on a river bar In the southeast part, the hills are rounded gentle-sloped, and covered with vegetation. In this area hiking can be challenging due to the low brush cover and no established human or animal trails.

**Established Trails:** None.
**Mountains:** Fang Mountain (6,726') is in the southeast corner of this section. It's a difficult climb due to loose and rotten rocks.
**Animals:** Moose frequent the area.
**Fishing:** Grayling can be found in Caribou Creek.
**Savage River Campground:** This campground has a total of 34 sites, some of which can accommodate motorhomes. There is also one handicap accessible site. Site assignment is first-come, first-served upon arrival at the campground, after check-in at the Park Entrance Visitor's Center.
**Total Overnight Campers allowed outside of campground: Four.**

Notes:

# Alaska Range - Upper Savage River Drainage Double Mountain Area

**Mile 22-23. Topography Maps Healy B-5, C-5**

In the southern part of section six, the Sanctuary River begins in the 6,000' and higher peaks of the Alaska Range, and then this river flows due north to the Sanctuary River Campground and the Park Road. The river's headwaters comprise three branches flowing from the range. The two western-most branches flow from the glaciers in Refuge Valley. The eastern-most branch flows from Windy Pass. After the branches meet, the Sanctuary flows through a wide river valley, past hills reaching more than 5,000', and to Double Mountain. In the next five miles, the river flows across the tundra flats to the Park Road.

**Established Trails:** None.
**Mountains:** Double Mountain (5899'). Climbers need to use caution due to loose rock.
**Animals:** Hoary marmots. Moose and grizzly can be seen in this section. If you reach the Refuge Valley in the south part of this section, you can see some small caribou herds. Dall sheep are found on the slopes of the Alaska Range.
**Fishing:** Grayling can be found in Caribou Creek.
**Sanctuary River Campground:** Seven tent sites.
**Total Overnight Campers allowed outside of campground:** Six.

Notes:

# Alaska Range - Upper Teklanika River Drainage Area

**Mile 25 to 38. Topography Maps :Healy B-5, B-6, C-5, C-6**

In the south end of section six, two branches make up the headwaters of the Teklanika River. One branch begins at glaciers on the north side of the Alaska Range. After the branches meet the river flows over a wide gravel bar through a glacial valley for approximately 10 miles. Near the end of the relatively narrow valley, the river flows past Cathedral Mountain (4,905 feet) to the west and the junction of Calico Creek, the second branch. Calico Creek flows through the deep valley for about five miles, ending at Calico Pass, which leads into the upper Sanctuary River. Past Cathedral Mountain, the Teklanika River flows through a much wider river valley and then another three miles to the Park Road.

The slopes in the headwaters of the Teklanika consist of scree and exposed rock with some dry tundra. Expect wet tundra and thick brush at lower elevations of the river. Once past Cathedral Mountain, spruce occasionally line the river, and heavy spruce forest lines the river bar past the Teklanika River ridge.

## Established Trails:
*Cathedral Mountain Trail* (2.9 miles). Trailhead at mile 34, south of Igloo Campground. Easy hike to 0.8 mile, then moderate to strenuous climb to 4,905 feet on volcanic rock. Summit is only at 1.8 miles.
*Upper Teklanika-Sanctuary Rivers Trail* (35.0 miles). At mile 37 of the park road, hikers drop down and cross Igloo Creek and hike east,

keeping close to the southern flanks of Cathedral Mountain. Hikers must improvise and follow the GAME TRAIL. Bears are very common. You have an excellent chance of seeing dall sheep rams. Spectacular glacier-carved scenery along the crest. Wildflowers and birds are extensive.

**Mountains:** Cathedral Mountain (4,905 feet)) is in the central part of this section. Several peaks in the 6,000 feet range are in the south end of this section.

**Animals:** Grizzly bear and moose are sometimes seen at the base of Cathedral Mountain. Dall sheep are found on the upper slopes. Caribou sightings are common in the valley.

**Campgrounds:** Igloo Campground and Ranger Station. Seven tent sites.

**Total Overnight Campers allowed outside of campground:** Six.

Notes:

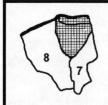 # Alaska Range - Upper East Fork River & Polychrome Glaciers

**Mile 43-50. Topography Maps–Healy C-6, B-6**

A wildlife preserve separates sections seven and eight. Since section seven has no road entrance, the easiest way is through Sable Pass.

Upstream from the East Fork River Bridge along the Park Road, the East Fork River branches into five major streams. The first two branches, the largest ones, flow south from small glaciers through glacial valleys. The other branches flow from narrow finger-glaciers called the Polychrome Glaciers. Halfway to their convergence, the streams enter an open tundra plain known locally as the Plains of Murie.

The entire branches of the East Fork river flow along gravel bars. Between the branches on the Plains of Murie, the vegetation consists of dry and moist tundra with low and high willow groves. The high hills that contain the Polychrome Glaciers and the glacier valleys of the first two branches consist of scree slopes and rock outcrops. Some ridges are occasionally climbed, though the rock cover and scree make this dangerous.

**Glaciers:** The Polychrome Glaciers are steep and covered with rock over much of their surface. Because of slope, loose rock, and crevasses, climbing can be dangerous

**Mountains:** Mount Pendleton (7,800'+). Access to the standard climbing route of Mount Pendleton is up on the Pendleton Glacier. Crevasses are a real hazard. Several other 7,000 foot peaks are in these sections and are towards the south end. Climbing is not advised.

**Animals:** Caribou travel across the Plains of Murie, occasionally in large groups. Grizzly bears can be found throughout the sections. In the upper hills, Dall sheep, marmots and pika can be found.

**Total Overnight Campers allowed:** Section 7–four, Section 8–six.

Notes:

_____

_____

_____

_____

_____

_____

_____

_____

_____

_____

_____

_____

_____

_____

_____

_____

_____

_____

_____

_____

_____

_____

_____

_____

_____

# Alaska Range - Upper Toklat River Valleys

**Miles 50-54. Topography Maps Healy B-6, C-6, Mt. McKinley B-1, C-1**

Sections nine and ten contain two glacier-carved valleys that were formed by the East and West branches of the Toklat River. Both branches originate from glaciers nestled against the north slopes of the Alaska Range. The Toklat's river bar widens to more than a mile at some points. Crossing these rivers varies from easy to extremely difficult. The easiest place to cross is near the glaciers.

**Established Trails:** East Branch of the Toklat trail starts just past the Polychrome overlook reststop.

**Mountains:** The mountains or large hills on either side of the river valleys rise to more than 7,000 feet and their slopes are scree-covered and dangerous. These mountains are unnamed.

**Animals:** Dall Sheep, marmots and pikas are in the higher elevations. Occasional caribou will travel around the river bars. In the late summer, soapberries ripen, and bears are often seen feeding on them.

**Total Overnight Campers allowed:** Sections 9-six. Section 10-six.

Notes:

_____

_____

_____

_____

_____

_____

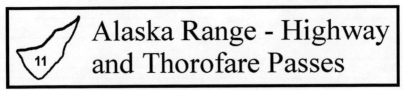

# Alaska Range - Highway and Thorofare Passes

**Mile 54-64. Topography Map B-1**

South of the Park Road, between the Toklat and Thorofare river drainages, are high and low hills with small creeks flowing south. These small creeks flow over gravel bars and are easy to cross. Scree slopes bound the streams and caution is advised.

Two passes, Highway and Thorofare, open south of the Park Road and divide the drainages. The hills are mostly scree slopes with patches of tundra, and some are climbable. The hills often give a great view of the drainage area and the higher mountains of the Alaska Range.

**Established Trails:** None.
**Mountains:** Gravel Mountain (5,936'), Stony Dome, and the base of Green Dome.
**Animals:** Caribou traverse the two passes parallel to the road. Grizzly bears are found in the low to middle elevations. Dall sheep can be seen in the hills.
**Fishing:** None.
**Total Overnight Campers allowed:** Two.
  Notes:

_____

_____

_____

_____

_____

# Alaska Range - Mount Eielson & Upper Thorofare River

**Mile 64-68. Topography Map B-1**

Most visitors and hikers visit the Eielson Visitor Center. All park buses stop here to allow people to stretch their legs and do a little hiking before resuming their tour of the park. Bathrooms, water, and a gift shop are in the visitor's center, but no food.

Section twelve contains two streams that join north of Mount Eielson. These streams are the Thorofare River and Upper Glacier Creek. The Thorofare River flows south from Sunset Glacier at the base of Sunset Peak. Sunrise Creek, flowing from Sunrise Glacier, enters the Thorofare about four miles downstream from the headwaters. The Thorofare River turns west and flows across the mile-wide Thorofare Bar at the base of Eielson Bluffs and Eielson Visitor Center.

After passing west of Mount Eielson, Upper Glacier Creek flows into the Thorofare River. In contrast to the wide glacial valley that the Thorofare River travels along, Upper Glacier Creek flows through a narrow channel between the eastern hills and the Muldrow Glacier moraine. This creek is crossable. Glacier Creek originates at the base of Anderson Pass, one of the few passes in this part of the Alaska Range. Halfway to the Thorofare Bar, Intermittent, Crystal, and Wolverine Creeks converge at Upper Glacier Creek.

The Thorofare River can be treacherous to cross, depending upon the location. Upstream from the Thorofare Bar, the river usually flows swiftly in one or two channels and finding secure footing is difficult. The river along Thorofare Bar (down stream from the Eielson Visitor

Center) is very braided, and crossing here makes the few extra miles well worth it.

**Mountains:** Scott Peak (8,828 feet) and Sunset peak (7,182 feet) both can be dangerous in early and late season depending upon route. Most routes include some type of glacier travel, and have well-deserved reputations for terrible weather. Other mountains which are easier and do not require much technical abilities are Mount Eielson (5285 feet), Read Mountain (7,165 feet), and Bald Mountain (5,285 feet). Anderson Pass provides a route to the south side of the Alaska Range, crossing it at 5,400 feet.

**Glaciers**

Many glaciers in this area can be safely climbed including Sunrise Glacier, the smallest glacier in the area, which is about three miles up a canyon from the junction of Thorofare River and Sunrise Creek. Also, Sunset Glacier, visible from the Eielson Visitor Center and only five miles from it, is climbable. To hike to Sunset Glacier from the Eielson Center, you must cross the Thorofare River, because of a large cutback, or climb for 500 feet to hike around it. Upper Glacier Creek may be running high but is usually not difficult to cross. Traveling upstream along this creek necessitates crossings, again due to cutbacks

Muldrow Glacier is the largest northflowing glacier in Alaska and the original route to summit of Denali. This glacier ends in this section of the park. In this unit, the glacier seems more gravel than ice, but under all the scree are all the same glacial hazards. Crossing the Muldrow to Pirate Creek can be very dangerous, especially near flowing water, which usually indicates an ice channel beneath

**Established Trails:**

*Mount Eielson*-14.0 miles-Trail head on the right of Eielson Visitor Center at mile 65. Easy to strenuous hike. Mount Eielson's summit is 5,802 feet. Good place to see bears, sheep, and caribou.

*Toklat River-Sunrise Glacier Trail*–This trail runs through section 12, but can not be reached directly from the Park Road. Must enter through section 10 or 13.

**Animals:** Caribou can be seen traveling along the river bars, or an occasional grizzly bear. Dall sheep are in the high elevations. Marmots and pikas play in the hills and lower regions of Anderson Pass.

**Fishing:** None.

**Total Overnight Campers allowed:** Four.

Notes:

_____

_____

_____

_____

_____

_____

_____

_____

_____

_____

_____

_____

_____

_____

_____

_____

_____

_____

_____

_____

_____

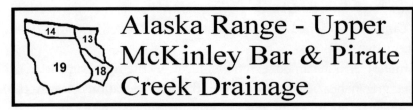

## Alaska Range - Upper McKinley Bar & Pirate Creek Drainage

**Mile 68-82. Topography Maps: Mt. Mckinley B-1, B-2, A-2**

Pirate Creek area extends west from the Muldrow Glacier to Coal Creek and south from the Park Road to the high hills north of the Muldrow Glacier. Muldrow Glacier is the south and east boundary of the region. The area between the Park Road and the McKinley River bar is gentle, with sloping tundra flat leading down to the river. The lower end of Thorofare River enters McKinley River on this broad bar. Upstream six miles from the junction of these rivers, the Thorofare River flows through Thorofare Gorge, a four mile-long run where the river becomes a single channel. On the McKinley Bar, the river braids across the one to two mile-wide bar. Turtle Hill, a gentle tundra ridge approximately 1,000 feet above the bar, divides the McKinley Bar and the East Fork of Clearwater Creek.

Turtle Hill and the slopes of the Park Road have a variety of tundra with willow groves and many tundra ponds. The Clearwater and other creeks south of Turtle Hill usually flow along river bars. The high hills have some scree slopes.

Numerous creeks flow into the Clearwater. These creeks, which include Coal and Pirate Creeks, originate in the hills to the south, which reach a height of more than 7,000 feet and are generally composed mainly of scree.

The McKinley River is among the most difficult to cross on the north side of the Alaska Range. Along the McKinley Bar the river can vary from two to 15 different channels. These channels can range from ankle to waist deep and at times are uncrossable. The Clearwater usually poses no difficulty.

The Thorofare River is especially dangerous to negotiate because of its single channel and speed. Try to cross the Thorofare below Thorofare Gorge.

**Established Trails:**
*Anderson Pass*: 13.0 miles, Section 13.
Start the hike two miles west of the Eielson Visitor Center at mile 67. Moderate hike with stream crossings. Good mountain scenery with frequent sightings of bears, caribou and Dall sheep along the way.
*Toklat River-Sunrise Glacier Trail*: This trail ends in section 13 but starts in section 10.
**Mountains:** Some hills in this area offer great views of the Alaska Range but there are no mountaineering peaks to climb.
**Animals:** Caribou can be seen on the McKinley Bar and Turtle Hill. Grizzlies are also common throughout this area. The tundra ponds in this area are home to beaver, muskrat and migratory waterfowl.
**Fishing:** None.
**Total Overnight Campers allowed:** Section 13–four, Section 14–four, Section 18–four, and Section 19–four.
Notes:

_____

_____

_____

_____

_____

_____

_____

_____

_____

# Alaska Range - McGonagall Pass

**Topography Maps Mt. McKinley A-2 & B-2**
**Near Wonder Lake at Mile 85**

The McGonagall Pass section holds historical significance. For many years it was the way mountaineers climbing the Muldrow Glacier accessed Denali. Dog sleds and packhorses were used to haul climbing gear. The two and a half-mile McKinley Bar Trail goes through a large spruce forest and ends at the river bar. Here, the McKinley River can be extremely hazardous. Plan on three or four hours to cross. Be very careful around any moving water on the Muldrow Glacier. After crossing the river, the rest of the way to the pass includes a traverse of Turtle Hill and its tundra ponds. Two miles below McGonagall Pass (5,700') you will find the fork to Oastler Pass (5,500') on the East Side of Oastler Mountain. From these passes are superb views of the upper Muldrow Glacier and Denali, and the other peaks of the Alaska Range.

**Established Trails:** The McKinley Bar Trail starts a half-mile east of Wonder Lake Campground. Overnight camping along this trail, in its vicinity or on the north half of McKinley Rivers is prohibited.
**Mountains:** The southern end of the section contains McGonagall Mountain and Oastler Mountain, both in the 6,500 foot range. These mountains are molehills compare to the 20,230 foot peak just ahead.
**Animals:** Moose may roam in the spruce forest along the McKinley River. Caribou wander throughout this area and are seen often on the McKinley Bar and Turtle Hill. Grizzlies are also common. The tundra

ponds on Turtle Hill and south of the road are home to beaver and the resting-place for migratory waterfowl.

**Fishing:** None.

**Total Overnight Campers allowed:** Four.

    Notes:

_____

_____

_____

_____

_____

_____

_____

_____

_____

_____

_____

_____

_____

_____

_____

_____

_____

_____

_____

_____

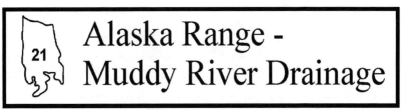

# Alaska Range - Muddy River Drainage

**Topography Maps: Mt. McKinley B-2, B-3, A-2, A-3**
**Mile 85 near Wonder Lake**

Section 21 encompasses three tributaries of the McKinley River-Muddy River, Clearwater Creek, and McLeod Creek. The eastern end of this section includes the western end of the Turtle Hill ridge and Clearwater Creek. The northern boundary is the McKinley River Bar, from approximately four miles upstream from the junction of the Clearwater to the beginning of Eagle Gorge. The western boundary is McLeod Creek and the southern boundary is the Alaska Range. This large area rises from an elevation of 1,600 feet on the McKinley River to more than 6,000 feet in the foothills of the Alaska Range. It is directly north of Denali and the Wickersham Wall.

Though the upper section of Clearwater Creek is a gravel bar; the last few miles of the large waterway flow through a narrow canyon. The Muddy River flows across a large gravel bar, as does the McKinley before Eagle Gorge. The upper few miles of the Muddy is similar to parts of Thorofare Gorge.

**Established Trails:** None
**Mountains:** This area has no peaks, but provides access to peaks near Denali.
**Animals:** Caribou and grizzly bears can be found in this area in the summer. The tundra ponds may have beaver and other aquatic mammals.
**Fishing:** None.
**Total Overnight Campers allowed:** Eight.

Notes:

# Alaska Range - The Far West End Area

**Topography Maps: Mt. McKinley A-3, B-3, A-4, B-4, A-5, B-5, Talkeetna D-4. (Three day hike from Wonder Lake)**

Section 22 is the largest section in Denali National Park. This section is not for the average day hiker; it is a two-three day-hike just to get to this section from Wonder Lake. The West End is the generic term given to these sections west of the Muddy River. Few people travel to this area during the hiking season. Though it often appeals to true wilderness lovers, access is difficult. Lower elevations in the north are comprised of dense taiga spruce stretching as far north as the eye can see. As you travel towards the Alaska Range and south, you will gradually enter the foothills of the range. Many large glaciers and their respective river systems flow north between notches in the foothills of the Alaska Range.

Taiga forests cover the flats, but above the 2,000-foot level you will find open dry tundra. This tundra and exposed rock dominate the flanks of the foothills, which are mostly scree slopes. Most streams and rivers flow over gravel bars for easy hiking.

Many large and small glaciers extend over the southern part of this region. The three largest glaciers in this section are Herror, Foraker, and Straightaway. Smaller glaciers include Birch Creek and the glaciers of Peters Dome. You can access the high peaks of the Alaska Range via Peters Pass to Peters Basin on the Peters Glacier

River and stream crossings are numerous in this unit. Foraker and Herron rivers and Slippery. Birch, and Highpower creeks in this section all have crossing ranging from difficult to very easy.

**Established Trails:** None
**Mountains:** The south area of section 22 contains the 10,000' foothills north of the Alaska Range. These foothills are not easy climb.
**Animals:** Caribou and grizzly bears are often spotted above the treeline. Black bears can be found in the taiga. Marmots are found in the foothills.
**Fishing:** None.
**Total Overnight Campers allowed:** unlimited.
   Notes:

_____

_____

_____

_____

_____

_____

_____

_____

_____

_____

_____

_____

_____

_____

_____

_____

_____

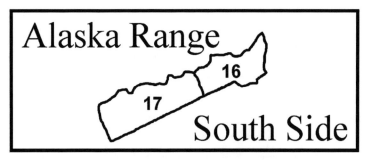

**George Parks Highway provides access between Cantwell and Broad Pass Topography Maps: Healy B-4, B-5, A-5, B-6, A-6, Mt. McKinley B-1. No direct access from Park Road**

The Nenana River on the west bounds sections 16 and 17. These sections are then bounded on the east by West Fork Glacier and bounded on the north by the Alaska Range Divide. Not many hikers make it to these sections. Hikers should go to the ranger's desk at the park's entrance for information.

**Established Trails:** None
**Mountains:** Mountaineering is not advised in this area, but some smaller peaks up to 6,000 feet offer good climbs.
**Glaciers:** Cantwell Glacier flows north to one branch of the Teklanika River and also flows south to form Cantwell Creek. The West Fork Glacier is the largest, trailing a scree line that travels to Anderson Pass.
**Animals:** Caribou, Dall sheep, and grizzly bear inhabit the area. Moose feed in the Windy Creek area where the vegetation is thick.
**Fishing:** None.
**Total Overnight Campers allowed:** Section 16–eight, Section 17–eight.
  Notes:

**Mile 1-15. Topography Maps: Healy C-5, D-5**

Mount Healy, which is also known as Healy Ridge, runs along a 10-mile ridge in the Outer Range. This ridge extends from the Nenana River in the east to the Savage River canyon in the west. Its jagged peaks range from 5,000' to over 6,000'. Numerous small creeks flow south to the Jenny and Hines creek drainages and north to Ewe and Dry creek drainages. The Savage River flows through a canyon north through the Outer Range. Mount Healy walls this canyon to the east and by Primrose Ridge to the west. This three mile long canyon ends in a gravel bar.

**Established Trails:** There are two trails in this area–Healy Overlook and Savage Canyon. Healy Overlook Trail begins in the park hotel area and climbs halfway up the East End of Mount Healy. The Savage Canyon Trail begins at the Savage River Bridge along the Park Road and winds down the West Side of the river. The latter is unmaintained. The south-eastern section of this area located around park headquarters and the hotel, is day-use only, and overnight camping is prohibited.

**Mountains:** Climbing Mount Healy (5,069') is possible, but beware of loose rock. Due to difficulty and exposure, a traverse of the ridge is rarely done.

**Animals:** Moose commonly roam the area's spruce forest at the lower elevations. Sheep range throughout the upper reaches of Mount Healy. Grizzly bear and some black bear frequent this area. Caribou sometimes migrate through this area early in the season near the Savage River.

**Fishing:** None.
**Total Overnight Campers allowed:** Section 24–four, Section 25–four.
  Notes:

_____

_____

_____

_____

_____

_____

_____

_____

_____

_____

_____

_____

_____

_____

_____

_____

_____

_____

_____

_____

_____

_____

_____

_____

# Outer Range - Primrose Ridge & Mount Wright

**Mile 15 to mile 22. Topography Maps: Healy C-5, C-6, D-5, D-6**

Primrose Ridge runs five miles east to west between the Savage and Sanctuary rivers, which parallels the Park Road. This flat topped ridge, contrasting with neighboring Mount Healy, reaches an elevation of 5,069 feet. Several small streams flow off the ridge to form Pinto Creek on the north side. Small streams to the south flow into the Savage or Sanctuary river drainages. Mount Wright is a dome shaped mountain between the Sanctuary and Teklanika rivers, which flow through narrow gorges on either side of Mount Wright. These river canyons are narrow and steep and should be avoided.

**Established Trails:** Primrose Ridge-4.1 miles, and Mount Margaret-2.3 miles.

**Mountains:** Mount Wright (4,275 feet). Hikes up Primrose Ridge and Mount Wright can hardly be called "mountaineering," but both afford incredible views.

**Animals:** Dall Sheep in the higher elevations.

**Fishing:** None.

**Total Overnight Campers allowed:** Four.

Notes:

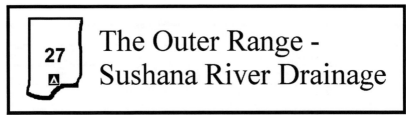

# The Outer Range - Sushana River Drainage

**Mile 25-31. Topography Maps: Healy C-6, D-6**

In section 27, the Sushana River originates from six streams flowing north out of a ridge from the Sushana Hills. The Sushana Hills' ridge reaches only 4,510 feet, and parallels the Teklanika River. This ridge forms the west wall of the Teklanika River canyon near Mount Wright. The Sushana Hills are part of the Outer Range, and the Sushana River flows north out of the park. North of the Sushana Hills along the river is a series of low hills interspersed with low tundra.

The higher elevations of this section are composed of dry tundra and exposed rock. In the lower elevations, the land consists of wet tundra.

The Teklanika River flows along a large bar in this area, and safe crossings are available. Crossing the Sushana River is only hazardous during spring high water conditions.

**Established Trails:** None
**Mountains:** Sushana Hills top out at 4,500 feet.
**Animals:** Sheep in the upper elevations. Caribou sometimes run through the river bar areas, and occasional grizzly are found in the lower elevations.
**Fishing:** None.
**Total Overnight Campers allowed:** Four.

Notes:

# Outer Range - Sable Mountain Area

**Mile 31-43. Topography Maps: Healy C-6**

Sable Mountain dominates sections 28 and 29. This area encompasses drainages and mountains in the Outer Range bordered by the Teklanika River and Igloo Canyon on the east, and by the East Fork River on the west. The mountain towers over Sable Pass and the Park Road. The other notable peak in this section is Igloo Mountain, which is more than 5,000 feet. Both mountain areas consist of dry tundra and exposed rock.

Two drainages are found to the north of Sable Mountain. These drainages include Tributary Creek, which flows into the East Fork River, and Big Creek, which flows into the Teklanika River. Many other streams drain east and west into these rivers. The East Fork River covers a wide gravel bar from the Park Road downstream for approximately eight miles where it enters the narrow gorge of East Fork Canyon for about seven miles. The hills of the Outer Range in this area are some of the most colorful and varied in the park.

In the southern area of section 29 is the Sable Pass Wildlife Closure Area. Entry into this area is prohibited except by travel on the Park Road.

**Established Trails (Section 29):**
*Sable Mountain Trail:* This trail is 3.3 miles past Igloo Campground.
*Igloo Mountain Trail:* The trailhead is at mile 34, just south of Igloo Campground.
**Mountains:** Sable Mountain (5,923')

**Animals:** Dall sheep can be spotted in the hills of the Outer Range. Grizzlies are common throughout these sections. Caribou can be found wondering along the river bars.
**Fishing:** None.
**Total Overnight Campers allowed:** Section 28–eight, Section 29–four.
Notes:

_____

_____

_____

_____

_____

_____

_____

_____

_____

_____

_____

_____

_____

_____

_____

_____

_____

_____

_____

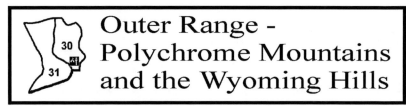

# Outer Range - Polychrome Mountains and the Wyoming Hills

**Mile 43–53. Topographic Maps: Healy C-6, Mount McKinley C-1**

Sections 30 and 31 primarily consist of the Wyoming Hills, which comprise the heart of the Outer Range. These hills border the park road and stretch 13 miles from north to south. The two peaks of these hills are Polychrome Mountain at 5,790 feet and Cabin Peak at 4,961 feet. These sections contain many small streams and a few small ponds throughout the hills. The shuttle buses stop here, and restrooms are available. This is an ideal hiking area for a few hours or several days. Hikers are rewarded with great views of the Polychrome glaciers on the south side of the park road.

**Established Trails:** None
**Mountains:** Polychrome (5,790'), Cabin Peak (4,961')
**Animals:** Dall sheep abound on the hills and there is a high concentration of grizzly bears throughout the region; marmots play in the higher, rocky elevations.
**Fishing:** None.
**Total Overnight Campers allowed:** Section 30-six, Section 31–four.
  Notes:

_____

_____

_____

_____

_____

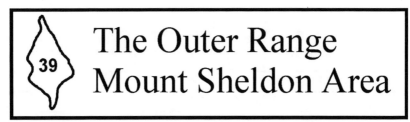

## The Outer Range Mount Sheldon Area

**Section 39. Topographic Maps: Mount McKinley C-1, D-1**

Mount Sheldon is located in the Outer Range between the Toklat River and lower Stony Creek. An impressive mountain, it overlooks the flats to the north of the range. To the west, lower Stony Creek flows between Mount Sheldon and an unnamed ridge to the west. At the northern end of this section Stony Creek enters the Clearwater Fork near the Stampede Mine Area.

Both the Toklat and Stony have gravel bars and braided channels for easier crossings. During high water, however, the Toklat varies from hazardous to uncrossable.

Mount Sheldon and other hills of the Outer Range are the "high spots" in this area, affording excellent views of the vicinity.

There is no direct access from the Park Road to this section. All access is through other sections.

**Established Trails:** None.
**Mountains:** Mount Sheldon (5,670').
**Animals:** Sheep can sometimes be found on Mount Sheldon. In the lowland moose, grizzly bear, and black bear often roam. Caribou also frequent the area.
**Fishing:** None.
**Total Overnight Campers allowed:** Four.

Notes:

# The Outer Range - Upper Stoney Creek

**Mile 53 to 68. Topographic Maps: Mount McKinley B-1, C-1**

The eastern part of section 33 is known as the Upper Stony Creek area; it falls between the Toklat River on the east, Boundary Creek to the west, north of the Park Road, and south of Mount Sheldon. Stony Hill, which is between Hight and Thorofare passes, is located in the western third of this area.. The creeks meet north of Stony Hill and Stony Creek and flow for approximately six miles until Boundary Creek enters them. Stony Creek can be hard to cross downstream but usually poses no problems to hikers. These creeks are the main drainages in this area, located between the 5,000-foot to 6,000-foot foothills of the Outer Range. Other small streams flow west and east. Thorofare Ridge towers over Eielson Visitor Center at 5,629 feet. The Park Road is south of Thorofare Ridge, and the upper reaches of Moose Creek are to the north.

Most of this area is above treeline. Dry tundra prevails and upper elevations have exposed rock and scree slopes. Some dwarf birch mixed in with dry tundra cling to the higher slopes. Some ridges afford a good climb, but scree may pose a hazard.

**Established Trails:** Stony Creek Base Camp Trails. Various distances.
**Mountains:** Stony Hill (4,508'), Thorofare Ridge (5,629').
**Animals:** Dall sheep roam on Thorofare Ridge. Caribou commonly migrate through Thorofare and Highway passes. Grizzlies are also common.
**Fishing:** None.
**Total Overnight Campers allowed:** Four.

Notes:

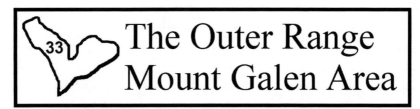

# The Outer Range
# Mount Galen Area

**Mile 68 to Mile 72. Topographic Maps: Mount McKinley B-1**

Mount Galen dominates this section. This rounded, dome shaped peak is northwest of Thorofare Ridge and is the last true peak of the Outer Range. West of Mount Galen, the land is lower and more rolling in character up to the Kantishna Hills. The upper part of Moose Creek flows between Mount Galen and Thorofare Ridge. A low pass exists between Moose Creek and an unnamed creek to the east that flows into Stony Creek. Most of the creeks in this area are easy to cross.

The vegetation consists of low to high brush along Moose Creek. Low brush fades away to dry tundra when climbing Mount Galen. Wet tundra and occasional thickets of willow and tundra ponds cover the tundra flats and hills surrounding Mount Galen.

**Established Trails:** None.
**Mountains:** Mount Galen (5,022') is a simple climb from the northwest side. The southeast side is much steeper and is covered in loose rock.
**Animals:** Caribou travel along the creek and tundra, and moose and grizzly also range over the area.
**Fishing:** None.
**Total Overnight Campers allowed:** Four.
Notes:

## 38 Outer Range - Lower Toklat & East Fork Rivers

**Topographic Maps: Mount McKinley C-1, D-1, Healy C-6, D-6**

In order to get to this section, you must hike completely though sections 31 or 32. It encompasses the Toklat and East Fork Rivers north of the Outer Range and south of the Denali Wilderness boundary. The two rivers meander over large gravel bars heading north. Tundra plains slowly rise from the rivers south toward the Wyoming hills.

Although the rivers flow over gravel bars, the Toklat and East Fork rivers significantly increase in water volume downstream and may be difficult to cross.

**Established Trails:** None.
**Mountains:** In the southern end are the Wyoming Hills which range from 4,000 to 5,000 feet.
**Animals:** Moose, caribou, and grizzly bear are throughout the area.
**Fishing:** None.
**Total Overnight Campers allowed:** Six.

Notes:

_____

_____

_____

_____

_____

_____

_____

_____

**Topographic Maps: Mount McKinley B-1, B-2, C-2**
**Mile 72-80**

Moose Creek starts in section 34 and flows west on a gravel bar between low, tundra-covered hills in section 35. You cannot get easily lost in this area because of the low tree cover and the rolling hills. As Moose Creek reaches the southern end of the Kantishna Hills, the main fork is joined by North Fork creek. A couple of miles beyond this junction, Jumbo Creek links up from the south in section 36. At this point Moose Creek enters the primary area of the Kantishna Mining District. The tundra of the lower elevations makes it difficult to travel cross-country. The higher elevations are less boggy and easier to hike

Moose Creek is the only large water body, and as you travel downstream it becomes increasingly difficult to cross.

The northern parts of these sections back up to the Kantishna Mining District, which mining area is active and privately owned. Please respect private property and stay away from mining claims.

**Established Trails:** *Moose Creek Station Trail* (Section 35)-3.5 miles. The trailhead is at mile 74. Easy to moderate hike to the Moose Creek Ranger Station (station not for public use).
**Mountains:** Mount Abba (3,195') is in section 34. Mount Galen (5,022') is just north of the Eielson Visitor Center
**Animals:** Moose range throughout the lowlands often sharing the ponds with beaver and assorted waterfowl. Caribou occasionally roam the area.
**Fishing** Some Grayling in Moose Creek.

**Total Overnight Campers allowed:** Section 34 & 35–four, section 36–two.

Notes:

_____

_____

_____

_____

_____

_____

_____

_____

_____

_____

_____

_____

_____

_____

_____

_____

_____

_____

_____

_____

_____

_____

_____

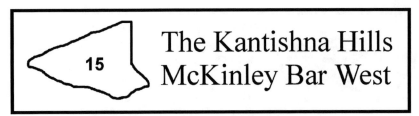

## The Kantishna Hills
## McKinley Bar West

**Topographic Maps: Mount McKinley B-2, B-3**
**Access from Wonder Lake Campground**

Section 15 is triangle-shaped, with Wonder Lake to the east, the Kantishna Hills to the north and McKinley River to the south. There is a series of low tundra hills interspersed with small and medium-sized tundra ponds. At the southeastern corner is an open grassy swamp. At drought or dry times, the swamp provides for easy, level walking. Make sure you have mosquito nets and plenty of insect repellant while hiking through this section of the park.

**Established Trails:** None.
**Mountains:** A series of low tundra hills from 2,500 to 3,000 feet.
**Animals:** Beaver and waterfowl are found in the numerous ponds in this section. Caribou, moose, grizzly and black bear also inhabit the area.
**Fishing:** None.
**Total Overnight Campers allowed:** Four.
Notes:

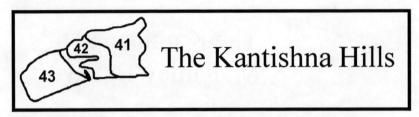

**Limited shuttle service is available past Wonder Lake Campground.
Topographic Maps: Mount McKinley C-1, C-2, D-1, D-2**

The Kantishna Hills are a series of low mountain ranges extending 30 miles. These hills have several prominent peaks, which include Brooker Mountain, Busia Mountain, Glacier Peak, Spruce Peak, and Kankone Peak. Most of the summits are above treeline and are surrounded by taiga forests, while dry tundra covers the tops. Numerous small streams flow either east into the Toklat drainage or west into the Moose Creek and Bearpaw drainages. Lower Moose Creek passes through a small mining community called Kantishna. In the north end of section 41, the abandoned Stampede mine site is located just north from the junction of Clearwater Fork and the Toklat River.

Most streams in these sections have numerous safe-crossing spots. Moose Creek, on the other hand, can be difficult to cross at high water. Most stream banks are either thick with brush or piled high with mining debris.

Mining Area:

The Kantishna Mining District is an active mining area and is private property. Most of the side streams in the Kantishna Hills have been mined. Abandoned and active trails and old, unimproved roads wind throughout the hills. Stay away from all mining claims and inactive mines.

**Established Trails:** None.

**Mountains:** Section 43–Brooker Mountain (3,774'), Busia Mountain (3,246'). Section 42–Wickersham Dome. Section 41–Glacier Peak (4,310'), Spruce Peak (4,753') and Kankone Peak (4,987')

**Animals:** Black and Grizzly bear roam this area. You may also spot an occasional moose. At nearby Wonder Lake and reflection pond moose are often seen early in the mornings.

**Fishing:** Grayling can be found in Clearwater Fork and Moose Creek.

**Total Overnight Campers allowed:** Section 41–12, section 42–12, and section 43–12.

Notes:

# Chapter 10

## *Denali National Park Kennel*

In 1921 Denali, then Mount McKinley National Park, had its first park ranger. Known as "the Seventy Mile Kid," Harry Karstens was an Alaskan adventurer, mountain climber (first to summit Denali), miner, guide and mailman. His main duties were to establish park boundaries and protect the park's populations of Dall Sheep and caribou from poachers. Since the park is covered in snow for seven or eight months a year, with brutal winters, dogs were the only animals that could help rangers do their job.

> "-45 degrees. Too cold to take horses out, hauled a load of coal from the railroad station to headquarters with dogs."
>
> *-Superintendent's Report, January 1924*

Through the 1930s and into the war years, sled dogs remained an essential mode of transportation, but the world was changing and with it transportation.

> "All patrols were made in the M-7 snow jeep which worked satisfactorily. However, park ranger Rumohr, an experienced dog team driver, says about the snow jeeps, 'The distance traveled in a day over unbroken trails exceeds the best a dog team could perform, but the dogs have less trouble with their carburetors.'"
>
> *-Superintendent's Report, January 1946*

The park continued to keep a small number of dogs for summer demonstrations. In the 1960s, the decision was made to revitalize the kennels, and Denali became one of the few places with sled dogs as a primary form of transportation. Dog-mushing had become nearly extinct in Alaska, but experienced people were found, old timers shared their knowledge, and the Denali National Park Kennels became a vital part of operations, summer and winter. In the winter, Denali rangers still conduct regular dog sled patrols and in the summer, the dogs, in daily dog sledding demonstrations, show their talents for visitors.

Visitors can meet sled dogs and visit the dog sledding museum. The demonstrations are at 10:00 am, 2:00pm, and 4:00pm. The park service provides shuttle buses that pick up at Riley Creek Campground, the Visitor Center, and the Denali National Park Hotel. The shuttle is strongly recommended since vehicle parking at the kennel is unavailable.

## Dog Sledding Terms

*Mush:* This term comes from the misuse of the French word "marche" ("to go"). Dog mushers heard the French Canadian trappers using the word marche to make their dogs run. They interpreted it as 'mush.' Modern dog drivers don't use this term, instead preferring "Hike" or simply "All Right" to move their dogs.

*Husky:* This is the name most dog drivers apply to all northern breeds.

*Alaskan Malamute:* Probably the oldest breed of sled dog, now used mostly for freighting and weight pulling than for racing, because of its size and weight. It can reach 100 or more pounds.

*Siberian Husky:* The "classic" sled dog. These are smaller than Malamutes, weighing 40 to 70 pounds. They were brought to Alaska from Siberia at the turn of the century.

*Alaskan Husky:* A term that applies to racing dogs of mixed breed. These dogs usually share ancestry with the Siberian Husky and some type of hound. Greyhounds, black and tans, and coonhounds have all been used to produce some of the fastest racing sled dogs of today.

*Gangline:* The main line from the sled to which all the dogs are attached.

*Gee:* The command given to the dogs to make a right turn. This is an old muleskinner's term.

*Haw:* The command used to make a left turn.

*Come Gee or Come Haw:* The command used to make the dogs turn 180-degrees.

*Whoa:* The command to stop.

*On By:* This phrase is short for "go on by" to send a team past another team from behind or to pass a trailside distraction.

*Handler:* There are two meanings to this term. One is the owner and trainer of the pull dogs. The term is also used to describe the person or persons helping a musher get his/her team to the starting line.

*Pedaling:* When the musher keeps one foot on the runner of the sled while pushing with the other foot to help speed the team along.

*Trail!:* Request from one musher to another for the right of way when one team wishes to pass another.

*Drop the Dogs:* Term used when the musher is going to lift the dogs out of the dog truck so they can exercise, be fed or watered or go to the bathroom. When finished, he will lift the dogs back into the dog truck. The complete process is called a "Dog Drop."

**Dog Sledding Tours and Expeditions (*See also* "Winter Activities")**

**Husky Homestead Tours**
Address: PO Box 48, Denali National Park, AK 99755
Phone: 907-683-2904
Email: *Info@huskyhomestead.com*
Website: *www.huskyhomestead.com*

Step back from the crowds and join an intimate group for a personal tour of the homestead and kennel of three-time Iditarod champion Jeff King and his wife, well-known wildlife artist Donna Gates King. You can meet champion sled dogs, Visit with puppies and see summer training in action, and enjoy a narrated kennel tour. Transportation is provided from area hotels

See arctic survival gear, sleds and racing equipment. Learn about state-of-the-art dog-powered training carousels and heated dog barns. Enjoy 20 years of Alaska dog-mushing stories with highlights including freight-hauling on Denali and crossing the finish line in Nome with a champion Iditarod team.

Jeff King is recognized as the "Winningest Musher in the World." His victories include not only the 1,160 mile Iditarod Sled dog race in 1993, 1996, and 1998, but also over two dozen first place finishes in races all across Alaska.

Donna is a well-known artist whose art portrays her intimate involvement with mushing and her love and respect of nature.

The Goose Lake Studio gallery and booking office, located between Denali Princess Hotel and Lynx Creek Pizza adjacent to Denali Windsong Hotel, will be open 8:00 AM to 10:00 PM daily.

Vans pick up at most area hotels as well as at the Goose Lake Studio gallery.

# Chapter 11

## *Climbing Denali*

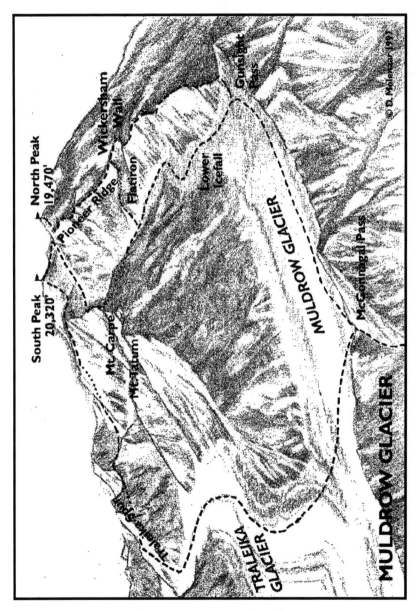

**The early routes up Denali**

Today, between 300 to 600 climbers a year reach the summit of Denali, most of whom are airlifted to base camp at 14,000 feet. Historically, four Denali climbs hold a mark of significance: one where the wrong summit was climbed, one where the true summit was climbed, and one achieved and accomplished by seven huskies and a sled.

Dr. Frederick Albert Cook (1865-1940) was a pioneer in American Polar exploration. He spent two decades in expeditions to both polar regions and subarctic Alaska between 1891 and 1909. Dr. Cook made two ascents on Denali: a failed attempt in 1903 and one "claimed" in 1906.

In Cook's written description of the successful ascent, his account becomes more grandiose and vague after he reaches the head of Ruth Glacier, which is several thousand of feet below the summit. Once reaching the summit, Cook tells about "the heaven-scraped granite of the top" and "the dazzling witness of the frosted granite blocks." The problem with this description is Denali does not have any exposed rock above 19,000 feet. He also mentions reaching the summit on a clear day, but fails to mention anything about the magnificence of Mount Foraker, otherwise known as Denali's Wife, only a few miles away.

Not only did Dr. Cook claim he climbed Denali, he also claimed he reached the North Pole. This claim was proven false. But, today, the FREDERICK A. COOK SOCIETY, a nonprofit, educational organization, recognizes his scientific and geographic accomplishments.

In 1910, an expedition known as the Sourdough Climb successfully climbed the lower peak of Denali. Unfortunately, from a distance the North Peak looks like the highest peak of Denali, but is actually 500 feet lower than the South Peak.

On June 7, 1913, the Karstens-Stuck expedition conquered the true peak. With Harry Karstens and Rev. Hudson Stuck were Robert Tatum and Walter Harper. From their vantagepoint atop the South Peak they could look across to the North Peak and see the flagpole left by the Sourdough Party. Harry Karstens went on to become the first superintendent of Denali National Park in 1917.

In 1979, Joe Redington (founder of the modern day Iditarod) and Susan Butcher (three-time winner of the Iditarod) were fresh from their ninth and 10th place finishes of the 1979 Iditarod. The two decided to take a team of dogs up Denali. After tackling the 1100-mile dog race, they thought climbing Denali with a sled team could be achieved. But, neither of them had climbing experience. So, with the help of expedition guide Ray Genet and photographer Robert Stapleton, seven huskies, 800 pounds of dog food and 800 pounds of people, Joe and Susan headed up the mountain.

Veterinarians said the dogs could not survive, but probably not many vets think a team of dogs could survive the 1100-mile sled race in-20 degree weather, either. As it turned out, the dogs were going not too slow, but too fast: Why was this a problem? The climbers could not keep up. Areas that could take four hours to climb were done by dogs in 45 minutes. The weather on the climb was horrible. Thirty days out of the 44-day expedition it was below zero and some days hit–40 with 100mph gales. Down glacial areas, sleds would sometimes overtake the dogs. During the final ascent, Joe and Susan found that seven dogs were too many, so they left three with a woman who had altitude sickness and camped below at 14,000 feet. Once the team reached the summit, they were blessed with a clear, windless day at–8 degrees and incredible panorama view of the Alaska Range.

## DNP Mountaineering Timeline

1903–First attempt of Denali: Judge James Wickersham and four partners reach 8,100' on a spur of what is now called Wickersham Wall.

1903–The First Cook Expedition: Made the first circumnavigation of Denali, covering hundreds of miles on foot and horseback.

1906–The Cook-Parker Expedition: An eight-man party with Dr. Cook and Professor Herschel C. Parker was the first to explore the southwest approaches to Denali.

1906–The Cook-Barrille Expedition: Also known as the "Famous Fake Ascent". Dr. Cook, Edward Barrille, and prospector John Dokkin claimed they made a speedy ascent via Ruth Glacier (named after Dr. Cook's wife). They actually only reached a 5,300 foot peak, 19 miles from the summit.

1910–The Sourdough expedition led by Thomas Lloyd. The members of this expedition carried a 16-foot spruce flagpole and planted it on the wrong peak.

1910-Claude E. Rusk and the Mazamas party made the first ascents of Mount Barrile and Pittock Pass of the Alaska Range.

1910–The Parker-Browne Expedition made the first ascent of Explorers' Peak of the Alaska Range.

1912–The second Parker-Browne Expedition led by Dr. Herschel Parker and Belmore Brown came within 200 yards and 150 feet of the top of Denali when a tremendous storm forced them back.

1913–The Stuck-Karstens Expedition was the first successful ascent of Denali on June 7, 1913.

1930–The first flight over the summit of Denali was made by Matt Neimenen and Cecil Higgins of Alaskan Airways.

1932–Joe Crosson made the first airplane glacier landing.

1932–Second ascent of Denali was made by Alfred Lindley, Harry Like, Erling Strom and Grant Pearson.

1932–Allen Carpe and Theodore Koven were the first men to lose their lives attempting to climb Denali.

1934–First ascent of Mount Foraker, Denali's "wife," was made by Charles Houston, T. Graham Brown, and G.C. Waterston.

1936–First photographic exploration of Denali, done by the National Geographic Society-Pan American Airways, made over 200 photos of Denali and Foraker from a large aerial camera.

1944–First ascent of Mount Deception. Grant Pearson led a 44-man expedition to a site where a C-47 plane had crashed on the side of the mountain.

1945–First ascent of Mount Silverthrone: Bradford Washburn led a five-man party for the U.S. Air force. Camped on the summit for five days.

1947–On June 6, Barbara Washburn stood at the top of Denali: the first woman to do so.

1949–The first Helicopter reconnaissance, sponsored by the Navy, landed a helicopter at 6,000 feet on Muldrow Glacier.

1951–The first ascent of Denali's West Buttress was led by Bradford Washburn and Henry Buchtel.

1952–The first ascents of Mount Brooks, Mount Mather, and Brooks Gap were completed by a Harvard expedition led by Thayer Scudder.

1954–First ascent of Mount Hunter by Heinrich Harrer, Fred Beckey, and Henry Meybohm.

1955–First ascent of Mt. Dickey: a five man team led by B. Washburn.

1956–First ascent of Mount Tatum, accomplished by a British Army Party led by Captain J. E. Mills.

1962–Second ascent of Denali by a woman, Anore Bucknell.

1962–First ascent of Mount Russell: Klaus Ekkerlein, Robert Goodwin, and Peter Hennig.

1963–First ascent of Denali via Wickersham Wall by Gmoser, later that year a seven man Harvard Party also accomplished this feat.

1967–First winter ascent of Denali by Blomberg.

## Successful Summits of Denali from 1987-1999

| YEAR | ATTEMPTS | SUMMITS |
|------|----------|---------|
| 1999 | 1183 | 503 |
| 1998 | 1166 | 418 |
| 1997 | 1110 | 566 |
| 1996 | 1148 | 494 |
| 1995 | 1220 | 523 |
| 1994 | 1277 | 575 |
| 1993 | N/A | N/A |
| 1992 | 1081 | 515 |
| 1991 | 935 | 553 |
| 1990 | 998 | 573 |
| 1989 | 1009 | 524 |
| 1988 | 916 | 551 |
| 1987 | 817 | 251 |

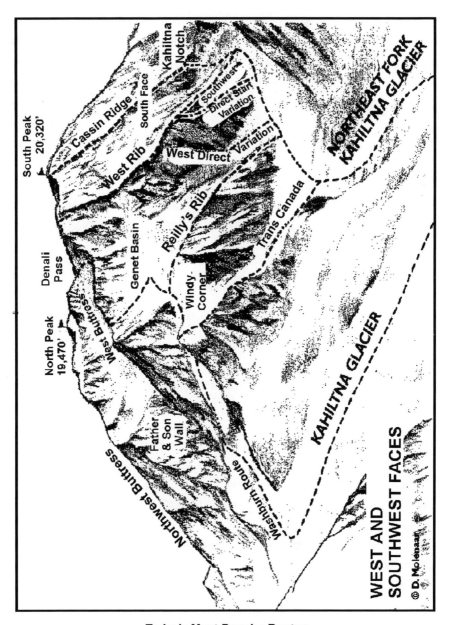

**Today's Most Popular Routes**

## Climbing Denali Today

The following information is from the National Park Service as a reference for planning technical or expedition climbs. Up to date information concerning climbing Denali and Mount Foraker can be obtained from the Talkeetna Ranger Station, Denali National Park and Preserve, P.O. Box 588, Talkeetna, Alaska 99676. Phone: 907-733-2231; Website: www.nps.gov/dena/mountain

### REGISTRATION AND EXPEDITION INFORMATION

1. A 60-day preregistration period is required for climbing on McKinley and Mount Foraker. A registration form is due at the Talkeetna Ranger Station 60 days prior to your climb date. The leader of your expedition is responsible for compiling the registration and deposits for all expedition members and submitting them in one packet to the Talkeetna Ranger Station.

2. A Mountaineering Special Use Fee of one hundred and fifty dollars will be charged to each expedition member attempting Denali or Mount Foraker. This fee is paid in two installments as follows: DEPOSIT-non-refundable, nontransferable deposit of $25 is due when you submit your completed registration form. Payment for this deposit may be made by money order, Visa or MasterCard. Personal checks will not be accepted as payment. BALANCE-the remaining balance of one hundred and twenty-five dollars will be due when you check in at the Talkeetna Ranger Station. Payment for the remaining balance may be made by money order, US currency, Visa or MasterCard. Personal checks are not accepted.

3. Registered climbers are required to check in and out at the Talkeetna Ranger Station. This includes expeditions originating on the north side of the Alaska Range. Expeditions should allow two hours for the check in process at the Talkeetna Ranger Station. Expedition members will be required to provide photo identification. Your expedition

may check in and out during our regular hours of operation: 8:00am-6:00pm, seven days a week. It is best to arrange for an appointment prior to your arrival.

4. Expeditions are permitted to add or substitute one new member to their expedition. This new member must pay the $25.00 deposit and be registered 30 days prior to the start date of the expedition.

5. If you plan to use a guide service, make certain that Denali National Park and Preserve authorizes the service. Illegal guiding is prohibited and your climb could be canceled at any time.

6. Read the National Park Service publication *Mountaineering–Denali National Park and Preserve*, which covers search and rescue requirements, clean climbing requirements, high altitude medical problems, glacier hazards and self-sufficiency. You should have a solid understanding of the potentially serious medical problems and the extreme mental and physical stresses associated with high altitude mountaineering.

## Search and Rescue Requirements

Denali National Park and Preserve recognizes that a certain number of park visitors each year will become ill, injured, or incapacitated in some way. It is the policy of Denali National Park and Preserve to assist those in need, when, in the opinion of the park personnel apprised of the situation, it is necessary, appropriate, within the reasonable skill and technical ability of park personnel and without jeopardizing the searcher and rescuer safety.

Search and Rescue operations are conducted on a discretionary basis. The level and exigency of the response is determined by field personnel based on their evaluation of the situation. Rescue is not automatic. Denali National Park and Preserve expects park users to exhibit a degree of self-reliance and responsibility for their own safety commensurate with the degree of difficulty of the activities they undertake.

Denali National Park and Preserve encourages self-reliance, preventative education and user preparation. We believe the prudent use of these elements to be the best possible means to safely enjoy the park.

## Mandatory Requirements

The following regulations must be complied with by anyone planning climbs or backcountry trips within the park:

*Registration.* The following is mandatory for Denali and Mt. Foraker: Each expedition member must register with the Talkeetna Ranger Station at least 60 days in advance. The group's forms should all be sent together. Since the rangers deal with over 300 expeditions each year, each party must have a distinct name, which should be used on all correspondence. Registration forms are available from the Talkeetna Ranger Station.

*Check In.* All Denali and Mt. Foraker climbers must stop by the Talkeetna Ranger Station for an orientation and briefing prior to their departure. This briefing will include information about sanitary practices and current weather, avalanche and glacier conditions. All other backcountry users should register and attend the orientation. Backcountry permits are required for any overnight use on the northside and can be obtained at the Backcountry Desk located in the Denali Visitor Center.

*Check Out.* Upon your return from the mountains you must immediately check out at the Talkeetna Ranger Station.

*Garbage.* EVERYTHING taken into the park must be brought out of the backcountry when you leave. Do not leave any permanent caches on the mountain. Abandoning surplus food, fuel, wands, and other equipment in caches or disposing it in crevasses is prohibited. By regulation, all garbage must be carried off and taken out of the park. KEEP THE MOUNTAIN CLEAN.

*Human Waste.* Follow the instructions provided by rangers on proper human waste disposal. Use pit toilets where provided. Elsewhere, biodegradable bags are used for latrines. Plan on bringing additional bags for this use. Citations are given for improper disposal of garbage and human waste.

## Guiding:

If you plan to climb with a guide, make sure the guide is authorized to operate within Denali National Park and Preserve. There are seven guide companies authorized to provide this service. If you have questions about your guide, please call the Talkeetna Ranger Station. Unauthorized guiding is illegal and your climb could be cancelled at any time. Fines can be imposed and criminal charges will be brought against the unauthorized guides.

## Arctic High Altitude Mountaineering

In the interest of personal safety all expedition members should be familiar with the potentially very serious medical problems and extreme mental and physical stresses associated with high altitude arctic mountaineering. You will be carrying heavy loads (often 60-90 lbs., 27-40kg.) at altitudes between 7,000 and 20,000 feet (3000-6000 meters). Temperatures may range from 90 degrees F (32 C) to-50F (-40C).

Conditions may vary from intense snow glare to severe snowstorms with whiteout and winds in excess of 100 mph (160 km/h). Expeditions usually last from two to five weeks. Prolonged confinement within cramped tents or snow caves due to bad weather often occurs.

Rescue of injured or ill climbers, if possible at all, may be exceedingly slow and uncertain if weather conditions are not ideal. You should be prepared and equipped to perform self-rescue. Each party must rely on its own resources and cannot count on the aid of other climbers or rescue personnel (See Search and Rescue).

## Climbing Clean

Leave nothing in the mountains. Expeditions have climbed Denali and have carried out everything brought in including their human waste. The most important part of clean climbing is planning ahead.

*Litter Removal.* Everything MUST be carried off the mountain. Each person must make a strong personal commitment to remove all of their garbage, excess food, fixed lines, and all other equipment. Sleds or haul bags make excellent descent towing bags, allowing an additional 50 to 75 pounds (20-30kg) to be taken out. Keep litter dry by consolidating it in plastic bags or waterproof stuff sacks.

*Caches.* Temporary caches should be buried under large snow blocks or loose snow at a minimum of three feet deep. When relaying loads, be careful to bury your food caches to protect them from ravens. More than one expedition has come to grief from these birds. Mark the cache with long wands, 1.5-2 meters above the surface. Clearly mark the cache with the name of your expedition and expected date of return. This will prevent other climbers and the Mountaineering Rangers from thinking the cache were abandoned. At lower altitudes, wolverines, grizzly and black bears have been known to destroy caches near the edge of glaciers. Secure these caches in three layers of garbage bags so no scent is emitted. At higher altitudes, high winds often scour the snow, exposing caches.

Do not leave permanent caches in the Park. Food caches left for another party must be clearly marked and buried at least a meter deep. This other party will be responsible for retrieving the entire cache. If only a portion of the cache is utilized, then the remainder becomes garbage. These caches often melt out, making the cache vulnerable to ravens, which peck it apart. Once they are broken open, the wind will scatter the loose material. Locating a reported cache can be very difficult. Caches left for others rarely serve their intended function, and almost always contribute to litter problems. An expedition will be cited and fined for littering if a cache is abandoned.

*Human Waste and Sanitation.* Intestinal disorders, vomiting and diarrhea may result from contamination of your food or drinking water caused by human waste. The resulting dehydration can become a serious problem at high altitudes. All drinking water is obtained from melted snow. Precaution must be taken when gathering snow from well used camps. Conditions become worse as the season progresses and improperly deposited waste melts out. For the health and safety of all, it is imperative for everyone to follow these simple steps:

1. Use pit latrines where they are provided. At other locations, dig a shallow hole in the snow or use a plastic bucket.
2. Line the hole or bucket with a biodegradable sack.
3. Stake the corners of the bag open with wands and use a snow block to cover the top when not in use. A little attention to prevent over-filling will make the process of disposal much easier.
4. Use this bag as the latrine for all members of the expedition while at camp.
5. Develop a separate urinal spot and mark with a wand.
6. When you move camp or the bag fills, simply tie it off and toss it into a deep crevasse. If no crevasses are available, the bag should be carried until a suitable crevasse is found. The wastes are usually frozen and will ride well on a sled. On steep technical routes, the bag can be tossed away from the climbing route or feces can be deposited on snow blocks and shoveled off the route.
7. Crevasse ONLY human waste. All other trash must be carried off.

*Fixed Lines.* The use of fixed lines as climbing aids has become a serious problem on popular technical routes in the Alaska Range. As alpine ascents have become more popular, very few parties leave fixed lines in place. Several lines are managed seasonally on the West Buttress headwall between 15,500 and 16,200 feet. Other than these, all other fixed ropes must be removed on descent. Old fixed lines are often in very bad condition and should not be used. One climber was killed when he relied on an old fixed line. Expeditions should make an effort to remove old lines and must remove their own fixed lines.

## General Information

### The Expedition

The expedition should consist of at least two to four members. A larger expedition of four or more provides greater inherent strength and self-rescue capability. Expeditions should not exceed 12 members. A group composed primarily of individuals who have not climbed together is a weak climbing group; such expeditions are not recommended. Each member should have solid mountaineering skills, glacier travel knowledge, and must have stamina, conditioning, excellent equipment and the mental fortitude to survive in severe arctic conditions. Experience has shown that even these qualifications do not guarantee safety or success. The more difficult routes are technically very demanding and all members attempting these routes should be highly skilled. All members must know the physical condition, limitations, and the experience of each team member.

### Solo Climbing

The major hazard facing a soloist on Denali is that even the most cautious and experienced climber is unable to determine the location and strength of the many snow bridges that must be crossed. Each year, a number of people take serious crevasse falls on the large Alaskan glaciers. Nearly all of these falls prove to be little more than an adrenaline rush for the entire climbing team... unless of course, the person who fell is either improperly roped or not roped at all. Unfortunately, experience plays little part in determining who falls through these snow bridges. Some crevasses may be faintly visible while others are totally undetectable. Some soloists have devised crevasse-spanning poles attached to their climbing harness that provide a degree of protection in case of a crevasse fall. Many are experienced enough to identify and avoid most mountain hazards, but hidden crevasses add a new dimension of risk to soloing. Virtually all experienced Alaska Range mountaineers are not willing to accept this level of risk.

A solo climber has virtually no self-rescue ability in the event of a serious accident or illness, and creates undue risks to the search and rescue party. Solo travel is strongly discouraged.

## Climbing Seasons

Weather conditions for climbing major Alaska Range peaks are usually best from May through July. Colder minimum temperatures and strong northwest winds commonly occur in May. Late June and July are warmer but more unsettled. By late July, travel on the lower glaciers is made difficult by snow bridges melting over crevasses and by more inclement weather with heavier snowfall and increased avalanche danger. The highest success rates occur in June. April is an excellent month for many of the lower peaks, with conditions often cold and clear, while the winter extremes still linger on Denali and Mt. Foraker. The coldest weather on Denali is found November through April with average temperatures ranging from-30F to-70F recorded at the 19,000-foot level. It is not uncommon to find it-50F at the 17,200 foot camp in early May.

Winter climbing in Denali borders on the ridiculous more because of its unfathomable risks than because of its mountaineering challenge. Some of the world's best climbers have either disappeared or perished form literally being flash frozen! In winter months, the jet stream, +100mph (160 km/h) will often descend over the mountain's upper flanks. Combine this wind with the naturally caused venturi effect, which doubles wind velocity in such areas as Denali Pass, and you will find one of the most hostile environments on this planet. The combined effect of ferocious wind and extreme cold easily and routinely send the wind chills off the charts.

## Routes

Of the more than 30 routes on Denali, the West Buttress, West Rib, Cassin Ridge and Muldrow are the most frequently climbed. The West Buttress and the Muldrow are the easiest ascent routes with primary climbing difficulties being crevasses, steep ice and exposed ice covered ridges. Approximately 1000 climbers attempt Denali each season with over 75% attempting the West Buttress. With this many climbers in such a short season, climbers can expect to encounter several hundred others.

The Talkeetna Ranger Station has reference materials for routes on Denali and other peaks in the park. This includes climbing areas such as the Ruth, Little Switzerland and and the Kichatna Spires. A good route guide for Denali, Mt. Foraker and Mt. Hunter is *High Alaska* by Jon Waterman (see Reference Materials). Other specific route descriptions maybe found in the American Alpine Journal. Valuable information often comes from members of previous expeditions. If you are unable to find information elsewhere, you can direct specific questions to the Talkeetna Ranger Station.

High quality photographs of peaks and routes taken by Bradford Washburn can be acquired through the University of Alaska, Fairbanks. For specific photo numbers you may need to contact Bradford Washburn directly.

## Approaches

From the south, the usual approach is by ski plane from Talkeetna to the Southeast Fork of the Kahiltna Glacier, or to the Ruth Glacier in the Don Sheldon Amphitheater. Some groups have skied in from the Peters Hills or the Anchorage-Fairbanks Highway. The conditions are usually good for skiing on these lowland approaches until the breakup in early May. Plan to have expedition gear flown in and allow at least a week for the ski approach. Specific route information can be obtained from the Talkeetna Ranger Station.

From the north, the approach for Denali and other peaks is by foot, ski, or dogsled. The park road is generally open by the second week in June where the approach can be made from Wonder Lake. Before the road is open you will have to fly to Kantishna (several more miles) or ski the road from the Park Headquarters. The approach from Wonder Lake to McGonagall Pass is 18 miles (29 km). The majority of expeditions planning climbs from McGonagall Pass arrange to have their supplies taken in by dog team in the spring. Parties that have prepared for this have the highest chance of success. A major challenge and potential danger is crossing the McKinley River. This broad, braided river typically runs higher from June through July due to glacier melt. Each member should be versed in river crossings and teamwork needed for deeper sections.

## Guide Services

Seven American guide services are authorized for Denali, Mt. Foraker and other peaks/mountainous areas within the wilderness boundary. These and other guide services have permits to operate within the new park additions outside the Wilderness. Each of the seven Denali services meets stringent standards established by the National Park Service to insure a quality operation. All operators are reviewed periodically to maintain high standards.

The guide services usually require a deposit several months in advance and a resume of your climbing skills. All chief guides leading on Denali have previous Denali experience. A list of the seven authorized guide services is available from the Talkeetna Ranger Station.

**Hiking Guides for Denali**
**Alaska Denali Guiding, Inc.**
P.O. Box 566
Talkeetna, Alaska 99676
Phone: 907-733-2649

**Alpine Ascents International**
121 Mercer St.
Seattle, Washington
Phone: 206-378-1927

N.O.L.S.
P.O. Box 981
Palmer, Alaska 99645
Phone: 907-745-4047

**American Alpine Institute**
1515 12th Street
Bellingham, Washington 98825
Phone: 360-671-1505

**Mountain Trip**
Box 91161
Anchorage, Alaska 99509
Phone: 907-345-6499

**Rainier Mountaineering**
535 Dock Street, Suite 209
Tacoma, Washington 98402
Phone: 206-627-6242

## Aircraft

Aircraft operated by commercial use permit holders are allowed to land in new park additions. The original park is designated wilderness and, as such, motorized vehicles are prohibited. Helicopters are not allowed to land in the park unless there is an emergency. Talkeetna is the base of operations for the air services.

## Medical Problems

*Cold Injuries:* Major hazards of a Denali climb are frostbite and hypothermia. Denali presents a combination of long exposure, severe weather, high altitude, low temperature and low humidity, which make it one of the most severe climates on Earth. Cold resistance is impaired by high altitude hypoxia and dehydration. Mountaineering literature contains numerous, vivid accounts of frostbite on Denali, (see Accidents in North America Mountaineering). Forty cases of frostbite (3-4%) are common for climbers on Denali each season. Several of these require extensive hospitalization, often with debilitating results. Adequate clothing, food and water are critical at all times.

*Acclimatization.* It requires one to two weeks to become acclimatized to a given altitude on Denali (depending on the individual). Individuals also lose this acclimatization in the course of a few weeks. Talkeetna is close to sea level, which is a major disadvantage for someone who has established some acclimatization and is waiting to fly in. The longer the wait, the more acclimatization is lost. Several days spent high on peaks before your arrival will not be enough to transfer that acclimatization to your climb here. You will lose acclimatization in transit.

Limit your ascent to 300 meters (1,000 feet) per day at elevations above 3000 meters (10,000 feet). The following schedule is the fastest recommended rate of ascent of the West Buttress given ideal weather. Expeditions should plan on 21 days.

Day 1: Base camp 7,200 feet
Day 2: Base of "Ski Hill" 7,900 feet
Day 3: Upper Kahiltna 9,600 feet
Day 4: Camp 11,000 feet
Day 5: Rest
Day 6: Bergschrund 13,000 feet or past Windy Corner 13,500 feet
Day 7: Basin 14,200 feet
Day 8 through Day 11: Rest in Basin and acclimatize.
Day 12: Move to 16,200 feet Ridge Camp or 17,200 feet High Camp
Day 13: Rest
Day 14: Summit

Many other factors figure into this plan, including the weight carried, weather, and each member's health. The extra rest days at 14,200 feet (4330 meters) have proven critical before ascending higher.

*Physiological and Physical Impairment.* Mountaineers preparing to climb Denali must be aware that everyone is physically weaker at high altitude. Expeditions can expect to move more slowly and not be able to carry very heavy loads. There are also other problems at high altitude less commonly known but potentially as dangerous, such as mental impairment, dehydration, fatigue, loss of cold resistance, and lack of recuperative powers. The major environmental variable responsible for these effects is the lack of oxygen (hypoxia) associated with high altitude.

*Mental Function.* Bradford Washburn has estimated that above 18,000 feet on Denali a person is reduced to roughly 50% mental capacity. Most high altitude climbers can recall situations in which thinking was impaired and judgement poor; many high altitude-climbing accidents are attributed to such lack of judgement. The effects are insidious, since climbers are not aware of the impairment at the time. A controlled exposure in a low-pressure chamber is often necessary to convince a climber (or pilot) of the effects of hypoxia. It is important climbers realize in advance that mental functions are reduced. Advance planning should be thorough to avoid a critical situation magnified by poor judgement and slow thinking. For example, impulsive decisions to move on or return must be considered carefully.

*Lassitude.* At high altitude motivation can diminish greatly. Joseph Wilcox, leader of a 1967 Denali party wrote, in his diary:

*"With five people crammed in the tent, morale decreased rapidly. There was no interest in cooking meals and by the next day no one was even interested in melting drinking water. We found ourselves very apathetic...not caring whether or not we got enough to drink or eat or if our gear was wet...we just lay there and waited with little or no sleep...by morning the cold had taken its toll...Jerry Lewis and I had numb feet and I had numb fingers."*

Here the motivation to do even the simplest camp chores almost disappeared, yet the tasks of melting snow, cooking, or drying clothes in the wind help determine the success and safety of the party. The will to survive and succeed must prevail. Inactivity during tent bound stormy days can be devastating to morale, and as tiring and debilitating as climbing. Keep the body limber and mind alert on storm days with camp projects in and out of the tent.

*Dehydration, Illness or Injury.* It is difficult for the body to recover from illness and injury above 14,000 feet. Descending to a lower elevation is often the only way to a complete recovery.

Diarrhea can serious when climbing above 14,000 feet because dehydration is further aggravated, and with impaired absorption the body receives little nourishment and weakened more. A person suffering from severe diarrhea should descend or be assisted below 14,000 feet, and should not go back up until gastrointestinal function returns to normal.

Dehydration is a major hazard of high altitude mountaineering. Dehydration may compound any illness or injury, making recovery more difficult. It contributes to frostbite directly by causing constriction of blood vessels in hands and feet. Climbers have difficulty drinking adequate amounts of water above 14,000 feet. Fuel for melting snow is not difficult to carry; yet the tendency is to take only a minimum. It is inviting tragedy not to have at least a week's supply of fuel if one plans to spend even one night above 17,000 feet. The fuel is used to provide each climber with at least three liters of liquid per person each day. Water bottles should be filled as often as possible and kept in sleeping bags at night to prevent freezing.

*Fatigue.* To a considerable extent, Denali creates a problem in logistics. Climbers feel they must make the best use of good conditions, even though doing so may overextend the physical and emotional capabilities of some or all of the party. Climbers must maintain a physiological margin of safety against fatigue and cold just as they do food, fuel and shelter.

*Sleep.* Standard sleeping medications should be avoided above 10,000 feet (3000 meters). Sleep medications cause a decrease in the respiratory response, lowering blood oxygen levels, which can cause Acute Mountain Sickness (AMS). Diphenhydramine or Acetazolamide are the drugs often prescribed for sleep at high altitude.

*Carbon Monoxide Poisoning.* Cooking in poorly ventilated areas, such as tents, old ice glazed igloos, or snow caves can produce Carbon Monoxide (CO) poisoning. An inexpensive CO detector is very beneficial and is at most hardware stores. Avoid the temptation to heat shelters with cooking stoves. Allow for good ventilation. Extra caution is necessary if two stoves are being used at the same time. Cook in the open as much as possible.

*Altitude Illness*

The difference in the barometric pressure at northern latitudes affects acclimatization on Denali and other high arctic mountains. Denali's latitude is 63 degrees, while the latitude of Mt. Everest is 27 degrees. On a typical summit day in May, the Denali climber will be at the equivalent of 22,000 feet when compared to the Himalayas at the same altitude. This phenomenon of lower barometric pressure at higher elevations is caused by the troposphere being thinner at the poles.

Other phenomena observed on Denali are the dramatic low-pressure weather systems that are generated in the Gulf of Alaska. Each season the camp at 14,200 feet experiences barometric changes that physiologically raise the camp by over 1000 feet in less than a 24 hour period.

Acute mountain sickness, high altitude pulmonary edema, cerebral (brain) edema, and retinal (eye) hemorrhages often occur together. They are all manifestations of failure to adapt to the stress of high altitude and are not individual diseases. Hypoxia (lack of oxygen) is the underlying cause in all cases. The extreme cold of Denali also apparently contributes to altitude sickness, especially pulmonary edema.

*Types of Altitude Sicknesses:*

*Acute Mountain Sickness (AMS)* is common and occurs usually above 8,000 to 9,000 feet. Symptoms appear a few hours after arrival at a new altitude and may worsen, then slowly improve. AMS should dictate slowing down or halting a climb, and the climber should be watched for more serious developments. Light activity, plenty of fluids, and no upward progress are the best treatment.

Aspirin or Tylenol can be taken for headaches and Acetazolamide (Diamox) can be started to speed acclimatization and prevent AMS.

Many parties experiencing early signs of AMS have been able to continue to complete a successful expedition by descending 2,000 to 3,000 feet (600 to 1000 meters) to allow one or two days acclimatization, then reascending. Like all forms of altitude sickness, it is minimized or prevented by taking more time to gain altitude.

*High Altitude Pulmonary Edema (HAPE)* seldom occurs below 9,000 feet (2750 meters). Symptoms begin to appear hours after a too rapid ascent. It is suspected that hard work and cold increases susceptibility to HAPE. Symptoms are increasing fatigue, shortness of breath at rest, weakness, and a dry cough. Later, bloody or frothy white sputum and bubbling in the lungs becomes obvious. Usually there is a low-grade fever, the pulse is often fast (90-130 beats per minute at rest), respirations rapid (20-40 per minute at rest) and lips and fingernails are blue.

Once HAPE is diagnosed or even strongly suspected, the party must start down. This is the only readily available treatment. Oxygen is effective, but usually not available, especially in the quantities necessary (12 to 36 hours of oxygen breathing). However, no medication, no amount of rest, and not even oxygen is a substitute for descending. The party is taking a greater risk by delaying evacuation than by starting down at night or in dubious weather. Getting down even one or two thousand feet usually has a dramatic beneficial effect, unless the illness has progressed too far, and then further descent to hospital care, oxygen and medical attention are necessary to save the life of the victim. Exertion by the victim must be minimal.

*Cerebral (brain) Edema (CE)* is less common. It is unusual below 12,000 to 13,000 feet (3600 meters). Symptoms include staggering as if intoxicated while walking, and sometimes a severe headache and vomiting. Hallucinations may occur. Behavior becomes irrational and simple tasks impossible. Lethargy leads to decreasing consciousness and the patient may drift into coma and die. Even more urgent than HAPE, CE demands immediate descent under almost any conditions.

The loss of coordination (ataxia) in CE can be detected by simple coordination tests, such as the heel to toe walking test. Draw a straight line in the snow and have the person walk on the line, placing the heel of each foot directly in front of (touching) the toe of the last. Anyone unable to walk normally along the line should be assumed to have CE, and possibly HAPE. Dexamethasone (DECADRON), if available, can be administered early in CE (a dose of four mg orally or injected every six hours is often prescribed), and the victim should be taken down the mountain.

*Summary*

There is no way of predicting who will develop altitude sickness since physical fitness offers no protection. The best treatment for any type of altitude illness is rapid descent to a lower altitude. Normally, anyone with altitude illness who starts down early after onset will recover rapidly and completely. As is the case with all medical problems, prevention is the most important aspect in the management of altitude sickness. Listen to your body and climb according to how you feel. Remember the adage "carry loads high and sleep low." Delay moving to a higher altitude with symptoms of AMS. Spend two to four days at 14,000 feet to acclimatize. Watch team members of your expedition carefully for signs of high altitude sickness. Don't ignore other members' complaints.

## Glacier Hazards

*Crevasses.* Glaciation is vast throughout the Alaska Range. With tree line at 1,500 to 3,000 feet, the extent of ice-covered lands is enormous. The glaciers in the park demand respect. Year-round snowfall constantly hides crevasses. Extensive networks of crevasses exist throughout the range, and climbers should be roped at all times. Snow covered crevasses are often hard to detect and many climbers have been surprised by serious falls. Be sure to thoroughly probe a campsite and wand its periphery before unroping. An avalanche probe or ski pole without the basket makes a good crevasse probe, while ice axes shorter than 70cm are inadequate.

*Roped Travel.* When traveling in teams of two on the lower glaciers, climbers should be roped at least 100 feet (30 meters) apart. A space of 50 feet (15 meters) apart is minimum for four on a rope. Many crevasse bridges easily exceed 60 feet (20 meters). Make sure your sled and pack are tied off to the rope as you travel. When in doubt about a crevasse crossing, use a belay.

*Icefalls.* Icefall activity is unpredictable. Avoid runout zones if possible and don't stop when crossing these zones. Locate campsites considerable distances from icefall areas. When choosing a campsite, consider what is high above your location and the possibility of an earthquake, which is common in the Alaska Range, disrupting inactive icefalls. Icefall activity increases with temperatures are above zero during the day and at freezing at night, which commonly occurs in July. Most of the glaciers have icefall zones. The Talkeetna Ranger Station can provide detailed information about safe routes.

*Avalanche.* Heavy snowfalls combined with widespread avalanche hazards are dangers climbers face in the Alaska Range. Every year climbers trigger avalanches and in many circumstances someone is seriously hurt or killed. Parties should be capable of estimating avalanche hazards and snow stability. Anywhere in the range, good judgement and a careful approach to route planning are key elements in avoiding avalanches. Each team member should carry avalanche transceivers, shovels and probe poles and be thoroughly trained in their use. Mountaineering parties should be equipped to deal with an avalanche accident and be a self-contained rescue team.

Jill A. Fredon and Doug Felser in their book, *Snow Sense: A Guide to Evaluating Snow Avalanche Hazard*, recommend the following when selecting routes or campsites:

1. Terrain Analysis
   Is the terrain capable of producing avalanches?
2. Snow Stability Evaluation
   Could the snow slide?
3. Avalanche Weather Forecasting
   Is the weather contributing to instability?
4. Route Selection/Decision-Making
   Do safer alternatives exist?

If the answer to any of these questions is 'yes,' then you would be well advised to go where the answer is 'no.'

If you decide that you do want to travel on or near steep slopes, then you must seek the key information needed to answer the questions above. By doing so, you can begin to base your hazard evaluation upon solid facts rather than assumptions, feelings, or guesses.

The Talkeetna rangers may be able to advise your party of current weather, snowfall accumulations and reported avalanche activity.

## Rescue

A climbing party high on Denali or other arctic mountains cannot depend on any assistance in case emergency. Due to acclimatization restrictions, it could be days before a ground party could arrive on the scene for a rescue. Clear air turbulence can often prevent air support, even on good days. For all practical purposes, a climbing party is alone and must depend upon its own resources if an emergency situation arises. Injured or ill persons must often be moved to lower elevations by the remainder of the group if at all possible. This is for the benefit of the injured person and to aid in rescue by a ground party or possible evacuation by aircraft.

Certain conditions (weather, avalanche hazard, terrain, etc.) may preclude any rescue attempt. The determination of when, or even if, a rescue attempt will be made is based on the collective judgement of those who are in charge of the rescue operation. The use of aircraft in a high altitude rescue operation or on steep terrain is difficult and hazardous. Do not delay evacuation if bad weather threatens or if an aircraft evacuation is doubtful. To delay the evacuation of a climber suffering from altitude illness to a lower altitude may prove fatal. Don't risk the opportunity to descend in the hope of a quick helicopter response.

A rescue by helicopter requires a great deal of risk, effort and expense. The average rescue costs $10,000; some run over three times this amount. When an injured or ill climber can be carried down to the lower glaciers and evacuated by fixed wing aircraft, the rescue costs are much less.

Helicopter assistance has been requested by expeditions in the past. Frequently, help was not possible because of severe weather, inadequate landing locations, or the helicopter availability. Parties were forced to handle emergencies on their own.

All climbing groups confronted with an emergency situation should first determine what they could do to handle the situation on their own. Next, they should try to enlist the help of other climbers nearby. Finally, and only when all other options have been tried, the group should request additional assistance.

If a rescue becomes necessary and the party has exhausted all means of evacuation, it may request assistance from the National Park Service via the party's radio or other means. In a rescue situation, parties must provide clear concise information, which may require transmitting in the blind.

Parties requesting assistance should provide:

1. Name of party
2. Location and elevation
3. Extent of illness or injury
4. Current weather
5. Names/locations of other climbers who can assist
6. Immediate plans/response

*Rescue Transmission.* All climbers must speak slowly in English. If you speak very little English, you should first initiate the call by saying, "Rescue, Rescue" and then say the name of your party. Next give your elevation, location, injury or illness and weather. (If foreign, you may wish to briefly transmit the same information again, in your language.) Transmit your brief message three to four times every 30 minutes until you get a response. When possible, the Park Service will record your message (and get it translated if necessary). Remember to warm the radio and batteries at least 30 minutes before each call. You may have to move to a different location to get out, since most radios are line of sight. Some parties adapt their radios to a portable battery pack, which can be kept warm while transmitting. Always be prepared to evacuate the injured member or attempt other means of help. The rescue signal of "standing upright with two arms fully raised over your head" indicates you need rescue. If by the time an aircraft arrives on the scene you have lost communication due to weak batteries, you should display this signal to the aircraft.

*Self sufficiency* Those who depend upon rescue efforts from experts are inviting disaster. Helicopters and/or acclimatized rescuers are often not available or the weather prohibits response. In the Alaska Range, travelers should be prepared with knowledge, equipment, strength and common sense to support their own expeditions.

The selfless assistance provided by other climbers has saved countless lives. This help has not been given without hardship and often causes aborted climbs for the rescue volunteers. All climbers must prepare to be self-sufficient, but when desparate situations occur, other climbers often come to the aid.

## Equipment and Supplies

*Footwear:* The single most important piece of gear is footwear, which must be of the highest quality. Boots must be of the warmest-rated double plastic models or the military vapor barrier type. Both have excellent records for use on Denali. All double boots must be equipped with a completely insulated overboot, including closed cell foam on the sole. Supergators are inadequate substitutes for overboots. Boots should be fitted with several pair of socks and should not be too tight as feet tend to swell slightly at higher altitudes. Many climbers use vapor barrier liners (VBL) against the skin or over a thin pair of socks. Feet that have been wet all day from the VBL's need to be placed in a dry environment each night (foot powder is very helpful in drying out the feet). Not allowing the feet to dry can lead to a serious condition known as immersion foot (trench foot). Many climbers have suffered with this debilitating condition, which is similar to frostbite. All footwear systems should be thoroughly tested before departing.

Single leather boots are inadequate for conditions and contribute to frostbite. Most of the severely frostbitten feet occurr on summit day. All members should be ready to leave camp at the same time so no one remains to get "cold feed". Once you have left your high camp you will have little opportunity to attend to your feet. Cold toes are common, but adequate circulation must be maintained with some degree of sensation in the tips of the toes at all times. If your toes become too cold at this point, you must either stop to rewarm your feet or make a hasty retreat. On most summit days the option to stop is not a possibility, but frostbite of the feet can sneak up slowly and its consequences are devastating.

*Clothing.* Outer layers of clothing must be adequate for the most severe arctic conditions. The best is necessary. These items should include:

1. Expedition weight down parka with a good hood and wind tunnel.
2. Down pants or expedition weight pile pants
3. Parka shell, loosely fitted, with a hood, wind tunnel and plenty of pockets.
4. Climbing bibs or wind pants that are fitted for layers.
5. Mittens fitted large with long sleeves and removable liners.
6. Light weight face mask or balaclava
7. Hat of double layer construction with good ear protection

The conditions experienced in lower glacier travel are often very hot when the sun is out, or wet when it is snowing. Several medium weight layers of synthetic clothes work best. A good sun hat and reflective white shirt are very helpful with the intense glare. Lightweight, wind-resistant clothing in layers allows for adjustments to be made according to conditions. Several changes of socks should provide thick, loose insulation. Booties are filled with down or synthetic fiber with insulated soles are good for wear around camp and while sleeping. Booties work exceptionally well inside the overboots for colder conditions or when there is deep snow in and around camp. Each climber should bring synthetic gloves and extra mittens. Thick pile tops and bottoms are needed for climbing prior to June.

Parties traveling through the lowlands during the summer months will need headnets, effective mosquito repellent, rain gear and mosquito netting for tents. The icy cold river crossings are made easier with neoprene booties worn in lightweight running shoes.

*Sleeping Gear.* An expedition quality sleeping bag is essential. Down or synthetic fiber filled bags rated to minus 20 degrees is the minimum acceptable. Many climbers use an overbag along with their sleeping bag. This is especially important for April and May climbs. Allow extra room in the sleeping bag for wearing layers of clothing, inner boots, and storing a water bottle. Almost as important as the sleeping bag is sufficient insulation underneath. Two closed-cell foam pads or a combination closed cell with inflatable foam pad are the standard. Adequate sleep is essential at high altitudes. Do not economize on weight by compromising sleeping gear.

*Snowshoes or Skis.* One pair of snowshoes or skis per person <u>must</u> be taken! Hidden crevasse bridges become unpredictable without the flotation of skis and or snowshoes and snow accumulations of greater than a meter can occur at any time. Only experienced skiers should attempt to ski. Skiers should practice with a heavy pack and sled to make sure they are prepared. Climbing skins are necessary. Snowshoes should be sturdy with traction devices for steeper sections and side hill traversing. Ski poles are also very useful with snowshoes. Anticipate that snowshoes tend to need more repairs than skis.

*Sleds and Haul Sacks.* Sleds or sacks are very useful for travel on the lower glaciers and for shuttling loads. A single climber can pull loads of 30 to 40 pounds with little difficulty. Most Denali climbers use lightweight plastic sleds available from department stores or through the Talkeetna based air services. Sleds can be rigged with rope breaks on the descent. Sleds and sacks can be used for carrying garbage on the descent, and for evacuating sick or injured climbers.

*Stoves.* Carry at least two stoves of proven efficiency at high altitudes and in extreme cold, with spare parts for cleaning and repairs. Almost all stoves use white gas, which is readily available. Disposable gas cartridge models are discouraged and are difficult to obtain in Alaska; domestic cartridges may not be pressurized enough for extreme cold. Plan on four to eight ounces of white gas per person per day, or more earlier in the season due to colder temperatures and drier snow. All fuel containers, empty or full, must be packed out. The rangers may ask to see your containers upon arriving at base camp.

*Food.* Plan three weeks of food for the West Buttress, consisting of 4,000 to 5,000 calories per person per day (this amount allows for a week of storm-bound days). Each climber should plan on consuming at least four liters of fluid per day as hydration hastens acclimatization and prevents dehydration. Be sure to repackage food before you depart for the mountain to minimize garbage. (Foreign climbers need to be aware that no freeze-dried meat may be brought into the United States; only commercially canned is allowed, other meats must be purchased upon arrival in the United States). Anchorage has numerous retailers who sell freeze dried, dried, bulk and other food commodities at prices equivalent to other areas in the United States.

If you access the mountain by air, plan a base camp food cache in the event that bad weather delays your flight out at the end of your climb. Be sure to bury this cache at least a meter and mark it with your name and expected return date. The lower glaciers melt considerably during the climbing season, and ravens can raid exposed caches. If the cache is not labeled with your expedition name and date, the mountaineering rangers will conclude that it was abandoned, and remove it.

If you are planning to traverse through the lowlands, you should be prepared to prevent giardia by filtering or boiling your water, or using water purification tablets. Giardia cysts have been found in lakes and streams on both the north and south sides of the Alaska Range. You should plan to cook 50 to 100 meters away from your camp to prevent the intrusion of bears due to cooking smells. After cooking, all food, garbage, pots and other utensils should be triple packaged in large plastic bags and placed 100 meters from the camp in a different location than where you cooked, but in a spot that can be observed from your tent.

*Snow Shovels.* Carry several shovels per party. Larger, sturdier types are essential. Avoid small, lightweight shovels since they are ineffective for moving large volumes of snow. The aluminum grain scoop (14 x 18in or 35 x 45cm) has proven indispensable. These scoops can be purchased at many hardware stores. Shovels are used for digging in campsites, constructing snow caves, removing snow from around tents, and occasionally for clearing the route after deep accumulations. A small, strong shovel such as a steel spade is ideal for digging snow caves or tent platforms in wind packed snow or at camps above 14,000 feet.

*Snow Saws.* Parties should carry several snow saws, since they are essential for building walls around your tent or constructing igloos and snow caves. They should be sturdy, with large, sharp teeth, a stiff blade and a large handle.

*Tents.* Tents should be of expedition quality and have an excellent track record. Allow extra room per person since many days are often spent storm-bound. Extra poles and repair materials are important, in case of damage caused by storms. Plan to take extra pickets, wands or deadmen for anchors. Never leave a tent without anchoring it securely. Tents are easily lost due to sudden gusts of wind while left unattended or drying. The rain fly should be used for its added strength. It also traps a layer of air for added warmth.

Operation of the stove should occur outside of the tent. Under extreme conditions, members of a party may be forced to cook inside the tent. If so, cooking must be done at the entrance, with plenty of ventilation. Never cook without adequate cross ventilation! Avoid lighting the stove while inside the tent.

Snow walls should be constructed around tents for protection from winds. However, even the best walls and tents will not provide comfort and rest during severe wind storms. Snow walls collapse and tents fail each year. Furthermore, the noise of flapping tents can become nerve-wracking, causing significant mental and physical fatigue. Winds in excess of 80 miles per hour are common and may last many hours or days. Always be prepared for a tent failure with tools needed to build a snow cave.

*Snow Shelters.* Acclimatization days are well spent constructing an igloo or snow cave. Often, the only shelters to survive a wind storm at the high camps are snow shelters. All party members should have experience in the construction of snow shelters. A small steel shovel is invaluable for digging into the hard ice found high on Denali or Mt. Foraker. Habitation within the snow shelter can be quite pleasant compared to the agony of a tent during cold evenings or stormy conditions. During construction, make sure the entrance opens at right angles to the wind. Candles and a small lantern for spring climbs provide added light and warmth. Always allow for good ventilation while cooking.

*Rope.* Take at least one 45 meter, 9mm Perlon water repellent rope per two people and a 45 meter spare for crevasse rescue. Use a 50 meter rope for three climbers. Fixed rope made of Polypropylene (solid core 9mm) only should be used on snow and ice. Static Perlon should be used over sharp ice and any rock for fixed line. All fixed rope must be removed upon descent.

*Ice Axes.* One ice axe per person is necessary, plus an extra per party (since they are easily lost in crevasse falls). An ice axe 70cm or taller is more practical for non-technical climbs such as the West Buttress or Muldrow Glacier routes. Picks and ice climbing tools are frequently broken on technical climbs since the extreme cold creates very hard ice. Tape the grip area on the head of the ice axe with closed cell foam and duct tape or hockey tape, which inhibit cold penetration to the hand.

*Crampons.* Bring one pair of crampons per person that can be adjusted to be worn with or without overboots. An adjustable pair should be carried as an extra for each party. A small file is essential on technical routes. Clamp-on crampons will work with most current overboots and are a significant advancement since lace-on crampons tend to place pressure across the top of the foot.

*Crevasse Rescue.* All party members must work together on similar techniques for crevasse rescue. Crevasse falls are imminent while traveling on glaciers in the Alaska Range. Each climber should be rigged for a crevasse fall with foot loops, mechanical ascenders or prusiks and a pulley ready to be used. Attach the pack and sled to the rope while traveling. Safety straps should be used on skis since they are easily lost in a crevasse fall. Each member should carry a picket in addition to their ice axe.

*Snow and Ice Anchors.* Snow pickets of two to three-foot length are critical for anyone traveling on glaciated terrain. The snow bollard or deadman anchors work well but require additional time to place. They may be the only anchors that will work in a variety of unconsolidated or slush snow conditions. A rack of ice screws are essential on steeper routes but only a couple per party are needed for the West Buttress or Muldrow.

*Eye Protection.* Snow blindness is common due to the extreme glare, even on overcast days. Sun glasses should provide maximum protection from ultraviolet and infrared rays, along with protection from side glare. Double lens ski goggles work well in bad weather and whiteout conditions. Extra glasses should be taken by each party.

*Medical Kits.* All members of the party should be familiar with the contents and use of the medical kit. Split kits should be carried when members in a party separate. It is of the greatest importance that members consult at length with a physician or take a course on the field treatment of common emergencies. The following is a list of medical kit contents for a high altitude expedition to Denali or Mt. Foraker suggested by Dr. Peter Hackett:

| ITEM | USE |
| --- | --- |
| Diphenhydramine | Allergies, Sleep |
| Promethazine | Nausea, vomiting |
| Ibuprofen | Headache, muscle aches & pains, burns, frostbite, sunburn |
| Codeine | Painkiller, cough suppressant |
| Dexamethasone | Severe AMS or HACE |
| Diamox | To speed acclimatization, treat mild AMS |
| Cephalosporin | Antibiotic |
| Labiosan | Lip protection |
| Immodium | Diarrhea |
| Antibiotic ointment | Skin infections and prevention |
| Acetaminophen | Headache, pain killer, fever |
| Sun Block | Sunburn prevention |
| Throat Lozenges | Sore throat |

*Radio.* Carrying a two-way radio is recommended for all parties, and essential for climbs off the beaten path of the West Buttress. Each season, climbers are rescued without significant delay because they used a radio to call for assistance. Some of the most lengthy and drawn out rescues were delayed by the lack of communication. In some accidents, climbers had to wait for weeks, or crawl for days to summon help. The Park Service will often drop a radio to a suspected injured party in order to provide clear communication. If you are climbing in the Ruth or on the Cassin, a radio can be a real life saver in an emergency.

The Citizen's Band (CB) radio is the radio preferred and carried by most climbers. Channel 19 (27.185 MHz) on the CB is monitored by air services and the Park Service in Talkeetna. Even though Denali is 60 miles from Talkeetna, its great height allows direct communication with the Talkeetna Ranger Station and as far away as Anchorage or Fairbanks (over 100 miles distant). While flying in the mountains, the Talkeetna pilots monitor Channel 19, as do rangers at the Kahiltna Base Camp and the 14,000' Ranger Station on the West Buttress. Daily mountain weather forecasts are broadcast from the Base Camp Operator. The standard 3-5 watt CB can easily be purchased from electronics retailers or rented from your air service in Talkeetna. Be sure to carry extra batteries and ensure the radio and batteries are warm before transmitting.

Communications from the north side of the Alaska Range are more difficult. If you are climbing the Muldrow or other routes in the vicinity, the CB is the best choice. Beginning in May, Channel 7 is monitored at Camp Denali near Wonder Lake, while Talkeetna's pilots who frequent the area will be monitor Channel 19. If you are considering a remote area, your best choice is a radio that can transmit on aircraft frequencies. This will allow you to communicate with the airlines or use the emergency locator transmitter frequency.

Cellular phones are being used on a limited basis with connecting repeaters from Anchorage to Fairbanks. Both cellular phones and CB radios are line of sight and are usually functional only above 13,000 to 14,000 feet (4000 meters) on most routes. The CB has the advantage of allowing communications between expeditions on Denali and other peaks. Always be prepared for radio failure and have a contingency plan ready in the event that your radio does not work.

*Signal Devices.* Because radio communication may not always be possible, other types of signal devices should be carried. Smoke and rocket-type flares have been used with limited success. Mirrors are much more limited, being dependent on adequate sunlight. The portable ELT (Emergency Locator Transmitter) has had good results, but lacks the capacity for two-way communication.

*Trail Markers (Wands).* Every expedition should carry a few (20) wands (dark green bamboo garden stakes) whether to mark a cache, or indicate the edges of a crevasse. Several wands should be carried on summit day to replace any that have been blown away in recent storms. Near-zero visibility can envelop the upper mountain very quickly, making Denali's broad summit plateau difficult to navigate. Once the trail to the summit is lost, effort should be made to retrace your steps back to the last wand. Wands should be 1 to 1.5 meters in length, spaced 100 to 150 feet (30 to 50 meters) apart. Several wands should be taped together to form a sturdy marker two meters above the snow to mark caches below 14,000 feet. Wands can be purchased from garden and hardware stores, and are available locally.

*Repair Kit.* Plan your kit around the equipment you carry, such as the stove, skis and tent. In addition, carry parachute cord, wire, duct tape, a screwdriver for skis, patching material for inflatable mattresses and tents, and a sewing kit.

## Talkeetna Ranger Station

In 1977, the National Park Service established a ranger station specifically for mountaineers in the small community of Talkeetna. Since 1984, the station has been staffed year-round to provide information and assistance to mountaineers before, during and after climbs. The mountaineering rangers have extensive experience in the Alaska Range and can provide thorough information.

A collection of over 150 high quality photographs of the Central Alaska Range by Bradford Washburn can be viewed at the ranger station. The station maintains a reference library including a complete set of American Alpine Journals, a map collection, and specific route information for other peaks, including the Ruth, Kitchatnas and Little Switzerland. Please feel free to use all of these resources while in Talkeetna to better prepare for your climb

# Chapter 12

## *Lodging around Denali National Park*

### Hotel and Inns in Healy and Near the Park Entrance
(Descriptions provide by properties management/prices and information subject to change)

**Denali Bluffs Hotel**
P.O. Box 72460 Fairbanks, Alaska 99707
Phone: 907-683-7000, 800-488-7002
Email: *denali@denalibluffs.com*
Website: *www.denalibluffs.com*

Denali Bluffs Hotel is dedicated to providing superior accommodations and service. The new 112-room hotel in Denali National Park is the closest to the park entrance (less than one mile at Mile 238.3 Parks Highway). Many rooms have a private balcony and most have breathtaking views of the surrounding Alaska Range. The lodge features relaxing sitting areas and a large stone fireplace that invite guests to linger. An activity desk is available in the Lodge for taking advantage of most park activities. Our shuttle service is available to meet you at the rail depot or take you to other park facilities.

The Mountaineer Cafe is available for your convenience. Various other dining choices are nearby. A well-appointed gift shop, vending facilities, and a coin-operated laundry are available for guest use.

## Denali North Star Inn

P.O. Box 240I, Healy, AK 99743

Phone: 1-800-684-1560, 1-907-683-1560

Located in beautiful Healy at mile 248.8 Parks Highway. Comfortable, reasonably priced rooms, and the finest dining in the Denali National Park vicinity. Reservations for Park and area tours. Authentic Alaskan gifts, barber shop and beauty salon. Recreation and exercise facilities, saunas, laundry, tanning beds. Eleven miles to Denali National Park entrance. Open year round. Shuttle service to Denali National Park train station.

## Denali River View Inn

P.O. Box 49, Denali National Park, AK 99755

Phone: 907-683-2663

Relax to the sound of the river in your clean, comfortable room. Peak season $134 plus tax, Spring/Fall $84 plus tax. Featuring two double beds and private bath, quiet atmosphere. Local courtesy transportation. Local craft gift shop and Espresso stand. Located one mile north of Park entrance on left at Mile 238.4 Parks Hwy. Deposit required. Visa, MasterCard, Discover, checks accepted.

## Motel Nord Haven

P.O. Box 458, Healy, AK 99743

Phone: 907-683-4500

E-mail: *nordhavn@ptialaska.net*

Let us pack your lunch for your Denali National Park visit! Local owners and staff give you top quality service. Scenic secluded location is just off Alaska Highway #3, twelve road miles north of Denali National Park entrance. Twenty-four large rooms, all non-smoking, feature queen beds, TVs, telephones, and private baths. Open year around. Summer rates $98-$117.

## Stampede Lodge
P.O.Box 380, Healy, Alaska 99743

Phone: 1-907-683-2242, 1-800-478-2370

Located just 10 minutes from the entrance to Denali National Park at the foot of Primrose Ridge is Denali's best hotel value, the Stampede Lodge. Year round, the Lodge offers Alaskan hospitality and easy access to all Park activities. Our comfortable rooms offer private baths and telephones for only $79.00 for two persons or $89.00 for three or four persons, the lowest rates in the park area! Our full service restaurant, the Bushmaster Grill, serves the best food in the Valley along with a fine selection of Alaska's best beers and wines. Our friendly staff will ensure that you will feel at home in our warm, cozy atmosphere. A full service Tour Desk is located in the lobby and can handle all your reservation needs for all Park activities including rafting, horseback riding, park tours, and flightseeing or any exciting winter adventures.

Winter adventures at Stampede Lodge include dog sledding, snow-mobiling, snow shoe hiking, Iditarod kennel visits, demonstrations on dog mushing, exploring winter wildlife and habitat, learning about the natural history of Denali, and Northern Lights viewing. During the day, our local Alaskan guides will show you the vastness of the Alaskan Interior as you experience our frozen winter world. Then, on a cold clear night, the heavens can come alive with the Northern Lights, the view of a lifetime!

## Totem Inn
P.O. Box 105, Healy, Alaska 99743

Phone: 907-683-2420

Totem Inn is located 12 scenic miles north of the Denali National Park entrance. We are Alaska-owned and operated, 24 hours daily, year-round. Deluxe rooms, summer rates: $80.00 to $110.00, Winter: $60.00 to $90.00. Semi-deluxe and economy rooms, summer: $40.00 to $65.00,

Winter: $30.00 to $55.00. Restaurant, motel, lounge. A clean, comfortable, friendly place to stay.

# Lodges

### Camp Denali and North Face Lodge
P.O. Box 67 Denali National Park, Alaska 99755
Phone: 907-683-2290
Email: *info@campdenali.com*
Website: *www.campdenali.com*

   Camp Denali's seventeen privately situated log and frame guest cabins capture unparalleled views of Denali. The cabins are a three to seven-minute downhill walk from the historic hand-hewn log lodge, homey dining room, central shower building and natural history resource center. Each cabin has a small wood stove, wall mounted propane lights and a hotplate for heating water. From every hand-built outhouse, framed by a heart in the door to patchwork quilts handcrafted by the staff, Camp Denali defines rustic elegance. Camp Denali's programs of active learning adventures, exploring the Denali wilderness by hiking and wildlife observation, is a hallmark in the national park system.

### Denali Backcountry Lodge
P.O. Box 810, Girdwood AK 99587
Phone: 800-841-0692
Email: *info@denalilodge.com*
Website: *www.denalilodge.com*

   Offers thirty comfortably appointed cedar cabins and a spacious lodge complete with dining and lounge areas. Each cabin is heated and enjoys its own private bath. Denali Wildlife Drive included in package price.

   Activities: Naturalist programs, guided and unguided hikes and walks, mountain biking, evening presentations, optional flightseeing, and even gold panning are all popular activities.

## Denali Princess Lodge

Healy, AK 99743

Phone: 800-208-0200

Website: *www.princess.com/dest/we_mckinley.html*

The Denali Princess Lodge features a luxurious lobby, extensive viewing deck with hot tubs, and highly rated dining experience on the bluff above the Nenana River, looking out towards Denali National Park. The Denali Princess Lodge has 350 rooms. All rooms have private baths, telephones, cable TV and courtesy coffee. The room rate includes courtesy transportation to and from the rail depot. All Park tours and activities depart from the Denali Princess Lodge. Dinner theater performs each evening.

## The EarthSong Lodge

P.O. Box 89, Healy, Alaska 99743

Phone: 907-683-2863

E-mail: *EarthSong@mail.denali.k12.ak.us*

Website: *www.alaska-online.com/earthsong/*

Nestled in the Alaska Range along Denali National Park's northern boundary, is an area of unsurpassed wilderness beauty. Come into our lodge, remove your shoes, and enjoy the warmth and comfortable atmosphere provided by your hosts, Jon and Karin. Summer rates: $115 to $135.

EarthSong Lodge offers a variety of summer and winter adventures, ranging from lodge-based accommodations to overnight camping trips. In the summer, guests stay in their own charming log cabin, complete with private baths, handcrafted log furnishings, continental breakfast and naturalist programs. Jon and Karin even offer a sled dog kennel tour and, for those who really want to feel what it is like to mush, there are dogcart rides. Backcountry winter sled trips use snug cabins and heated tents to assure comfort and safety.

## Kantishna Roadhouse

P.O. Box 130, Denali National Park, AK 99755
Phone: 800-942-7420, 907-479-2436
E-mail: *kantshna@polarnet.com*
Website: *www.kantishnaroadhouse.com*

Welcome to our lodge and to a long Alaskan tradition of hospitality. The original roadhouse at Kantishna was built in the early 1900s, serving as a private residence, a community center, a post office, and informal accommodations for those visiting Kantishna. You can still see the old log structure and other remnants of the past at the back of our property. Many nights were spent spinning tales of the trail over a hot cup of coffee and a hearty meal. Today, we still talk of the trail, but in more comfortable surroundings. Through years of hard work, the Kantishna Roadhouse has evolved from a gold miner's tent camp into a modern Alaskan resort with a rustic flavor. In 1986 a modern tent camp was established to cater to a federal mineral survey crew assaying surrounding claims. Word of this unique camp experience spread, and its popularity grew. Additional guest cabins have been built every season to accommodate growth. The beautiful log lodge was built in 1993, adding an expanded dining area, a new library resource room, a handcrafted bar, and a spacious lobby.

## McKinley Chalet Resort

Healy, Alaska 99743
Phone: 907-683-2215, 907-276-7234.

A full-service resort with pool, sauna, recreation center with nightly videos, a deli and an excellent scenic restaurant. Make reservations for either McKinley Chalet Resort of Denali National Park Hotel c/o A.R.A. Outdoor Room, 825 West 8th Avenue, #240, Anchorage, AK 99501.

## White Moose Lodge

P.O. Box 68, Healy, Alaska 99743

Phone: 800-481-1232, 907-683-1231

Website: *www.alaska-online.com/whitemoose/*

Conveniently located at Mile 248 Parks Highway, 11 miles north of Denali National Park's entrance, our 12-room motel provides clean, comfortable and affordable accommodations in an informal, friendly and picturesque setting. Each room is non-smoking with two double beds, private bath and TV. Enjoy our complimentary continental breakfast on the picnic table looking out on rugged Mount Healy.

# Bed and Breakfasts Near Healy and the Denali National Park Entrance

## Carlo Heights Bed & Breakfast

Owner: Rick Swenson

P.O. Box 86, Denali National Park, Alaska 99755

Phone: 907-683-1615

Website; *alaskasbest.net/carloheights/carloheights.html*

Email: *carloheights@alaskasbest.net*

Rick Swenson's Carlo Heights Bed and Breakfast, located 11 miles south of Park headquarters, offers spectacular views in a private setting. The fully modern log-frame home/B&B is also ideal for families and business or tour groups of up to 12 people. Full kitchen, barbeque, laundry and pet boarding facilities.

## GrandView Bed and Breakfast

P.O. Box 109, Healy, AK 99743

Phone: 907-683-2468

E-mail: *grndview@mtaonline.net*

Nestled on five private acres in the foothills of the Alaska Range. Spectacular "panoramic" mountain view. All accommodations have kitchens. Deluxe suites available. Our guests say it best: "We have stayed in B & Bs throughout Europe, the US, Canada and New Zealand, but Grand View is superlative. The view is unsurpassed and we enjoyed the nice touches."

## Pat and Windell's B and B
P.O. Box 50, Healy, Alaska 99743
Phone: 907- 683-2472, 1-800-683-2472
E-mail: *pwindell@mta.online.net*

Experience real Alaskan hospitality with long time Alaskans Pat and Windell Speer. Their comfortable home has a beautiful view of nearby Mt. Healy. Rooms are spacious and comfortable with private baths and your choice of a light or hearty breakfast. Pat and Windell's is located 12 miles north of Denali National Park entrance in a quiet, residential neighborhood. The Speers can arrange for an afternoon tour of Alaska's only working coalmine.

## Touch of Wilderness Bed and Breakfast
P.O. Box 397, Healy, Alaska 99743
Phone: 907-683-2459
E-mail: *touchow@usibelli.com*

Trees and a panoramic view of the Alaskan Range surround our two-story cedar house. Relax in one of eight warmly decorated bedrooms, or sit by the fire in one of two large common rooms. Wake to a hearty Alaskan breakfast. Come experience the wilderness with all the comforts of home. We will be waiting to hear from you.

## Valley Vista Bed & Breakfast
P.O. Box 395 Healy, Alaska 99743
Phone 907-683-2842
E-mail: *valleyvista@usibelli.com*

Secluded, private and affordable accommodations, only 12 miles north of the Denali National Park entrance. Guests of Valley Vista Bed & Breakfast will feel welcome and relaxed in our clean, modern home. We are just minutes away from the entrance to Denali National Park. There are spectacular views of the Alaska Range from the living room and guestrooms. The guestrooms are located on the top floor of our two-story house and have a shared bath. Our home is decorated with Alaskan artwork and handmade quilts.

Your hosts, Colin and Amy, are both lifelong Alaskans who enjoy sharing their Alaskan knowledge with guests. Colin was raised in Healy and has a great deal of knowledge about the local area. Amy was raised in the Kenai Peninsula. Both are graduates of the University of Alaska, Fairbanks. Our family includes two children, Zoë and Abel, and a friendly Dalmatian named Macy. Children are welcome in our non-smoking home.

## Otto Lake Bed & Breakfast

Hosts: Lyle and Beth Westphal
P O Box 45 Otto Lake Road, Healy AK 99743
Phone: 907-683-2339

Open year round, this B & B has private and shared baths, microwave, refrigerator, TV, VCR and a library.

## Alaskan Chateau Bed and Breakfast

Hosts: Teresa Chepoda and John Usibelli
P.O. Box 187, Healy, Alaska, 99743
Phone: 907-683-1377
E-mail: *chepoda@mtaonline.net*

Located on two wooded acres minutes from Denali National Park. We offer private suites with private baths, queen beds, telephone, refrigerator, microwave, coffeepot and TV. A hearty continental breakfast is served to guests in their rooms.

# Cabins Near Denali National Park's Entrance and the Town of Healy

## Denali Cabins

P.O. Box 229 Denali National Park, Alaska 99755
Phone: 907-683-2643, 888-560-2489
Email: *dencabins@aol.com*

At Denali Cabins the surrounding views are spectacular, the rooms are comfortable and there are activities in and around Denali National Park for everyone! Our front desk will provide you with all the information about local helicopter tours, flightseeing, rafting, hiking and shuttle schedules for Denali National Park. Relax in one of our two outdoor hot tubs!

We are located at Mile 229 on the George Parks Highway (that's 229 miles north of Anchorage and 131 miles south of Fairbanks). You may drive here in your own car, a rental car, a motorcoach, or we'll even meet you at the Alaska Railroad depot and provide your transportation while you're with us.

## Denali Crow's Nest Cabins

P.O. Box 70, Denali National Park, Alaska 99755
Phone: 888-917-8130
Email: *crowsnet@alaska.net*
Website: *www.denalicrowsnest.com*

If unique accommodations, fine dining and incredible views are high on your priority list while visiting Denali National Park, look no further than Denali Crow's Nest and the Overlook Bar and Grill. Situated high on Sugarloaf Mountain, the Crow's Nest offers solitude off the beaten path. All of our 39 log cabins offer panoramic views of the Alaska Range and comfortable accommodations in a quiet, wilderness setting. Our facility is perfect for the Alaska traveler seeking quality accommodations and proximity to Denali National Park.

## Denali Lakeside Lodging
Host: Jan St. Peters
P.O. Box 323 Healy, AK 99743
Phone: 907-683-2511
E-mail: *lakeotto@mtaonline.net*

Choose between four non-smoking accommodations located on Otto Lake, 12 miles from Denali National Park. Our duplex offers a two-story unit with double and queen beds upstairs, foldout queen downstairs. Full kitchen, bath, washer, dryer. Sleeps six. Children welcome. Or choose our log cabin, decorated with antiques. Kitchen, bath, double bed and foldout queen. Sleeps four. Adults only.

## Denali Sourdough Cabins
P.O. Box 118  Denali National Park, Alaska 99755
Phone: 800-354-6020
Email: *denalisourdough@hotmail.com*
Website: *www.denalisourdoughcabins.com*

Experience the beauty and majesty of Denali with a night of peace and tranquility at Sourdough Cabins. All cabins are fully furnished, heated and nestled in a peaceful spruce forest. Activities: *Flightseeing*-fixed-wing and helicopter. Flightseeing is a great way to view the park. Don't miss seeing Denali from the air. *River rafting*- Enjoy floating leisurely down the upper Nenana River or experience the thrill of shooting the rapids on the lower stretch of the Nenana. *Horseback Riding*-Enjoy the beauty of the Denali area on a half-day, full day or even an overnight horseback trip. *Alaska Cabin Night*-all-you-can eat dinner of fresh Alaska salmon, halibut, ribs and all the fixin's. A musical revue follows dinner.

## Healy Heights Family Cabins
P.O. Box 277 Healy, AK 99743
Phone: 907- 683-2639
E-mail: johnson@healycabins.com

Website: *healycabins.com*

Family-owned. Modern cedar cabins with private baths on 12 wooded acres atop a scenic ridge, overlooking the Alaska Range. All with microwave, refrigerator, coffee maker and toaster. Some have full kitchens. 15 minutes from Denali National Park Entrance…away from the crowds. A peaceful, relaxing setting for the entire family. Coffee and tea provided. Nonsmoking. No pets.

## McKinley Creekside Cabins

P.O. Box 89, Denali National Park, AK 99755
Phone: 1-888-5DENALI, 907-683-2277
Email:*cabins@mtaonline*
Website: *www.mckinleycabins.com*

McKinley Creekside Cabins are conveniently located 13 miles south of the Denali National Park entrance. Situated on Carlo Creek, beneath breathtaking mountains, McKinley Creekside Cabins boast an ideal location with convenient access to all the park's activities, yet allow you the privacy to experience Denali in its natural setting. The best value in Denali, rates starting at $79.00. Located at milepost 224 Parks Highway.

## The Perch

Restaurant, Bar and Cabins
HC2 Box 1525 Denali National Park, Alaska 99743
888-322-2523 1-907-683-2523
Email: *theperch@yahoo.com*
Website: *www.alaskaone.com/perchrest/*

After a long day of park adventures, come and relax in our beautiful restaurant and lounge. Enjoy remarkable views of the Alaska Range while you sip wine and talk about the day's events. We are an Alaskan family owned and operated business. We have 20 cabins along Carlo Creek six of them priced at 65.00 per night.

### Ridgetop Cabins

HC 1 Box 3000 Healy, AK 99743

Phone: 907-683-2448

E-mail: *ridgetop@mtaonline.net*

Brand new private cabins with a spectacular view. Quiet location only three miles from all services: restaurants, gas station, groceries and more. Private baths, continental breakfast, one queen and one twin bed in each cabin. Denali National Park entrance is only 18 miles south. No smoking.

## Private Campgrounds & RV Parks Near the Park Entrance

### Otto Lake Campgrounds

P.O. Box 195, Healy, AK 99743

Phone: Summer 907-683-2100, Winter 907-683-2603

E-mail: *ottolake@mtaonline.net*

Walk-in tent sites in the coves of the lake, and primitive wooded RV sites equipped with firepits and picnic tables. There are rainbow trout and silver salmon in Otto Lake, where you can fish from your site or rent a boat. Paddleboats and canoes are available. A tackle shop is "fishing-ready" right down to fishing poles. The wildlife in our area is abundant. We are located just on the north side of the Alaska Range, right on the border of Denali National Park, at Mile 247 George Parks Hwy.

### Carlo Creek Lodge Campgrounds

HC 2 Box 1530, Healy, Alaska 99743

Summer Phone: 907-683-2576, Winter: 907-683-2573

Location: 12 miles south of Denali National Park entrance on mile 223.9 of the Parks Highway. Private covered campsites each with a picnic table and a fire pit with an adjustable grill. eight individual long, hot showers. A small general store, gift shop, a pay phone, and information are all in the main lodge at the campground to make your stay more convenient.

## Denali Grizzly Bear Cabins & Campground
P.O. Box 7 Denali National Park, AK 99755
Phone: 907-683-2696
   South entrance Denali National Park on Nenana River. Cabins, Rent-a Tents, propane, laundry, gifts, groceries, liquor, phone. Surrounded by snow-capped mountains.

## McKinley Campground
Denali National Park, AK
Phone: 907-683-2379
   All sites include a picnic table and a fire ring. There is also a small convenience store, gift shop, ice, propane, showers, laundry facilities, firewood, playground and a nightly movie on ALASKA! We are within one mile of a clinic, post office, and restaurants. The campground has 89 sites with electricity, water, sewer, basic camping, and small and large tent sites. Located: 11 miles north of the Gateway to Denali National Park and Preserve, located at milepost 248.5 Parks Highway.

# Lodging, Campgrounds, & RV Parks on you way to Denali

# Cantwell

## Adventures Unlimited Lodge
Cantwell AK 99729
Phone: 907-561-7723
Email: *mis@goalaska.com*
   Open year round, this lodge has rooms, cafe with home cooked breakfast, lunch and dinner, and homemade pies. Activities include Denali National Park and Preserve tours, fishing, hiking and mountain biking. Winter activities include snowmachining, dog sled tours,

northern lights viewing and cross-country skiing. Located at milepost 99.5 Denali Highway.

## Backwoods Lodge

P.O. Box 32, Cantwell, AK 99729
Phone: 800-292-2232
E-mail: *Backwoods_Lodge@Yahoo.com*

AAA approved, cedar log lodge in a peaceful setting surrounded by mountains. 27 miles south of Park crowds. See Denali from pond with canoe. All rooms non-smoking, have queen bed(s), private bath, phone, TV, microwave, refrigerator, coffee, tea, cocoa and snacks. BBQs on covered porch.

## Cantwell Lodge

"Home of the Longhorned Sheep"
P.O. Box 87, Cantwell, AK 99729
Phone: 907-768-2300 Reservations-800-768-5522

Located two miles west of the Parks Highway and Denali Hwy junction. Offers lodging and dining for summer tourists. The bar, liquor store and laundromat are open year round. There are RV electric hookups and showers. Located at milepost 135.5 Denali Highway.

## Gracious House Lodge and Flying Service

P.O.Box 88 Cantwell, Alaska 99729
Phone: 907-822-7307, 877-822-7307

There are 20 modern cabins or motel units, most with private baths. Bar and café features ice cream and home-baked pies. Tent sites and parking for self contained RVs available overlooking the nearby lake. Air taxi and guide services available for sportsmen, tourists, and photographers. Located at milepost 82 Denali Highway.

## Lazy J Cabins and Cafe

P.O. Box 104, Cantwell, AK 99729

Phone: 907-768-2414

Cozy log cabins, only 20 minutes from the Denali National Park entrance at mile 210. Located one mile from the beginning of the Denali Highway. All cabins are surrounded by a beautiful view of Alaska's mountains and wildlife, with spectacular displays of the northern lights in winter. The cafe has homemade pastries and daily specials. Laundry and hair salon are on the premises.

# Nenana

## Alaskan Retreat B&B

PO Box 38, Nenana, Alaska 99760

Phone: 907-832-5431

E-mail: *gayle@mtaonline.net*

This beautiful Alaskan home is centrally located in Nenana Alaska. Nenana is one scenic hour drive from Fairbanks by car. You can easily explore the town by foot from the B&B. Whether you want to have a bite to eat, see the sites, meet the locals or just stretch your legs, Nenana is a great place to do it. Located at milepost 305 Parks Highway.

## Rough Woods Inn

P.O. Box 515, Nenana, AK 99760

Phone: 907-832-5299

Rough Woods Inn is located in the heart of historic Nenana, Alaska. Nenana is the home of the world renowned Nenana Ice Classic and the site where President Harding drove the golden spike for completion of the Alaska Railroad.

## Tripod Motel

Nenana, AK 99760

Phone: 907-832-5590.

Rooms start at $39.95 all with private baths and TV; kitchenettes available. Located at milepost 304 Parks Highway.

# Palmer

## Fairview Motel
P.O. Box 745, Palmer, AK 99645
Phone: 907-745-1505

## Abundant Acres B & B
HC04 Box 7471-A, Palmer AK 99645
Phone: 907-745-0757

## A-Lazy Acres B & B
P.O. Box 4013, Palmer AK 99645
Phone: 907-745-6340
Email: tazzman@matnet.com

## Colony Inn
P.O. Box 118, Palmer AK 99645
Phone: 907-745-3330

This structure was built to house teachers and nurses in the days when President Roosevelt was sending settlers to Alaska to establish farms. When innkeeper Janet Kincaid purchased it, the inn had been empty for some time. She restored the place, including the wood walls, which now create a cozy ambiance in the common areas. The 12 guestrooms are nicely appointed, and 10 include a whirlpool tub. Meals are not included, but the inn's restaurant offers breakfast and lunch. The inn is listed in the National Register of Historical Places.

## Fairview Motel, Restaurant & Lounge
P.O. Box 745, Palmer AK 99645
Phone: 907-745-1505
Email: *rehus@mtaonline.net*

## Gold Rush B&B

HC 05 Box 6914P, Palmer, Alaska 99645
Phone: 877-745-5312, 907-745-5312
Email: *stay@alaskagoldrush.com*
Website: *www.alaskagoldrush.com*

Located at the base of beautiful Hatcher Pass, near Palmer, Alaska. Offering 1800s period Gold Rush Rooms & Suites, Alaskan Theme Cabins and a hearty breakfast served up with genuine Alaskan Hospitality.

## Hatcher Pass Bed & Breakfast

HC05 Box 6797-D, Palmer AK 99645
Phone: 907-745-6788
Website: *www.hatcherpassbb.com*

Hatcher Pass Bed & Breakfast welcomes you to a truly Alaskan log cabin getaway. Enjoy a private cabin with all the modern amenities situated at the base of beautiful Hatcher Pass. Located ten minutes from Palmer, fifteen minutes from Wasilla, and a little over an hour from Anchorage, we offer you an opportunity to escape from the city and relax.

## Hatcher Pass Lodge

Box 763, Palmer, Alaska 99645
Phone: 907-745-5897
Website: *www.hatcherpasslodge.com*

Situated above treeline at 3,000 feet in the Talkeetna Mountains, Hatcher Pass Lodge offers overnight guests and day visitors the full spectrum of outdoor experience in Alaska. Hatcher Pass Lodge sits at the heart of a dazzling winter playground blessed with seven months of snow. Breathtaking slopes of the Talkeetna Mountains lure skiers of all abilities. Miles of groomed ski trails are set, some as high as 4,000 feet in the Gold Cord Bowl, an October Training Site for the U.S. cross-country Ski Team. This lodge has a total of nine cabins and three rooms. The seven larger cabins can sleep up to six people and have queen-size beds. Breakfast, lunch, and dinner are served.

## Iditarod House Bed & Breakfast

P.O. Box 3096 Palmer AK 99645
Phone: 907-745-4348
Website: *www.iditarodhouse.com*

Enjoy the Matanuska-Susitna Valley and Anchorage from a serene country setting. The Iditarod House Bed & Breakfast is the ideal choice for the Alaska traveler seeking quality, affordable accommodations. Located one easy mile from Palmer, Alaska, these modern, comfortable rooms are 40 minutes from Anchorage, 15 minutes to Wasilla, and about 3 1/2 hours from Denali National Park. Your hostess is a retired Iditarod sled dog musher.

## Motherlode Lodge

1150 S Colony Way, PMB 183, Palmer AK 99645
Phone: 907-745-6172
Website: *www.motherlodelodge.com*

Visit Motherlode Lodge (30 minutes from Palmer, in the Talkeetna Mountains at Hatcher Pass) for gold mining country including the historical Independence Mine State Preserve. Criss-crossed by old mining trails, summer or winter, Hatcher Pass is spectacular both in its beauty and the variety of wilderness sports activities available: hiking, mountain biking, berry picking, gold panning, llama trekking, gold mining history tours, snow shoeing, snowmobiling, dog mushing, northern lights viewing, snowboarding, skiing of every kind imaginable including cross country skijoring and snow cat skiing and tours.

## Tara Dells B & B

HC05 Box 6718 Trunk Road, Palmer AK 99645
Phone: 907-745-0407

Website: *www.taradells.com*

Five wooded acres near Wasilla Creek make the setting for these accommodations. Owners Andy and Donel Dowling have over 50 years in Alaska, with lots of experiences to share. They provide their visitors with videos and pictures of Alaskan-style fishing and hunting.

## RV Parks and Camping

### Homestead RV Park

P.O. Box 354, Palmer, AK 99645

Phone: 907-745-6005

Overlooking the Matanuska Valley, this wooded park has 64 sites.

### Mt. View RV Park

P.O. Box 2521 Palmer, AK 99645

Phone: 907-745-5747

Located in the Chugiak Mountain Range, nestled up against Lazy Mountain. Guests are not surprised to find moose and sheep walking through the park. 68 sites.

### Fox Run Campground

P.O. Box 4174 Palmer, AK 99645

Phone: 907-745-6120

## Paxson

### Paxson Alpine Tours and Cabins

MP 185.6, Richardson Hwy, Paxson, AK 99737

Phone: 907-822-5972

E-mail: *paxtours@alaska.net*

Website: *www.alaskan.com/paxsontours/*

Luxurious riverside log cabins with full baths, TV/VCR, mountain views, private decks. Located midway between Denali and Wrangell-St.

Elias National Parks. Evening wildlife float trip departs at 7pm. Great way to see Alaska up close. Suitable for all ages. Extended fishing and sightseeing trips by reservation.

## Paxson Inn & Lodge

Richardson Highway, Paxson, AK 99737
Phone: 907-822-3330
Website: *paxsoninn.themilepost.com*

Located at the junction of the Denali Hwy and Richardson Hwy, this facility has rooms with baths, full RV hookups, restaurant, cocktail lounge and fuel. Located at milepost 185 Richardson Highway.

## Tangle River Inn

Denali Highway, Paxson, AK 99737
Phone: 907-822-3970
E-mail: *info@tangleriverinn.com*

Jack Johnson and his family built their homestead, which now encompasses the Tangle River Inn, in 1953. He and his father laid most of the trails, now used for hunting, fishing & other recreation. A map of the extensive trail systems in the area, provided by the Bureau of Land Management, is available at the Inn. Located at milepost 20 Denali Highway.

## Tangle Lakes Lodge

P. O. Box 670386 Chugiak, Alaska 99567
Phone: 907-688-9173
Website: *www.alaskan.com/tanglelakes/*

More bicyclists are discovering the Denali Highway, not only for its incredible scenery and wildlife, but also its lack of vehicle traffic. For those riding through Alaska on a budget, the Denali Highway offers several fantastic campgrounds. For those that prefer lodging each night, the Denali Highway features six lodges along its route. We are proud to say that Tangle Lakes Lodge has become one of the favorites along the way for our bicycling travelers! In addition to fine food, Tangle Lakes Lodge also offers a good selection of fine wines. Cozy log cabins and a sauna down by the lakeshore make this a very relaxing stop after a hard day on the road. Located at milepost 22 Denali Highway.

# Talkeetna

### Caribou Lodge
P.O. Box 706, Talkeetna, AK 99675
Phone: 907-733-2163
Website: *www.cariboulodgealaska.com*
   Behold the majesty of Denali. Feel the tranquility. Touch the wilds of the Alaskan Bush. Located on a remote lake, above the timberline. Fantastic views of Denali and the Alaska Range as well as the beautiful Talkeetna Mountains. Recreation limited only by your imagination. Hiking, gold panning, fishing. Wildlife abounds. Open year round.

### Chinook Wind Cabins
P.O. Box 356, Talkeetna, Alaska 99676
Phone: 800-643-1899 907-733-1899
E-mail-*mrdavis@mtaonline.net*
   Chinook Wind Cabins provides accommodations ideally situated for anyone seeking a quality experience in Talkeetna. Open year-round, we offer five cabins-each with private bath. We are located within walking distance of every restaurant; gift shop and tour operator in town.

### Denali Anglers
P.O. Box 77, Talkeetna, AK 99676
Phone: 907-733-1505
Email: *fishalaska@denalianglers.com*
Web Site: *www.denalianglers.com*

We have eight units located on the river in Talkeetna, four deluxe cabins and four lodge suites. These units are on the shore of the Susitna River with views of the Alaska Range. Fully equipped for day and multi-day stays. Open year-round.

## Denali View Bed & Breakfast

Mile 3 Talkeetna Spur Road, Talkeetna, AK 99676
Phone: 907—733-2778
Website:*www.denaliview.com*

Spectacular view of Denali. Private bath, queen beds, full breakfast, completely modern. A bed and breakfast where hospitality is our top concern. Cabin also available. Located 12 miles south of Talkeetna.

## High Lake Lodge

P.O. Box 704, Talkeetna, AK 99676
Website: *www.highlakelodge.com*

Alaska wilderness lodging, fishing, hiking, flightseeing, photography, wildlife viewing, and canoeing in the Talkeetna Mountains. Cabin rentals. Unguided hunts. Open year round. Ice fishing, cross-country skiing, and snowmobiling in winter. "Good Times-Lasting Memories."

## Latitude 62 Lodge/Motel

P.O. Box 478-MS, Talkeetna, AK 99676
Phone: 907-733-2262

Fine dining, cocktails, and 12 modern rooms with private baths. Open year-round. Offering guided and drop-off riverboat fishing trips, guided snowmobile and dogsled rides. Experience true Alaskan hospitality.

## Swiss Alaska Inn

P.O. Box 565-MS, Talkeetna, AK 99676-0565
Phone: 907-733-2424
Website: *www.swissalaska.com*

The Swiss Alaska offers casual dining in pleasant surroundings with a full breakfast, specializing in famous omelets and Swiss-style French toast; delicious lunches including buffalo burgers, hamburgers, home-made soups and chili; and fresh Halibut or Salmon dinners. The dining room seats 50 people and offers a picture perfect view of Denali and a relaxed informal lounge. Modern, comfortable smoking and non-smoking rooms with private baths available.

## Talkeetna Hostel International
NHN I Street, P.O. Box 952, Talkeetna, AK 99676
Phone: 907-733-4678
Website: *www.akhostel.com*

An Alaskan Hostel in Talkeetna that offers clean affordable accommodations. Kitchen and hot showers. Two hours from Denali National Park. Walking distance to downtown Talkeetna, the airport, train, and more.

## Talkeetna Alaskan Lodge
P.O. Box 727-MS Talkeetna, AK 99676
Phone: 888-959-9590 907-733-9500
Email: *info@talkeetnalodge.com*
Website: *www.talkeetnalodge.com*

The Talkeetna Alaskan Lodge provides guests the opportunity to soak up the beautiful scenery and soak in our outdoor hot tub. The lodge also has a tour service desk, nature trail system and convenient access to outdoor activities for all ages and seasons. Shuttle service between the Lodge and the Railroad Depot. Located at milepost 12 Talkeetna Spur Road.

## Talkeetna Cabins
P.O. Box 124, Talkeetna, AK 99676
Phone: 888-733-9933 907-733-2227
E-mail: *talcabin@alaska.net*

Enjoy the tranquility of staying in our log cabins ideally located in downtown Talkeetna. Four cabins with complete kitchens and private baths.

## Talkeetna Roadhouse
P.O. Box 604 Talkeetna, Alaska 99676
Phone: 907-733-1351

Since we're halfway between Anchorage and Denali on the Alaska Railroad, an overnight stay in Talkeetna is a wonderful way to break up the eight-hour trip. Our rooms are cozy and typical of an old style Alaskan Roadhouse (meaning the bathrooms are "just down the hall"). In the morning you will smell hot cinnamon rolls just out of the oven mingling with the aroma of freshly ground coffee. The big tables in the cafe are always full of lively conversations and a true taste of the town.

## Trapper John's Bed and Breakfast
P.O. Box 243, Talkeetna, AK 99676
Phone: 907-733-2353, 800-735-2354

"Talkeetna-A taste of the real Alaska!" Enjoy exclusive use of our 1920s log cabin, decorated with trapping memorabilia. Sleeps four. Private setting, full kitchen. Short walk to beautiful downtown Talkeetna. Enjoy full sourdough pancake breakfast served in host's cabin.

# Trapper Creek and Petersville Road

## Denali View Chalets
P.O. Box 13245
Trapper Creek, Alaska 99683
Phone: 907-733-1333
E-mail: *roxie@alaska.net*

Open year round. Clean, comfortable, modern facilities with the privacy and convenience only a cabin or chalet can provide. Great view of Denali.

## Forks Roadhouse

P.O. Box 13109, Trapper Creek, AK
Phone: 907-733-1851

Forks Roadhouse was built by Mrs. Isabel McDonald and Frank Lee to supply miners and is a must to see. The Forks still in operation and is the oldest operating roadhouse in Alaska today. Cold beer available.

## Gate Creek Cabins

P.O. Box 13390, Trapper Creek, AK 99683
Phone: 907-733-1393
E-mail *gRawie@worldnet.att.net*
Website: *www.alaskan.com/gatecreekcabins/*

Modern family-size log cabins, heated and fully furnished for your comfortable stay of a day, week, or longer. Located on plowed road for easy year-round access. On lake with free use of canoes or paddleboats. Mountain view. Family pets welcome.

## McKinley Foothills B&B and Cabins

P.O. Box 13089, Trapper Creek AK 99683
Phone: 907-733-1454
E-mail: *mckinley@matnet.com*

These secluded, furnished log cabins have kitchenettes: and full breakfast provided. Summer activities include gold panning, fishing, birding, hiking and mountain biking. Winter brings skiing, snow machining and dog mushing tours. Located at Mile 17.2 Petersville Road.

## North Country Bed & Breakfast

P.O. Box 13377 Trapper Creek, Alaska 99683
Phone: 907-733-3981

An Alaskan Bed and Breakfast with a terrific view of Denali; snowmachine and sledding tours available.

### Trapper Creek Inn & General Store
Trapper Creek, AK
Phone 907-733-2302
Conveniently located north of Anchorage at Mile 114.8 on the Parks Highway. Travelers' supplies, delicatessen, deluxe lodging, economy prices, laundromat, large RV Park.

## Wasilla

### Windbreak Cafe & Hotel
2201 E. Parks Hwy Wasilla, Alaska 99654
Phone: 907-376-4484
E-mail: *windcafe@corecom.net*
$65 and up per night

### Mat-Su Resort on Lake Wasilla
1850 Bogard Rd. Wasilla, AK 99654
Phone: 907-376.3228
Website: *www.alaskan.com/matsuresort/*
Capture Alaska's pristine beauty on the shores of Lake Wasilla. Our main lodge (complete with decks, and boat and float plane launch) features all the amenities that make your stay comfortable. You can watch the salmon spawn, rent paddle and rowboats, swim, snowmobile, play 18-hole "ice golf", ice fish, and cross country ski. We even have volleyball, horseshoes, and lovely covered picnic pavilions plus our own gallery of trophy-winning Alaskan wildlife. Rates: May to September from $95, October-April from $65

### Best Western Lake Lucille Inn
1300 West Lake Lucille Drive, Wasilla, AK 99654
Phone: 907-373-1776, 800-528-1234
Resting on the shores of picturesque Lake Lucille, the Best Western Lake Lucille Inn welcomes you. The most modern and luxurious hotel

in Wasilla, the Best Western Lake Lucille Inn features deluxe rooms and suites, some with private balconies overlooking the lake, and a personable and knowledgeable staff that can assist you with your special needs and itinerary. Experience fine dining in our Shoreline Restaurant while admiring a spectacular view of snow capped mountains and the natural beauty of Lake Lucille.

### Agate Inn Bed & Breakfast
4725 Begich Circle, Wasilla, AK 99654
Phone: 800-770-2290
Email: *agate@alaska.net*

### Yukon Don's Bed & Breakfast Inn
1830 E. Parks Hwy. #386, Wasilla, AK 99654
Phone:800-478-7472
Email: *yukondon@alaska.net*
Website: *www.yukondon.com*

Originally homesteaded by A.J. Swanson in the early 1900s, this land was purchased by the Federal Government to be included in Roosevelt's New Deal Colony lottery in 1935. In 1960 Bob and Merlie McCombs purchased the farm and operated a dairy. Life here was a rugged, rural existence in what today is an idyllic country retreat. Transformed into a B&B Inn in 1986 by the Tanner family, it is now Alaska's most acclaimed bed and breakfast inn. Each of our seven rooms and cabin are decorated in authentic Alaskan decor and offer queen beds, private phones, ample room and unforgettable views.

# Willow

### Ruth Lake Lodge
P.O. Box 87 Willow, Alaska 99688
Phone: 907-495-9000

## Gigglewood Lakeside Inn

HC 89 Box 1601, Willow, Alaska 99688

Phone: 800-574.2555

Website: *www.gigglewood.com*

In the heart the Susitna River Basin's prime fishing region, Gigglewood Lakeside Inn is a beautiful log bed and breakfast, which captures the mood of the Alaska wilderness. Set above an unforgettable backdrop of lake reflections, the call of loons and grebes welcome you to this special place in harmony with nature.

## Willow Island Resort

71.5 Parks Hwy, Willow, AK 99688

Phone: 907-495-6343

Website: *www.willowislandresort.com*

The Willow Island Resort is a scenic roadside resort offering cabins, secluded campsites, full RV facilities, and more recreational activities than any resort of its kind in Alaska. If you're looking for an Alaskan roadside angling experience without the "Combat Fishing" feel, then look no further! Let our on site experts, the Willow Creek Rafting Co., cater to your angling needs. You can rent your own and float Willow Creek at your own pace, take along one of the guides to show you where all of the hot spots are, or take advantage of drop-off service. The Willow Creek Rafting Co. also specializes in remote, fly-out fishing and drop-off hunting adventures.

## Alaska Creekside B & B

Mile Post 47 Park Highway, Willow, AK 99688

Phone: 907-495-6556

Open year round, this B & B located on Willow Creek in a wooded setting has smoke-free rooms with private baths and advertises fishing "right out the front door."

## Alaskan Host Bed & Breakfast

Milepost 66 1/2 Parks Highway, Willow, AK 99688
Phone: 907-495-6800
Website: *www.alaskanhost.com*

Alaskan Host Bed and Breakfast opened its doors in 1996. Kathy and Jim Huston are hosts in this spacious home on two hundred acres with a private lake and hiking trails. Moose and other Alaskan wildlife are frequent visitors to the peaceful estate. The house is decorated with Alaskan wild game mounts, furs, and Alaskan videos and books. Children are always welcome.

## Susitna Dog Tours B & B

Milepost 91 1/2 Parks Highway, Willow, AK 99688
Phone: 907-495-6324

Relax off the beaten path in our beautiful log home. Susitna Dog Tours Bed & Breakfast is conveniently located at mile 91.5 of the Parks Highway, midway between Anchorage and Denali National Park.

## North Country RV Park

Deception Creek
Willow, AK 99688
Phone: 907-495-8747

# Chapter 13

## *Restaurants Near Denali National Park*

### Restaurants Near the Park Entrance
(Write-ups provided by properties)

### McKinley/Denali Salmon Bake

P.O. Box 90, Denali National Park, Alaska 99755
Website: *www.denalipark.com*
Email: *kevin@denalipark.com*
Phone: 907-683-2733

Our restaurant is a rustic Alaskan style wood and log building and heated with locally cut birchwood. We have indoor and outdoor seating with a majestic view of the mountains and crackling fires in wood-burning stoves. Your choice of meals at a price to fit any budget.

*Breakfast* features all-you-can-eat homemade sourdough and blueberry pancakes, reindeer sausage, French toast, eggs, homefried potatoes, hot & cold cereals, fruits, juices, and more. *Lunch* features two dozen gourmet burgers & sandwiches, steaks, broiled salmon, BBQ ribs, deep fried halibut, homemade soup, pie & ice cream, and a full beverage bar providing for all appetites and tastes. *Dinner* features gourmet burgers & sandwiches along with charbroiled steaks, broiled Alaska king salmon, halibut, BBQ beef ribs, and chicken. We also have an extensive salad bar with a large variety of salads and vegetables, homemade soups, beverages, desserts, and a full cocktail bar.

## The Perch Restaurant, Bar and Cabins
HC2 Box 1525 Denali National Park, Alaska 99743
Phone: 888-322-2523, 907-683-2523
Website: *www.alaskaone.com/perchrest/*
Email: *theperch@yahoo.com*

After a long day of park adventures, come and relax in our beautiful restaurant and lounge. Enjoy remarkable views of the Alaskan Range while you sip wine and talk about the day's events. We pride ourselves in providing excellent food, personalized service and comfortable accommodations-all with an original Alaskan flair. We serve breakfast, lunch and dinner, seven days a week throughout the summer season. Menu includes: fresh Alaskan seafood including: Halibut, Salmon, King Crab and Rainbow Trout. Steaks, light fare including pastas, poultry, salads and home-made soups, fresh baked breads, and a children's menu. We have 20 cabins along Carlo Creek six of them priced at $65 per night.

## Crow's Nest
P.O. Box 70, Denali National Park, Alaska  99755
Phone: 1-907-683-2723, 888-917-8130
Email: *crowsnet@alaska.net*

If unique accommodations, fine dining and incredible views are high on your priority list while visiting Denali National Park, look no further than Denali Crow's Nest and the Overlook Bar and Grill.

## Lynx Creek Pizza
238 Parks Highway, Denali National Park, AK 99743
Phone: 907-683-2548

When you're tired of fish, drop by this casual pizza place, which is just a few miles from the entrance to Denali National Park. Behind the log cabin walls you'll find a curious menu, which includes pizza,and sandwiches and Mexican dishes. Order you food in the front and bring it out back to the picnic tables. A hangout for both locals and tourists.

**Totem Restaurant** at the Totem Inn
P.O. Box 105, Healy, AK 99743
Phone: 907-683-2420

**The Mountaineer Café** at Denali Bluff Hotel
Milepost 238 Parks Hwy
Denali National Park, AK 99755
Phone: 907-683-7000, 800-488-7002
Website: *www.denalibluffs.com*

Open 5:00 AM to 10:00 PM. A continental breakfast buffet is available with individual breakfast items. Box lunches are available for day-long park excursions, and soup and sandwiches are available throughout the day.

**Stampede Lodge-Bushmaster Grill**
Healy, Alaska
Phone: 907-683-2242, 800-478-2370

Good food with Alaska beers

**Alaska Cabin Nite at McKinley Chalet Resort**
Milepost 238 Parks Highway, Denali National Park, Alaska 99755
Phone: 800-276-7234, 907-276-7234

Treat yourself to a real taste of Alaska. The moment you step through the door at Alaska Cabin Night Dinner Theater be ready for good-time entertainment. Fannie Quigley and her group of unforgettable characters treat you the hilarious stories of the Gold Rush featuring foot stomping, knee-slapping music. The all-you-can-eat, family style meal is sure to please. Enjoy a feast of Alaska salmon and barbecue ribs served with three scrumptious side dishes, rolls and a tasty dessert.

**Other restaurants:**

| | |
|---|---|
| Clear Sky Lodge | 907-582-2251 |
| Cruiser's | 907-683-2282 |
| Denali North Star Inn | 907-683-1560 |
| Denali Princess Dinning | 907-683-2282 |
| McKinley Chalet | 907-683-8200 |
| Wally's Healy Service & Deli | 907-683-2404 |

# Chapter 14

## *Summer Activities Around Denali National Park*

### Fishing Around Denali National Park

#### License Information

If you decide to take a chance on fishing in Alaska without buying a license first, you could wind up paying for it. Sport fishing without a license in Alaska carries a fine of $100, and it's one of the most common violations issued by Alaska Fish and Wildlife Protection troopers.

#### *Fees*

To make things easy and affordable, non-residents have their choice between one-day, three-day, seven-day and 14-day licenses for $10, $20, $30 and $50, respectively. Nonresident season licenses cost $100 and are good for a year. If you plan to fish for king salmon, you will have to purchase a king salmon tag in addition to a sportfish license. Nonresident king salmon tags cost the same as whatever license you buy. For example, a one-day king salmon tag costs $10 and a 14-day king salmon tag costs $50. Licenses and king salmon tags are available at just about any sporting goods stores and many roadside convenience stores. You can also get a license by mail from the Alaska Department of Fish and Game Licensing, 1111 W. Eighth St., Room 108, Juneau, AK 99801.

*Anglers under 16*

Nonresident anglers under 16 do not need a license or king salmon stamp, but are required to possess a king salmon annual harvest record if they are fishing for king salmon. The harvest records are free.

## Fishing Seasons

Peak fishing dates for Denali and the surrounding areas

| | |
|---|---|
| King salmon: | June 1 to July 13 |
| Silver salmon: | Aug 1 toSeptember 5 |
| Red salmon: | June 5 to June 15; July 15 to August 15 |
| Chum salmon: | July 20 to    August 5 |
| Pink salmon: | June 20 to August 15 |
| Rainbow: | June 1 to July 30; September 20 to October 10 |

Best time June 1 to July 1; then again in September until it freezes.

| | |
|---|---|
| Dolly varden: | May 20 to June 20 |
| Grayling: | May 20 to June 20 |

## Fishing Guides and Places to Fish
### (information provided by operators)

## Healy & Park Entrance

OTTO LAKE RV PARK
Lot 3 Otto Lake, Healy, Alaska 99743
Phone: 907-683-2100

There are rainbow trout and silver salmon in Otto Lake; fish from your site or rent a boat. Paddleboats and canoes are available. Our tackle shop is fishing ready right down to the fishing pole if you did not bring one.

## Houston

FISHERMAN'S CHOICE CHARTERS
P.O. Box 940276-MS, Houston, AK 99694
Phone: 800-989-8707, 907-892-8707
Email: *info@akfishermanschoice.com*
Web Site: *www.akfishermanschoice.com*
    We know where the fish are; we go where the fish are! With three rivers to choose from, Fisherman's Choice achieves a better than 90% success rate! USCG Licensed Guides. Location: Little Susitna, Deshka & Talkeetna Rivers

## Palmer

FISHTALE RIVER GUIDES/SALMON FISHING
P.O. Box 155-MS Palmer, AK 99645
Phone: 800-376-3625 , 907-376-3687
Email: *charter@fish4salmon.com*
Web Site: *www.fish4salmon.com*
    Catch bragging-size salmon on beautiful Little Susitna River. Fun, easy, road-accessible riverboat trips. Day and multi-day fishing.

## Talkeetna

DENALI ANGLERS
P.O. Box 77, Talkeetna, AK 99676
Phone: 907-733-1505
Email: *fishalaska@denalianglers.com*
Web Site: *www.denalianglers.com*
    Riverside lodging and guided fishing excursions in south-central Alaska. Fishing for trout and salmon on the Talkeetna and Susitna Rivers.

LATITUDE 62 LODGE
P.O. Box 478-MS, Talkeetna, AK 99676
Phone: 907-733-2262

Offering guided and drop-off riverboat fishing trips, and guided snowmobile and dogsled rides. Experience true Alaskan hospitality.

MAHAY'S FISHING EXPEDITIONS
P.O. Box 705-Talkeetna, Alaska 99676
Phone: 907-733-2223
Email: *mahays@alaska.net*
Website: *www.mahaysriverboat.com*

Mahay's offers you some of the finest stream fishing in the state of Alaska. From our location we have over 200 miles of prime fishing territory. You can fish for all five species of salmon-king, sockeye, chum, pink and coho, in addition to rainbow trout, dolly varden and arctic grayling.

TALKEETNA RIVER GUIDES
P.O. Box 563, Talkeetna, Alaska 99676
Phone: 800-353-2677, 907-733-2677
E-Mail: *trg@alaska.net*
Website: *alaska-online.com/trg*

Located at the confluence of three world-class salmon rivers, with easy access to many others. Fish for five species of Pacific Salmon, as well as grayling, Dolly varden and rainbow trout ... amidst stunning landscapes teeming with wildlife. Our expert guides are avid fishermen themselves, fully licensed and adept at finding the best fishing holes around. All of our excursions are fully equipped for both fly-fishing and spin cast fishing.

**Wasilla**

EAGLE TALON CHARTERS
P.O. Box 874506, Wasilla, AK 99687

Phone: 907-357-LURE
Email: *info@eagletaloncharters.com*
Web Site: *www.eagletaloncharters.com*
Guided fishing charters, unguided drop-offs, and sightseeing in the Big Susitna drainage.

HUSKY TOURS LODGE
P.O. Box 872351-MS Wasilla, AK 99687
Phone: 907-373-4099
Email: *huskytours@neptune.com*
Web Site: *www.akcache.com/huskytours*
Explore our trails and river system, viewing wildlife, spawning salmon, snowshoeing, fishing, and canoeing. Tour the valley while relaxing in a custom van. Beautiful log lodge overlooking Little Susitna. Dogmushing, dogsled rides.

SALMON READY
HC 31 Box 5221-MS, Wasilla, AK 99654
Phone: 877-355-2430 907-355-2430
Email: *fishon@salmonready.com*
Web Site: *www.salmonready.com*
Fishing guide and outfitter specializing in fishing on the Little Susitna River and other Mat-Su Valley streams and rivers.

WASILLA LAKE B&B
961 N. Shore Drive-MS Wasilla, AK 99654-6546
Phone: 907-376-5985
Email: *wasillalake@alaskan.com*
Web Site: *www.alaskan.com/wasillalake*
Lake accommodations at their finest! Three comfortable guestrooms; deluxe, two bedroom furnished apartment. Exquisite view, hearty breakfast. Good fishing. Boat use. Resort-like atmosphere.

# Rafting Around Healy and the Denali National Park Entrance

## Denali Raft Adventures

Milepost 238 Parks Highway, Denali National Park, AK 99755
Phone: 888-683-2234
E-mail: *denraft@mtaonline.net*
Website: *www.denaliraft.com*

Denali Raft Adventures has been in business for 24 years, making it the oldest and most experienced raft company in the Denali National Park area. Through our years of experience on the Nenana River, we have developed a program that provides rafters with the safest rafting experience available, in an activity that has inherent risks, that can't be eliminated without destroying the unique character of the activity. Trips include: McKinley Run (two hours), Canyon Run (two hours), Healy Express (four hours), Full Day (eight hours), Paddle Rafts (two or four hours), and overnight trips.

## Denali Outdoor Center

P.O. Box 170, Denali National Park, AK 99755
Phone: 888-303-1925, 907-683-1925
Email: *docadventure@hotmail.com*
Web Site: *www.denalioutdoorcenter.com*

Denali's premier outdoor recreation provider. Mountain bike rentals, two and four hour whitewater, plus scenic rafting and kayaking river trips.

*Canyon Run*: Take on Razorback, Iceworm, Cable Car and Royal Flush Rapids on this two-hour whitewater adventure. Journey through 10 miles of the Denali National Park frontier while challenging class III & IV whitewater. Choose an oar-boat or paddle raft for extra excitement.

*Scenic Wilderness*: Enjoy the Alaskan splendor as we float the boundaries of Denali National Park. View the Yanert Fork River, Mount Fellows and Mushers Monument while watching for a variety of wildlife on this two-hour trip with mild class II rapids. Families and the less adventurous will discover the joys of rafting.

*Nenana Half Day*: This four-hour trip combines the mild Wilderness stretch and the rapids of the Canyon. Enjoy Alaska's scenic beauty and hit over 10 major rapids for a complete afternoon of river running.

## McKinley Raft Tours
P.O. Box 138, Denali National Park, AK 99755
Phone: 907-683-2581

McKinley Raft Tours offers three different kinds of experiences, from the quiet beauty of a float trip to the rush and excitement of the Nenana's famous white water. Group rates are available.

## Nenana River Adventures
Milepost 238, Healy, AK 99743
Phone: 800-789-RAFT
Email: *raftak@mtaonline.net*
Website: *www.alaskaraft.com*

Nenana River Adventures is located on the north bank of the Nenana River next to the bridge at Milepost 238 of the Parks Highway. All our trips in the Denali area begin here. For our expeditions we'll meet you at 9:00 a.m. For our day trips we have five scheduled departures daily so meeting times will vary.

Our Nenana Gorge and Upper Nenana scenic floats run 11 miles of river and take three to four hours, with approximately two hours spent on the water and 90 minutes for transportation and getting dressed in our drysuits or wetsuits. Our Class IV paddle raft trips run 22 miles of river and last approximately five-six hours. Our 22-mile paddle trips do take a mid-point break so bring a picnic lunch.

## Tooloouk River Guides & Outfitters
P.O. Box 106, Denali National Park, AK 99755

Phone: 907-683-1542
Website: *www.alaska-online.com/tooloouk/*
  Offering trips to the following areas:

*Hulahula River- Arctic National Wildlife Refuge, Brooks Range*
10 days/9 nights.-Mid- June
Talkeetna River-Talkeetna Mountains, Alaska Range
7 days / 6 nights–early June
5 days / 4 nights–July and August
4 days / 3 nights-July and August

*Chitina-Copper Rivers-Wrangell-St. Elias National Park and Preserve*
12 days / 11 nights-July 10-21
Copper River only-8 days / 7 nights.............July

*Fortymile River-Interior Alaska*
8 days / 7 nights.............August

*Yanert Fork / Nenana River-Denali National Park*
3 days / 2 nights.............Open Schedule
2 days / 1 night...............Open Schedule

## Talkeetna

**Talkeetna Outdoor Center**
P.O. Box 748, Talkeetna, AK 99676
Phone: 907-733-4444
Email: *journeys@alaska.net*
Website: *www.alaskajourneys.com*
  We offer an awesome three-day whitewater rafting trip through the Talkeetna Canyon-flight accessed, full of salmon, grizzly, and great paddling!

**Talkeetna River Guides**
P.O. Box 563 Talkeetna, Alaska 99676
Phone: 800-353-2677
Email: *trg@alaska.net*
Website: *www.talkeetnariverguides.com*

TRG has been in this area for more than twenty years and welcomes the opportunity to share a more intimate side of Denali with you. We use high quality equipment, and our skilled guides will gladly point out interesting features along the way. Trips are made aboard large, safe rafts, through wilderness areas without any white water:

*Two hour-Talkeetna River*
Departure Time: 1:00, 4:30 & 7:30 PM from Main Street Office

*Three hour-Talkeetna & Susitna Rivers*
Departure Time: Call for schedule

*Six hour-Chulitna River*
Departure Time: Call for schedule

*What to expect:* Although clear weather may afford us a beautiful view of Denali, wildlife activity and the many nuances of this wilderness environment truly come to life on cloudy and rainy days. We provide rain gear, boots and binoculars so you can enjoy your trip, rain or shine.

# Horseback Riding in and near Denali National Park and Healy, AK

**Denali Saddle Safaris (DSS)**
P.O. Box 435-IN Healy, AK 99743
Phone: 907-683-1200
Email: *trlrides@mtaonline.net*

Website: *www.denalisaddlesafaris.com*

Rides offer stunning panoramic views of the Alaska Range and the surrounding Healy Valley. Denali National Park surrounds us on three sides, but we are unable to ride into the park. DSS are the only horseback outfitter in Denali with views of Denali on our half-day and longer rides. Our experienced staff takes you on a journey traveling 3,200 feet in elevation with breathtaking views of the entire area.

### Tumbling B Ranch

P.O. Box 225, Denali National Park Alaska, 99755
Phone 907-683-6000
Email: *tbr@mtaonline.net*
Website: *www.tumblingbranch.com*

Tumbling B Ranch offers stunning trips into the heart of the Alaskan Mountain Range and the Nenana River Valley. No riding experience is needed to enjoy the close up encounters with wildlife and scenic grandeur tours provide. The Ranch is located in the heart of the Alaska Mountain Range, 12 miles north of the entrance to Denali National Park. The Tumbling B caters to smaller groups and prides itself in having a friendly, knowledgeable staff.

### Kantishna Roadhouse

P.O. Box 130, Denali National Park, AK 99755
Phone: 800-942-7420, 907-479-2436
Email: *kantshna@polarnet.com*
Website: *www.kantishnaroadhouse.com*

Kantishna Roadhouse invites adventurers to spend a few hours on the trail viewing this beautiful valley by horseback. Trail rides are guided by a professional wrangler so you don't have to be a horse expert to enjoy this activity. There are excellent photo opportunities from the ridges, easily reached by this leisurely method of travel. The front desk has information on rates and times for guided rides.

# Horseback Riding Around Denali National Park

## Wolf Point Ranch

P.O. Box 232, Cantwell, AK 99729

Phone: 907-768-1150

E-Mail: *wolfpt@mtaonline.net*

Few visitors to Denali National Park take the time to genuinely experience the wonders of the backcountry. Wolf Point has custom packtrips that leave the tourist crowds behind and traverse the heart of the Alaska Range, home to Denali. We are surrounded by a vast wilderness stretching virtually without end. Possibilities for excellent mountain riding are limitless.

Wolf Point offers five-day packtrip adventures, limited to only six participants per trip. After a get-acquainted dinner the night prior to departure, you will spend the next five days amidst mountains, glacial streams, dall sheep, moose, caribou, bears, wolves, and a host of other wildlife.

Highly experienced guides, excellent saddle stock, top quality gear, hearty meals and all the odds and ends to make your trip a safe, enjoyable adventure are provided.

## D&S Alaskan Trail Rides

P.O. Box 1437-MS Palmer, AK 99645

Phone: 907-733-2205

Email: *akrides@mtaonline.net*

D&S offers guided scenic horseback trail rides and horse-drawn wagon rides in Alaska's spectacular Denali State Park. Witness majestic snow covered Denali and the surrounding rugged peaks and glaciers of the Alaska Mountain Range. D&S has experienced, gentle horses for first time riders, and kids are welcome! Located at Mile 133 George Parks Highway. Open May through September. Hourly and day rates.

# Denali Country Ranch(DCR)

14901 Wildien Drive Anchorage, AK 99516

Phone: 907-345-3083

Website: *www.ranchweb.com/denali*

Denali Country Ranch is an active-guest riding ranch, offering fully guided riding opportunities and enjoyment for just about any experience level. DCR traverses the last frontier Alaskan-style through forested river bottoms and across high alpine meadows, photographing wildlife and taking in the view.

From the front or back door of the ranch, DCR offers hourly or daily horseback rides into pure wilderness. With prior arrangement and reservation, a fully guided and outfitted multi-day pack trip into the Alaskan backcountry is available.

Fishing is readily available, both to the hiker and as a part of a horseback trip. The Butte Lake camp is one of several options originating out of the ranch. Arctic grayling, lake trout and arctic char are the most commonly found species in nearby lakes and streams.

Denali Country Ranch is located on a remote section of the Denali Highway, about 20 miles west of the old ghost town of Denali. We also operate a camp on the only private land on Butte Lake, a remote alpine lake about ten miles southeast of the ranch. We have a cabin, boats, a chef, and fishing tackle at the camp. Access to the camp is an incredibly scenic three-hour horseback ride. The lake provides excellent lake trout and arctic grayling fishing.

Guided horseback riding into the country around the lodge is available at all times. While horseback riding is also available to the daytime guests, lodge guests have priority in access to the horses. Rates to the general public are $55/hr first hour and $45/hr for additional hours. Rates to our ranch guests are $45/hr first hour and $40/hr for additional hours.

DCR can arrange transportation to and from Anchorage and Fairbanks. Under some circumstances, we will furnish group transportation, including airport or hotel pick-up, at competitive rates.

## Saddle Trails North (STN) / Adventures Unlimited Denali Country Ranch

14901 Wildien Drive, Anchorage, Alaska 99516
Phone: 907-345-3083
Email: *info@saddletrailsnorth.com*
Website: *www.saddletrailsnorth.com*

Come enjoy an Alaskan wilderness horseback experience of a lifetime! Adventures Unlimited Denali Country Ranch, a family owned and operated guest ranch, can offer you the opportunity to truly explore Alaska's beauty and splendor from the back of one of our unique Alaskan mountain horses.

The country ranch's location offers virtually limitless options for both trail rides and true explorations, similar to the treks made early in the 1900s by prospectors in search of gold. Horses settled this country. Though the prospect of finding gold might not be high, the prospect of finding peace and a fresh perspective is *very* high.

## Flightseeing
(information provided by operators)

Many people discover Denali National Park by car, bus, bike, or by foot. But to see the south side of Denali and where most of the mountain climbers set up base camp, you must use a small plane. These flightseeing planes are a little pricey but well worth the money, especially if your adventure includes a landing on the Kahiltna Airfield where over 1,000 hikers attempting to summit Denali set up base camp. Below is a listing of flightseeing services in the Healy/Denali National Park area and Talkeetna.

## Denali National Park and Healy

### Kantishna Air Taxi
Box 46 Denali National Park, Alaska 99755

Phone: 907-683-1223
Email: *glflyboy@mtaonline.net*
Website: *www2.gorp.com/katair/*

Kantishna Air Taxi, based at the Kantishna International Airport, is at the end of the 94-mile gravel road deep within Denali National Park. Granted an exclusive concession permit by the National Park Service, Kantishna is the only air operator based within the boundaries of Denali National Park.

## Pere Air

Denali Natonal Park, Alaska 99755
Phone: 907-683-6034, 877-683-6033
Email: *Guy@pereair.com*
Website: *www.pereair.com*

*"PereAir"* is based 10 miles north of the Denali National Park entrance, in the rain shadow of the Alaska Range. Here, on average, it rains 50% less than on the south side. Often, we are flying tourists around Denali while rain and low clouds ground planes on the south side. Tours include: Summit Flight: 1.4 hours, Round the Mountain: 1.5 hours, Basic Tour: 1.1 hours.

## Era Helicopters Flightseeing Tours

Denali National Park, AK 99755
Phone: 800-478-1947
Website: *www.era-aviation.com*

Soar above the mountainous backcountry and over glaciers thousands of years old with Era Helicopters, Alaska's most experienced helicopter operator. Choose between Mt. McKinley's *"Denali Excursion"* the *"Peak Experience,"* or the *"Glacier Expedition"* fully narrated helicopter tours. All offer a personalized glimpse at an extraordinary world. Era also offers naturalist-guided heli-hiking tours.

# Talkeetna

## K2 Aviation

Box 545-B, Talkeetna, Alaska 99676
Phone: 800-764-2291, 907-733-2291
Email: *info@flyk2.com*
Website: *www.flyk2.com*

K2 has over 35 years of flying experience in Alaska. We enjoy taking our visitors for breathtaking flightseeing tours around Denali, landing on the glaciers surrounding Denali, providing climbers with expedition information, and creating wilderness adventure packages for independent travelers.

K2 is a respected and familiar name in both the climbing community and the tourism industry, having provided glacier-flying service since 1979. K2's experienced and professional staff has earned a solid reputation for excellent service and safety. Packages vary from one to two hour flights and can include glacier landings.

## Hudson Air Service Inc.

P.O.Box 648, Talkeetna, Alaska 99676
Phone: 907-733-2321, 800-478-2321
Email: *hasi@customcpu.com*
Website: *www.hudsonair.com*

Hudson Air is at the Talkeetna State Airport, 115 fast highway miles north of Anchorage. Hudson offers flightseeing, mountaineering support, fly-out hunting and fishing trips, aerial photography, wildlife viewing, and charter service. Hudson's is the only air service in Talkeetna authorized to fly for the National Park Service and has helped in a number of rescues on Denali in the past several years.

## Talkeetna Air Taxi

P.O. Box 73, Talkeetna, Alaska 99676

Phone: 907-733-2218, 800-533-2219
Email: *info@talkeetnaair.com*
Website: *www.talkeetnaair.com*

Don Sheldon founded the original flying service of Talkeetna, Talkeetna Air Service, in 1947. Mr. Sheldon was the pioneer of McKinley high altitude glacier landings. The story of Sheldon and his daring rescues of climbers on the mountain have attracted people to Talkeetna for decades. Several other aviators well known in the industry and throughout Alaska have owned Talkeetna Air Taxi, including Lowell Thomas Jr., former lieutenant governor of Alaska and son of the famous radio broadcaster. Over fifty years later, Talkeetna Air continues to lead the way exploring Denali National Park. Paul Roderick, Chief Pilot and owner, is a climber with experience on McKinley and other peaks in the region, giving him firsthand knowledge of the area.

### Doug Geeting Aviation
P.O Box 42, Talkeetna, AK 99676
Phone: 800-770-2366
Website: *www.alaskaairtours.com*

Packages include visiting the Kahiltna Base Camp, landing at Little Switzerland, landing at the Don Sheldon Mountain House, circling Denali, and taking wildlife-glacier tours.

## Golf

### Black Diamond Golf
P.O. Box 11 Healy, Alaska 99743
Phone: 907-683-4653
Email: *marilyn@usibelli.com*
Website: *www.blackdiamondgolf.com*

Black Diamond is a challenging course with Alaskan Hazards, such as a tundra marsh or the occasional moose hoof print. It's a relatively short course. Designed for accessibility and fun.

(Authors note: As you might imagine, golf isn't a major pastime around Denali, but we found one provider.)

## Climbing Denali
(information from service providers)

If you are considering climbing Denali, choose one of the following guide services:

### Alaska-Denali Guiding, Inc..
P.O. Box 566, Talkeetna, Alaska 99676
Phone: 907-733-2649
Email: *adg@alaska.net*
Website: *www.denaliexpeditions.com*
Alaska-Denali Guiding, Inc specializes in Denali expeditions, mountaineering trips, hiking trips and custom trips in Denali National Park and throughout Alaska. In 1983 we began Alaska-Denali Guiding, Inc. as a way to share the beautiful mountain and wilderness country that we have always loved to explore on our own. We have been very fortunate to find a niche that suits us and our clientele perfectly: quality time to climb or hike in Alaska's wilderness with a focus on the natural history and learning outdoor skills.

### Alpine Ascents International
121 Mercer Street, Seattle, WA 98109
Phone: 206-378-1927
Email: *Climb@AlpineAscents.com*
Website: *www.alpineascents.com*

Alpine Ascents has carefully selected each Denali guiding team to make the individual climber's experience is unsurpassed. Our staff of lead guides is a unique combination of famed climbers, but also instructors and regional experts. Our staff includes climbers Todd Burleson, Peter Athans, Vernon Tejas, Wally Berg, Willi Prittie, Tom Bridge, Martin Zabaleta, Jim Williams, Jamie Pierce, Bill McCormick, Sean Sullivan and Scott Darsney. The most unique aspect of our climb is the climber–to–guide ratio of 6:2, with some of the most experienced lead guides in the industry. Over the past two seasons, four of five teams summitted.

Denali climbs require highly experienced guides. Many Alpine Ascents guides have historical climbing achievements synonymous with their names. The role of a guide is to impart knowledge, use calculated judgment and assist an individual climber's development. Thus, we stress our acute ability to provide students and expedition members with personal attention, realizing the commitment to assist each team member in obtaining their goals.

## American Alpine Institute.
1515 12th St N-3, Bellingham, WA 98225
Phone: 360-671-1505
Website: *www.mtnguide.com/programs/denali.htm*

The Institute gives its clients careful and detailed counsel in preparations for climbing, and when appropriate, has clients first achieve intermediate goals to fully prepare. Climbs on Denali obviously involve many factors that we cannot control, among them temperature, wind, snowfall, and changeable climbing conditions. The key to success therefore is doing an excellent job working on those areas that a climber can do something about: skill in dealing with cold conditions, skill in climbing at an appropriate technical level, and personal conditioning. To have abilities in these areas well developed and then to combine them with a carefully designed and guided itinerary is the most direct line to safety and success.

Composed as they are of individuals with appropriate skill, experience, and training, AAI expeditions are strong and enjoy a rate of safety and success rarely matched by other teams. With well-prepared climbers, we do not have to rely on perfect conditions in order to move. Able to remain poised high on the mountain in poor conditions, our teams often make successful summit bids in small windows of good weather when other teams are out of position. AAI doesn't pretend to guarantee good health, good weather, or success on these expeditions, but it is committed to building strong teams and creating high potential for safe and successful climbs. The average individual success rate on Denali is 51% overall and 56% in guided groups other than AAI. The Institute's success rate for individuals for the last six years is 81% and for expeditions it is 86%.

In the context of technical climbing skills, the mountain offers quite varied lines of ascent, from several which require intermediate alpine mountaineering skills to others which rank among the world's most difficult alpine routes. By any route, however, the mountain requires great physical effort, skillful and cautious mountaineering and expedition practices, and patient acclimatization and climbing over a three-week period. We have chosen the West Buttress, West Rib, and Cassin Ridge for our ascents of McKinley. All three have more limited objective dangers than other challenging routes on the mountain, and together they offer three distinct levels of technical challenge. The West Buttress requires intermediate level mountaineering skills; the West Rib is more difficult and includes sections with sustained climbing on exposed 55-degree faces; and the Cassin is very challenging, with 65-degree hard ice, mixed climbing on steep ground, and rock. In addition to appropriate technical skills, all routes require winter backcountry experience in very cold conditions, and top physical conditioning.

## Mountain Trip
P.O. Box 111809, Anchorage AK 99511

Phone: 907-345-6499
Email: *MtTrip@aol.com*
Website: *www.mountaintrip.com*

Mountain Trip has been guiding climbers up Denali for over 25 years, with an excellent safety and success record. The 2001 season will be our 26th. For climbers wishing to do a nontechnical, but physically challenging, climb of Denali, we offer two options: round trip climb of the West Buttress route or a traverse climb. The duration of these routes is between 16 and 26 days. The Traverse ascends the West Buttress route and, after the summit climb, you descend the north side via the Harper and Muldrow Glaciers.

The Muldrow Glacier takes you to historic McGonagall Pass. This is the beginning of a 20 mile exhilarating hike to Wonder Lake, the highlight of which is often the river crossings, which are always thrilling.

## Rainier Mountaineering, Inc.

535 Dock Street, Suite 209, Tacoma, Washington 98402
Phone: 206-627-6242
Website: *www.rmiguides.com*

Rainier Mountaineering, Inc. was incorporated in 1968. Rainer is owned and operated by Lou and Peter Whittaker together with Joseph Horiskey. A staff of highly skilled and experienced mountain guides teaches the very latest in modern snow and ice climbing techniques. Our commitment to set the standards and fill the need for quality, professional instruction is reflected in the programs we offer. At 20,320', Denali is the crown of the Alaska Range and the highest mountain in North America. Completion of any RMI seminar or equivalent formal instruction is proper background for joining this expedition. Guided Denali expeditions have operated since 1975. RMI is an authorized concessionaire of Denali National Park. Please contact RMI for dates, rates, equipment list and additional information.

# Chapter 15

## *Winter Activites–Denali National Park and Surrounding Areas*

# Aurora Borealis (The Northern Lights)
## (by Sam McConkey)*

Imagine yourself as an early Alaskan settler out on an ice field at 40 degrees below zero, checking your game traps and fishing rigs when, suddenly, the night sky is filled with light of such intensity, moving with such speed, that it could only be a sign from the gods. The lights dance rapidly and randomly to and fro all the while changing color and even, you think, making sounds like whips cracking hundreds of miles over-head. The awesome power of these curtains of light fill you with fear and inspiration. What are they? What do they mean? Am I about to hear a booming voice from the heavens?

I will tell you from experience that the same amazement occurs each time I behold the Northern Lights. No matter how many times you see them, the thrill of their appearance is never anything less than spectac-ular. These divine phenomena make you rush outside in frigid temper-atures (usually in nothing but a bathrobe) simply to catch a glimpse. The drama of the Northern Lights captivates me and often brings tears to my eyes. Those of you who have experienced them will probably agree. Many of you may even say I've understated their power. In any event, let my descriptions serve as simply a prelude to a truly life-chang-ing experience. Seeing the Northern Lights is something everyone should do at least once in their lifetime.

*What Are the Northern Lights?*

The "Northern Lights" is actually a misnomer of sorts, because these lights exist in the southern reaches of the earth as well. The technical terms for these phenomena are The Aurora Borealis (northern) and the Aurora Australis (southern). The scientific explanation of the auroras is that they result from a very complex chemical reaction between particles emitted from the sun and gasses in the earth's atmosphere. Of course, science aside, their heavenly beauty makes me certain they are a glimpse of what lies beyond our miniscule, earthly lives. At the risk of completely oversimplifying the process, sunspots (powerful magnetic fields on the sun) emit electrically charged particles that enter the earth's atmosphere and cause a visible reaction with the atmospheric gasses above the earth. The magnetic properties of these particles result in their concentration around the magnetic poles of the earth, thus the northern and southern lights. These reactions occur in circular pattern around the poles, like a crown of light or a curtain. Of course, the curtain is huge, so we cannot see the entire thing all at once from the earth. Imagine lying on your back on the floor and looking up at your window curtains. When a breeze comes through the window, the curtain dances. The size of the circular curtain changes also. Sometimes, the curtain expands so much that the lights are visible in the continental United States.

Aurora activity varies from year to year because the sun is more or less active according to an eleven-year cycle. This cycle correlates with sunspot activity. The peak years include 1990, 2001, and 2012. The low activity years include 1996 and 2007.

*So, How Can I See the Lights?*

I often tell people the Northern Lights are nature's reward to those of us willing to face up to 40 degrees below zero in Alaska's winter. Unfortunately for most tourists, the lights aren't visible until late fall (late September), after the close of the tourism season. The lights are visible through the winter and can be seen as late as early March. The cold weather has nothing to do with the lights, of course. Like the stars, they are always there; you just cannot see them until it gets dark. In the land of the midnight sun, that means winter.

If you are in Alaska when the skies begin to get dark again, venture as far north as possible to get a good look at the Aurora, away from any big city. The clear, dark nights of February, March and April are best for

Aurora Borealis sightings. Look for the lights between midnight and 3 a.m., especially during the new moon phase of the month. If you get a chance, film northern lights with Denali as a backdrop.

It will be worth it, I promise you.

# Skiing

## Big Lake

*Susitna Expeditions, LTD*
P.O. Box 520243-MS Big Lake, AK 99652
907-892-6916 fax: 907-892-7727 AK: 800-891-6916
Email: *kayaker@mtaonline.net*
Web Site: *www.susitnaexpeditions.com*
Explore beautiful Byers Lake and Denali State Park. Backcountry ski tours.

## Palmer

*Hatcher Pass Lodge*
P.O. Box 763-MS Palmer, AK 99645
Phone: 907-745-5897
Web Site: *www.hatcherpasslodge.com*
Lodge above timberline at 3,000' elevation. Cross country skiing.

## Talkeetna

*Talkeetna Outdoor Center*
PO Box 743 Talkeetna, AK 99676
Phone: 800-349-0064, 907-733-8352
Email: *journeys@alaska.net*
Website: *www.alaskajourneys.com*
Cross-country ski rentals in winter.

## Wasilla

*Glacier Snowcat Skiing & Tours*
P.O. Box 874234-MS Wasilla, AK 99687
Phone: 800-770-3118, 907-373-3118

2000 vertical feet of POWDER! Nine-12 runs in our heated, 12-passenger snowcat. Skiing or snowboarding, we guarantee excitement! Come and experience the best Mat-Su has to offer.

## Willow

*Susitna Dog Tours and B & B*
HC 89 Box 464-MS Willow, AK 99688-9705
Phone: 907-495-6324
Email: *susdog@matnet.com*
Web Site: *www.alaskan.com/vendors/susdog.html*

Trails for snowshoeing, cross-country skiing and skijoring. Many photo opportunities. Year-round accommodations. Located at milepost 91.5 on the Parks Highway.

## Remote

*Within the Wild Alaskan Adventure Lodges*
2626 Galewood Street-MS Anchorage, AK 99508-4041
Phone: 907-274-2710 fax: 907-277-6256
Email: *alaskawild@gci.net*
Web Site: *www.withinthewild.com*

Within the Wild Alaskan Adventure Lodges owns/operates three backcountry lodges and offers remote cross-country skiing, dog mushing, snowmachine touring.

# Snowmachine/Snowmobile
## (information provided by operators)

## Healy & Denali National Park Entrance

*Stampede Lodge*
P.O.Box 380, Healy, Alaska 99743
Phone: 907-683-2242, 800-478-2370

Winter adventures at Stampede Lodge including dog sledding, snow machining, snow shoe hiking, Iditarod kennel visits, lectures and demonstrations on dog mushing, winter wildlife and habitat, natural history of Denali and Northern Lights viewing. During the day, our local Alaskan guides will show you the vastness of the Alaskan Interior as you experience our frozen winter world. Then, on a cold clear night, the heavens can come alive with the Northern Lights, the view of a lifetime!

## Cantwell

*Snowmobile Tours*
P.O. Box 83 Cantwell, Alaska 99729
Phone: 907-768-2600

Located Southeast of Denali National Park, GrayJay Snowmobile Tours offers completely outfitted, guided adventures by snowmobile into the Alaska wilderness. The area around Cantwell, offers world class snowmobiling conditions. You'll find incredible scenery and plenty of opportunity to see wolves, caribou, moose and other wildlife. Our snowmobile adventures will be the highlight of your Alaska vacation!

## Talkeetna

*Latitude 62 Lodge/Motel*
P.O. Box 478-MS Talkeetna, AK 99676
Phone: 907-733-2262

Fine dining, cocktails, and 12 modern rooms with private baths. Open year-round. Offering guided and drop-off riverboat fishing trips, guided snowmobile and dogsled rides. Experience true Alaskan hospitality.

## Trapper Creek

*Alaska Adventure Vacations*
P.O. Box 2661 Palmer, Alaska 99645
Phone: 907-745-1747

Email: *akadventure@akcache.com*

These trails pass through the old gold mining country of Petersville. From there break out into big open country above timberline. This provides for great views of the Alaska Range and Denali. This trip is a must for folks wanting to see Denali "up close and personal." The starting point is approximately 2½ hours from Anchorage, and this is a long one-day trip.

*Tokosha Mountain Lodge*
P.O.Box 13188-MS, Trapper Creek, AK 99683
Phone: 907-733-2821, 907-733-1985

Fantastic views of McKinley. Cabins, meals, lounge. June through September—boat, raft, or fly. December 31 through March—dogsled, snowmobile, or fly. Established 1978. Reservations required.

## Wasilla

*Arctic Northern Lights Tours*
HC 31 Box 5213 D Wasilla, AK 99654
Phone: 907-357-2142
Email: *info@akshowtours.com*
Web Site: *www.aksnowtours.com*

Scenic Alaska snowmachine tours, guided trips to view wildlife and the great Alaska outdoors. Have lunch in a rustic backwoods lodge. It is the trip of a lifetime!

## Willow

*Extreme Alaska Adventures*
P.O. Box 564, Willow, AK 99688
Phone: 907-250-6308
Email: *bedard@mtaonline.net*
Web Site: *www.extremealaska.com*

Snowmobile through beautiful river valleys and over the snow-laden Alaska range, sail down the mighty Yukon River, and race along the Norton Sound coastline on your way to the Gold Rush town of Nome. "Experience the wilderness, accept the challenge, ride the extreme."

## Remote

*Within the Wild Alaskan Adventure Lodges*
2626 Galewood Street-MS Anchorage, AK 99508-4041
Phone: 907-274-2710
Email: *alaskawild@gci.net*
Web Site: *www.withinthewild.com*

Within the Wild Alaskan Adventure Lodges owns/operates three backcountry lodges and offers remote float trips throughout Alaska. Fishing, hiking, bear viewing, cooking classes, cross-country skiing, dog mushing, snowmachine touring.

# Dog Sledding

## The EarthSong Lodge

P.O. Box 89, Healy, Alaska 99743
Phone: 907-683-2863
Email: *EarthSong@mail.denali.k12.ak.us*
Website: *www.earthsonglodge.com/winter.htm*

EarthSong Lodge Dog Sled Adventures is a concessionaire licensed to operate overnight trips in the heart of Denali National Park Wilderness, the only guides that can mush you to spectacular Wonder Lake and the park road corridor. No one else can get you closer to the spectacular North Face of Denali.

We specialize in bringing travelers to face to face with the Alaska they have come so far to see. Not only can we bring you closer to majestic Denali, but also our trips are fully interactive. You will mush a dog team deep into the heart of Alaska's most sacred place-Denali National Park in the winter. From river bars and mountain passes, to the Alaska Range glacier system, you will see a piece of wilderness most people will only see in the pages of magazines and books.

We also offer cross-country ski expeditions and spring mountain climbs in the Alaska Range. Our trips are for guests with skill levels from beginner to advanced. We have activities for all ages and abilities year-round from overnights in our cozy cabins with basic sled dog demonstrations to seven-day backcountry adventures, EarthSong Lodge can cater to your Alaskan fantasy vacation.

Day Trips-$100-$200/ person, Overnight Packages-$300-$350/person per night. Below are some adventure packages:

Five Day Sledding/Skiing/Cabin Package

Two Day Sledding/Skiing Package

Dog Sled Expedition: seven days, six nights

## Denali West Lodge

Jack and Sherri Hayden

P.O. Box 40AC Lake Minchumina, Alaska 99757

Phone: 907-674-3112

Email: *minchumina@aol.com*

Website: *www.denaliwest.com*

It may be Greek to you, but those lead dogs know what it means, and they'll be happy to teach you a thing or two about driving a dog team. We've successfully taught hundreds of novice mushers, ranging in age from 14 to 78. This is an exciting, active vacation with friendly dogs. Step on the runners with us and mush off through the north woods on a real Alaskan adventure.

• We take just six guest mushers at a time.

• Each guest will have his or her own team of our experienced huskies.

• No previous mushing experience necessary.

• Trips are February through early April.

## Husky Homestead Tours

Address: P.O. Box 48, Denali National Park, AK 99755
Phone: 907-683-2904
Email: *Info@huskyhomestead.com*
Website: *huskyhomestead.com*

Step back from the crowds and join an intimate group for a personal tour of the homestead and kennel of three-time Iditarod champion Jeff King and his wife, well-known wildlife artist Donna Gates King.

Meet champion sled dogs

Visit with puppies and see summer training in action

1 ½ hour narrated kennel tour

Transportation provided from area hotel

Come to understand the special relationship between musher and dog. See arctic survival gear, sleds and racing equipment. Learn about our state-of-the-art dog-powered training carrousels and heated dog barn. Soak in 20 years of Alaska dog-mushing stories (from freight hauling on Denali to crossing the finish line in Nome with a champion Iditarod team).

Jeff King is recognized as the "Winningest Musher in the World." His victories include not only the 1,160 mile Iditarod sled dog race in 1993, 1996, and 1998, but also over two dozen first place finishes in races all across Alaska.

Donna is a well-known artist whose art portrays her intimate involvement with mushing, and her love and respect of nature.

Also included is a kennel of more than 60 friendly, energetic Alaskan huskies ready to share with you their enthusiasm for the sport of sled dog racing and love of the outdoors.

Our Goose Lake Studio gallery and booking office, located between Denali Princess Hotel and Lynx Creek Pizza, adjacent to Denali Windsong Hotel, will be open 8:00 AM to 10:00 PM daily.

Our vans will pick up at area hotels and the Goose Lake Studio gallery.

Prices: $30.00/adult$15.00/children under 12.

# Winter Fun South of Denali

## Denali State Park

Cross-country ski with Susitna Expeditions: This company offers guided backcountry ski trips for skiers of all abilities (half-days or multi-day trips). Ski along the Iditarod Trail or explore the backcountry wilderness of Denali State Park

Ice fish on numerous lakes including Rocky, Horseshoe, Kalmbach, Marion, Diamond, Prator, Loon, Bear Paw and Cheri Lakes. Big Lake offers three different species including dolly varden/arctic char, rainbow trout, and burbot.

Snowmachine, dog mush, and cross-country ski the 160 acres of the Little Su River Campground off Armstrong Road at Mi. 57.3 Parks Hwy.

## Hatcher Pass

Enjoy groomed Nordic cross-country ski trails at Independence and Gold Cord Mines (pay $5 trail fee at Hatcher Pass Lodge). Explore other favorite trails up to Reed Lake, Reed Lake Falls, and Bomber Glacier. Or, take the Gold Mint trail.

## Houston

Snowmachine the 120-mile groomed trail system originating at Big Lake. Trails from Big Lake to Skwentna and beyond.

## Palmer

Cross-country ski on the groomed trails at Crevasse-Moraine (10K), Lazy Mountain (4.5K), Matanuska River Park (2.5K) and Colony High School (6.5K). Sled on the Crevasse-Moraine Trail, located off the Palmer-Wasilla Highway.

Snowmachine from Jim Creek all the way to Knik Glacier. Explore the many trails in the Knik River area.

Matanaska-Susitna Borough Trails
350 E. Dahlia, Palmer AK 99645
Phone: 907-745-9690
Email: *wtemplin@gci.com*

Trail Systems follow old logging trails through the kettle and kame moraine left by the retreating glacier up the valley. Trails-25 km groomed/3 lit, shared snowshoe.

## Sutton

Snowmachine to Knob Hill. Start at Alpine Inn, Mi. 61 Glenn Hwy. Lunch at Jonesville Café. Snacks, beverages available at Sutton General Store.

Ice-fish for rainbow trout at Wishbone Lake. Access is by snowmachine, snowshoes or skis.

Snowmachine or cross-country ski the King River Trail System. Access is at Mi. 67 Glenn Highway.

Sled and picnic at Jonesville Mine. Large hills perfect for sledding. Slipper Lake is nearby. Mi. 1.5 Jonesville Road, Sutton.

Try skating/rainbow trout fishing/snowmachining at 17 Mile Lake. Access is at 58 Mile Road.

Explore other trails suitable for snowmachining, skiing and dogsledding. Check out the Permanente Road and Puritan Creek Trails.

## Talkeetna

Take an invigorating dog sled ride with one of the Upper Susitna Valley sled dog tour companies. For a true Alaskan backcountry experience, stay at one of the remote lodges in the upper Susitna Valley, traveling by dog team, snowmachine, or ski plane to the wilderness.

Sled down Talkeetna's "Ski Hill" in your toboggan, tube or saucer. Located at Mi. 12.5 Talkeetna Spur.

Enjoy "Winterfest," a month long Christmas celebration every December that includes the famous Wilderness Woman Competition and Bachelor Auction.

View northern lights away from the big city. The clear, dark nights of February, March and April are best for Aurora Borealis sightings. Look for the lights between midnight and 3 a.m., especially during the new moon phase of the month. Filming northern lights with Denali as a backdrop.

Ski spectacular trails maintained by the Denali Nordic Ski Club on the hillsides just south of Talkeetna. Trailhead at Mi. 12.5 Talkeetna Spur Road.

Ice-fish for landlocked salmon and rainbow trout at Christiansen Lake, off Comsat Road at Mi. 12 of Talkeetna Spur Road.

## Trapper Creek

Explore the Petersville Road system of backcountry lodges by snowmachine and plan to spend the night at Denali View Chalets, Gate Creek Cabins, or Tokosha Mountain Lodge.

## Wasilla

Cross-country ski or snowshoe through the woods at Lake Lucille Park—access from Endeavor St., Mi. 2, Knik Goose Bay Road—and Bumpus Ballfields, a 120-acre city reserve—access from Mystery Ave., Mi. 1, Church Road.

Explore trails by snowmachine or dog team: Point Mackenzie to Rebel's Roost to Alexander Creek, or Cottonwood Creek to Knik Lake via Hay Flats and Scout Ridge.

Snowmachine on trails out of Chickaloon (Mi. 67), Purinton Creek (Mi. 90.1), Hicks Creek (Mi. 96.6), and Eureka Summit (Mi. 102).

Spend the weekend at Lake Louise, a popular year-round resort featuring numerous snowmachine poker runs and winter festivities. The junction to Lake Louise is located at Mi. 159.8 Glenn Hwy.

## Willow

Celebrate two weekends of winter fun at the Willow Winter Carnival—last weekend of January, first weekend in February. Highlights include: sled dog, skijoring, snowshoe and cross-country ski races, dog weight pull contests, sawing contests, snowmachine events, and a golf tournament.

Take a guided snowmachine excursion with Willow Island Resort up to Hatcher Pass or over 40 miles of groomed trails at Nancy Lake.

Ice fish at Kashwitna Lake, Mi. 76.4 Parks Hwy. for rainbow trout. Rainbows also await your lure at Honeybee and Lynne Lakes, accessed at Mi. 67.3 Parks Hwy.

Mush dogs and take a kennel tour at Lucky Husky Racing Kennels or Susitna Dog Tours and B & B.

Stop at Sheep Creek Lodge for snowmachine trail and activity guide and services.

# Chapter 16

## *State Parks and Recreation Areas Near Denali*

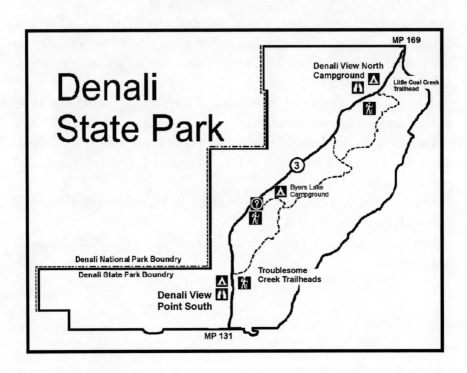

Denali State Park was established in 1970, and is located just south-east of Denali National Park or about 130 miles north of Anchorage. This park is situated between the Talkeetna Mountains to the east and the Alaska Range to the west. The Curry and Kesugi Ridges, a 35 mile-long north/south alpine ridge, dominates the area. The park's 325,240 acres provide visitors with a great variety of recreational opportunities, ranging from camping, kayaking, canoeing, and hiking in the summer to cross-country skiing and snowshoeing in the winter.

## Alaska Range Glaciers

The best view of some of the Alaska Range's glaciers is experienced while hiking the Little Coal Creek Trail. Spectacular valley glaciers, steep ice-carved gorges, and a year-round mantle of snow and ice above 8,000 feet can be viewed from the trail. The valley glaciers include the Ruth, Buskin, and Eldridge which are from 14 to 38 miles long and up to four miles wide. They flow from the high peaks and melt into the broad U-shaped Chulitna Valley, into the silty Chulitna River.

## Alaska Range

Denali State Park has spectacular scenic views of the Alaska Range. At milepost 135 of the Parks Highway, an interpretive bulletin board names the mountains and other terrain features. Other excellent high-way views of Denali are at milepost 147, 158, and 162. Day hikers can explore Kesugi Ridge or backpackers can hike the Peters Hills, for an unencumbered view of Denali.

## History

Pre-eminent Alaskan artist Sydney Laurence, in the early part of this century, captured the beauty of Denali and the Alaska Range from the Peters Hills on large canvas oil paintings. When the railroad trip from Seward and Anchorage to Fairbanks took two days, travelers in the early

1900s sometimes stayed an extra day at Curry to ascend the east side of Curry Ridge and gaze upon Denali and its wonders from Curry Lookout.

## Wildlife

The park's varied landscape is home to a diverse wildlife. Moose, grizzly and black bear are found throughout the park. Caribou occasionally reach the park's northern end. Smaller animals include lynx, coyote, red fox, snowshoe hare, land otter, and flying and red squirrel. Ermine, marten, mink and wolverine from the weasel family also make their home in the park. Muskrat and beaver can be found near the small ponds, while pika and marmot may be found in rocky areas above timberline. Porcupines can be found along the parks trails.

## Birds

More than 130 bird species use the park for breeding or during migration. Year-round residents include the raven, the gray jay, willow ptarmigan, and flocks of black-capped and boreal chickadees. However, most birds migrate long distances to frequent the park such as arctic tern, which flies from the Antarctic to breed in Denali. The golden plover nests on Denali's tundra after wintering in faraway Polynesia. Water birds such as the trumpeter swan, the common loon, and the osprey are attracted to the park's myriad lakes, ponds and streams. In early summer, the woods are alive with the sound of music from a host of small song birds, like the golden-crowned sparrow, Wilson's warbler, and ruby-crowned kinglet.

## Fishing

Fishing Denali's clear streams is a great delight to many park visitors. All five species of Pacific salmon spawn within the waters of the park and share the streams with rainbow trout, arctic grayling, and dolly varden. Small numbers of lake trout inhabit Byers, Spink, and Lucy Lakes.

Burbot and whitefish can also be found in Byers Lake. Many of the rivers in the area rivers are clouded with glacial silt and provide poor sport fishing.

## Public Use Cabins

Denali State Park has two public log cabins on Byers Lake. The cabins are available for daily rental year-round by pre-paid reservation through the Mat-Su Area Headquarters in Wasilla at 907-745-3975, or the Public Information Center in Anchorage at 907-269-8400. PUC #1 features handcrafted log work and a sod roof and is accessible by car. PUC #2 has a spectacular view of Denali, and is accessible by a half-mile walk or by canoe.

### *Hiking in the Back Country*

Trails around Byers Lake and the trail along Troublesome Creek receive very little maintenance attention. Proper footwear and hiking attire is advised. Hikers seeking the best access to country above timberline are advised to begin at the Little Coal Creek Trailhead.

## For More Information

A staffed visitor contact station at the Alaska Veterans Memorial, at mile 147.1, and bulletin boards at developed facilities throughout the park display detailed information on the park's history, natural resources, hiking routes and other advice for the traveling public. For specific inquires, contact the Denali State Park rangers through the Mat-Su/CB Area Headquarters at: Alaska State Parks-Mat-su/CB Area, HC 32, Box 6706, Wasilla, AK 99654-9719; phone 907-745-3975.

## Petersville State Recreation Area

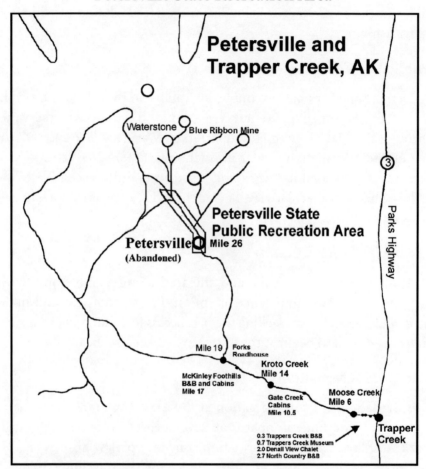

## History of Petersville

Gold was discovered in this area in 1898, and the first known mining activities began in 1906. An estimated 200,000 ounces of gold have been produced since, mostly by small-scale and hand mining. The Peters Hills and Petersville was named after Henry Peters, one of the first prospectors in the area.

Today, most of the mining is gone and most of the lands have been or are being reclaimed.

In the 1920s, the world-renowned Alaskan artist Sydney Laurence painted from the Petersville area. Captain James Cook walked and camped here while searching for a trail into the Interior of Alaska

## Petersville–Petersville Road Scenic Drive

*This sections is submitted by Dennis R. Garrett, owner and operator of the Blue Ribbon Mine located at the end of the Petersville Road.*

GETTING READY TO GO:

Petersville Road is the "other" road to Denali; the southern gateway to Denali, certainly the road less traveled. It's a rugged mining road, designed for true explorers of Alaska who want to discover the backcountry on their own terms.

This trip will take about two hours one-way, covering about 34 miles. I recommend you have a four-wheel drive sports utility vehicle, but it is not mandatory. The road conditions are usually favorable for travel between July 1 and August 31, while June and September are "iffy". Due to the area's proximity to the Alaska Range, there is usually a great deal of snow on the road beyond Mile 14 the rest of the year. (That explains the area's popularity with snowmachiners who flock to it throughout winter.)

You should also travel with necessary survival equipment, including a spare tire, towrope, raingear, wading boots, mosquito repellant, matches, food, blankets and other gear.

IF YOU NEED SOMEPLACE TO STAY:

Trapper Creek Inn & General Store is located at Mile 114.8 Parks Highway. Further up the road, Mary's McKinley View Lodge is also available at Mile 134.5 Parks Highway. Lodging on Petersville Road includes Trapper Creek B & B (Mi. .03), Denali View Chalets (Mi. 2),

North Country B & B (Mi. 2.7), Gate Creek Cabins (Mi. 10.5), McKinley Foothills B & B/Cabins (Mi. 17.2), and the Forks Roadhouse (Mi. 18.7). Most of these places have a beautiful view of Denali.

For those interested in roughing it, you can camp in any of the numerous pullouts along the side of the road and nearly anywhere you want beyond Mile 19, where there is almost no private property. Check with the State Division of Forestry for information regarding campfires.

NOW LET'S GO…FOR THE GOLD!

To begin your road safari to gold country, travel the George Parks Highway to Milepost 114.9 where the community of Trapper Creek is located. If you don't have a full tank of gas, you can fill up in Trapper Creek. You can also visit Trapper Creek's Old Historic Post Office.

Turn onto Petersville Road. The first three miles of this road are paved. Miners built the Petersville Road in the 1920s. You will notice many farms in the area. The "59ers," people who came up to take advantage of a federal land grab from 1948 through the 70s, established the farms.

Mileposts for Petersville Road

Mi. 0.7 Petersville Road: Trapper Creek's Spruce Lane Farms Museum and Gifts is an authentic log cabin museum with a view of Denali. Here you can get some background on the area's gold mining history and the homesteader movement. There are local gifts for sale and you can even pet the ponies before you continue your road safari.

Mile 6: Moose Creek. Here you can stop and have a picnic lunch and check to see if there are any trout or grayling in the creek. Also, enjoy good berry picking toward summer's end.

Mile 14: Kroto Creek—a good place to park your vehicle and snow-machine trailer in the winter since this is where road maintenance ends.

Various points between Mile 6 and Mile 19 offer views of the Alaska Range and tundra lakes—some with swans, ducks, geese, moose, etc.

Mile 19: Forks Roadhouse. The cold beer is good, and the remains of an old bridge can be seen on Peters Creek behind the roadhouse. It's called simply 'The Forks' by locals and regulars. I've seen people fishing and canoeing here.

Mile 26: You will pass through the long-abandoned mining camp of Petersville, which was also the Post Office for the mining camps in the 20s and 30s. The buildings are closed and off-limits; it's not really a good place to stop. Just keep moving. As you continue on, from Mile 28-30, you enter the spectacular Peters Creek canyon; a one-lane road that hugs one side of a deep gorge with waterfalls all around you. Views of the Alaska Range complete the picture.

One option before entering the canyon would be to turn right onto the trail at the mouth of the canyon. You'll go up to the top of the Peters Hills. This is where I have seen some of the most phenomenal views of the Alaska Range including Denali, Mt. Foraker, and Mt. Hunter. You can also see stunning views of the Chugach and Talkeetna Mountains, the Matanuska-Susita Valleys, and much more—all set in pristine alpine tundra. The breeze is refreshing. Surrounding you are many deep, clear lakes that were created when the ancient glaciers that sculpted this magnificent landscape sliced the top of this mountain off. Watch for migratory birds and small mammals early in the summer, and ptarmigan and bears feeding on the berries later in the year. This is a great area to begin a mountain biking trek, as there are many rugged trails and roads.

Mile 32: You will cross Peters Creek and enter the Petersville State Recreational Mining Area, an area set aside by the State of Alaska for the citizens to pan and mine for gold. If you don't know how, it's easy to learn and fun to do. This is also another outstanding area to camp.

Just past the bridge you come to another fork: the left fork takes you to the Cache Creek area; the right fork takes you to the Blue Ribbon Mine and Denali State Park. If you decide to head down the Cache Creek Road, we recommend that you visit the Dollar Creek Ventures of George and Delores McCullogh. They have a very nice, historic mine.

Call 907-733-2628 for information and reservations, or visit them on the Web at *www.dollarcreek.com*.

If you take the right fork, you'll travel a little ways beyond the bridge, where you'll come to the Peters Creek crossing. Bears and salmon can often be seen here. The idea of crossing the creek with your vehicle may, at first, appear daunting. However, the creek is generally quite shallow, except where strong currents have cut deep channels into the gravel bed of the creek. Stay away from these areas. Instead, cross only where the water is rough, and only when the water is relatively shallow, say two to three feet. Don't hesitate or stop in mid-stream, just keep your momentum and move forward.

After crossing the creek, you encounter yet another fork: the left takes you up Peters Creek, and the right takes you to Blue Ribbon Mine. You are also leaving the Petersville State Recreation area and entering privately held state mining claims. By law, you may freely travel through, or hunt, fish, even camp on mining claims without the owner's permission. However, remember that the gold and other minerals are the property of the claim owner, and any unauthorized removal can result in criminal charges and civil liabilities. This is also true for disturbing claim markers, corners, or vandalizing equipment and camp facilities. Please respect private property.

As you continue on, the road becomes narrower, at times indistinct. The only evidence of a road or trail, which sometimes is swallowed up by the stream, is the occasional piece of surveyors' ribbon hanging from a branch. The seemingly impenetrable brush suddenly opens up, and then it quickly surrounds you again.

Mile 34: You see a sign: Welcome to the Blue Ribbon Mine! (Unless it's very foggy you will have seen the mine long before now). To visit the mine, turn left here and drive for about 1.5 miles. Please feel free to take all the photos you want. For information and reservations about mine tours, or recreational gold panning and mining, contact the Blue Ribbon Mine via e-mail or call 907-355-8664. You can also write to

Dennis Garrett at The Alaska Freegold Company, P.O. Box 423, Willow, Alaska 99688.

## Bugs, Bears, and Hiking in the Area

The best places to hike are the areas higher on the flanks of the Peters and Dutch Hills, which are free of the dense scrub growths of willow and alder. These are the areas with the least amount of bugs due to the steady breeze. In areas where there is a clear trail, please stay on the trail to minimize impact. Alpine areas are relatively fragile and slow growing. The large dug-up areas you see along the hillsides are the work of Grizzly bears digging up ground squirrels for food.

## Nancy Lake State Recreation Area

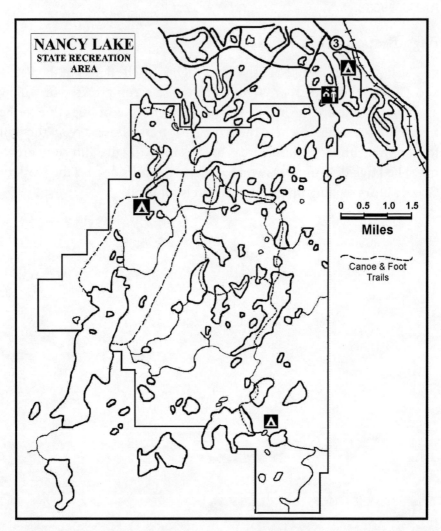

Nancy Lake State Recreation Area is one of the few flat, lake-studded landscapes in Alaska preserved just for recreation purposes. The recreation area's clear waters are ringed with unspoiled forests. Canoe, fish, hike and camp in the summer; cross-country ski, dog mush and snow-machine in the winter.

Nancy Lake State Recreation Area is a located at milepost 67 of the Parks Highway, or approximately a 90 minute drive north of Anchorage. To enter the recreation area, turn west onto Nancy Lake Parkway at Mile 67.3 of the Parks Highway. From there, the Nancy Lake Parkway travels 6.5 miles southwest to South Rolly Lake Campground.

## History

Massive glaciers once scoured the Susitna River Valley, including what is now the recreation area. When the ice retreated some 9,000 years ago, it left a rolling landscape dotted with hundreds of lakes and ponds.

Archaeologists believe that people lived in the region after the glaciers receded. The Tanaina Indians, and possibly Pacific Eskimos hunted, trapped and fished this region. Two prehistoric villages have been identified just outside the recreation area.

In 1917, the Alaska Railroad was built along the East Side of the lower Susitna Valley. The nearby towns of Wasilla, Houston and Willow grew as more homesteaders settled on lands opened up by rail access.

Through the years, most of the Nancy Lake area has remained wild and natural. The area is too wet for ideal cultivation and is not mineral-rich, so it has escaped large-scale settlement by humans. Today, those assets make it a prime place for recreation.

## Climate

Summer temperatures rise into the 70s and low 80s. Summer night-time temperatures may fall into the 40s. Winter temperatures may fall to 40 degrees below zero, and seldom rise above freezing until mid-March. The first snow usually arrives by late October. Snow depth in late winter averages three to four feet. Lakes are usually free of ice by late May.

## Public Use Cabins

The public can reserve cabins that are located by Red Shirt, Lynx, Nancy, James and Bald lakes. The cabins are insulated and equipped with wooden bunks, counters and wood-burning stoves. Each cabin has an outhouse.

Campers need to bring all personal items, including drinking water and firewood, and leave the site neat and clean when they leave.

## Berries

Beginning in late July, the first wild berries begin to ripen. Currants, cranberries, and blueberries frequently provide a bountiful harvest. Varieties of raspberry, crowberry and other berries can also be found. Pickers should learn to identify the baneberry, which looks edible, but is very poisonous.

## Wildlife

The recreation area's combination of lakes, wetlands and forests create ideal habitat for many mammals and birds. Perhaps most noticeable to the summer visitor are water dwellers, especially beaver and waterfowl. Beavers are active in lakes and ponds throughout the park, and visitors can see evidence of their work. These animals are vital to maintaining critical water levels in the ecosystem; their dams and lodges must not be disturbed.

Black bears are common throughout the park while grizzly bears are only occasionally sighted. Adverse encounters with bears are unlikely if proper precautions are taken. Please report any sightings to the park rangers.

Moose are commonly found in the park, although their numbers are dependent on the food supply. They prefer brushy areas or shallow ponds with tender aquatic plants.

While canoeing in this area, the explorer may be approached by a curious, common loon. These black-headed master divers are one of the trademarks of the area. Loons sitting on the shore should always be given a wide distance because they come ashore to nest, and will often desert their nests when disturbed.

Like Denali National and State Parks, the arctic terns is also a summer resident to Nancy Lake. Unlike the loons, these birds are graceful fliers as well as tenacious nest defenders. If a hiker disturbs a nest site, he is likely to be repeatedly dive-bombed by screeching terns.

The Independence Mine is at milepost 35 on the Parks Highway. Originally used by miners, Hatcher Pass Road provides a 50-mile loop from Palmer or Wasilla over a rugged mountain pass to Willow. The road climbs to an elevation of 3,886' at the summit. Old mines are visible from the gravel road as you climb the mountain. Explore a 271-acre abandoned gold mine at Independence Mine State Historical Park. Over 13 structures built in the late 1930s and early 1940s remain standing.

The drive over the pass takes about three to four hours. Visitors take to the slopes to hike, pick berries and recreational gold pan in summer, and to sled and alpine ski (by snowmachine) in winter. During winter months, the road over the pass is closed to highway traffic. About ten miles of Hatcher Pass Road remains open from Palmer or Wasilla Fishhook Road for trail access to the historical park and a variety of winter sports, including cross-country skiing, snowboarding and snowmachining in designated areas. Alpine lodging and dining high in the Talkeetna Mountains is available year-round near Independence Mine.

Once out of the pass, explore the unique communities along the Gold Loop, which include Willow, Houston, and Big Lake.

# Chapter 17

# *Businesses & Towns Near or In Denali National Park*

## Businesses

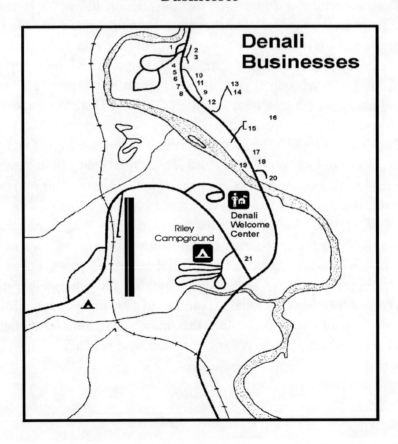

## Lodging

13 Crows Nest Cabins
15 Denali Cliff Hotel
6  Denali Princess Lodge
8  Denali Riverview Inn
16 Grand Denali
1  McKinley Chalet Hotel
4  Sourdough Cabins

## Restaurants

11 Blackbear Coffee
5  Lynx Pizza
9 Salmon Bake
17 Smoke Shack
14 Overlook Bar & Grill

## Activites

1  Cabin Night Theatre
2  Northern Lights Theatre
7  Denali Outdoor Center
19 Denali Raft
18 ERA Helicopters
6  Pere Air
20 Nenana Raft

## Stores

3  Denali Mt. Works
10 Canyon Gifts
12 Denali Outlet Store
21 Merchantile

## Towns Near or In Denali National Park
### 1) Kantishna
### 2) Healy

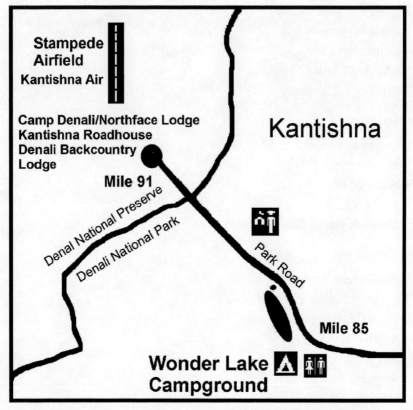

1) Kantishna (population: 2 in the winter, 135 in the Summer)

## History

Prospectors Joe Quigley and Jack Horn sparked the rush of stampeders into interior Alaska's Kantishna Hills when they discovered "paying quantities" of gold at Glacier Creek in 1905. After staking the creek, Quigley and Horn returned to Fairbanks where news of their strike created quite a commotion. Thousands of gold seekers streamed into the Kantishna Hills during the fall and winter of 1905. "Practically every creek that heads into the Kantishna Hills was staked from source to mouth and intervening ridges were not ignored." Several mining camps were established, complete with rowdy saloons and gambling halls. Winter camps include places named Glacier City, Diamond, Roosevelt, and Square Deal, while the primary summer camp was Eureka (later to be renamed Kantishna). During the first summer, Eureka was home to about 2,000 people.

Miners lucky enough to stake land along Glacier and Eureka Creeks found good-paying deposits, but little gold was found elsewhere. As in most stampedes, the large majority of treasure-seekers ended up empty-handed. By the spring of 1906, only about 50 miners remained.

Known production of metals from Kantishna Hills from 1905 through 1985—when all mining was stopped by the federal government—amounted to nearly 100,000 ounces of gold, 309,000 ounces of silver, five million pounds of antimony and about 1.5 million pounds of combined lead and zinc. Total value of the metals has been estimated at nearly $24 million and some geologists suspect that the Kantishna Hills still contain gold, silver, and antimony deposits worth up to $1.2 billion.

## Today

Most of the mining in Kantishna is gone and tourism now keeps it going. Four lodges and a small airstrip currently make up this town.

But, some areas in the Kantishna still contain active mining, and much of the town is private property. The Stampede mine site is inactive, but it is still private property and poses many hazards to hikers. Hikers, please respect the private property in this area, and stay away from mining claims unless the owner invites you.

Most of the side streams in the Kantishna Hills have been mined out, but with a little luck, a gold pan will still turn up some gold dust. So, if you are feeling lucky, take a gold pan and experience what the Yukon prospectors in the early 1900s.

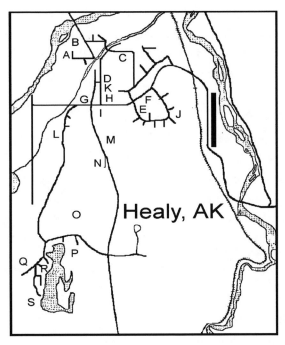

**2) Healy, Alaska–population 466**

## Lodging

| | | | |
|---|---|---|---|
| C | Aspen Haus | J | Midnight Sun B&B |
| Q | Denali Hostel | B | Motel Nord Havan |
| G | Denali North Star Inn | H | Mountain View Inn |
| A | Dry Creek B&B | K | Stampede Inn |
| F | Grey Fox Inn | I | Totem Inn |
| L | Healy Heights Cabins | N | White Moose Lodge |
| R | Homestead B&B | P | Otto Lake RV |
| M | McKinley RV | R | Homestead B&B |

## Gas Station & Grocery

D    Wally's

Healy lies at the mouth of Healy Creek on the Nenana River, 78 miles southwest of Fairbanks. It is located on a spur road, just north of the entrance to the Denali National Park and Preserve on the George Parks Highway.

## History

Healy was developed by the Usibelli Coal Mine in 1918, which has grown to become Alaska's largest coal mining operation. The mine supplies 800,000 tons of coal a year to Golden Valley Electric, the University of Alaska Fairbanks, the military, and South Korea. The Usibelli Coal Mine began a successful environmental reclamation program in 1971. Dall sheep now graze where there was once a strip mine.

## Culture

Healy is a non-Native coal mining town that has evolved into an economically-diverse community. Tourism also greatly affects the economy during summer months.

# Chapter 18

## *Towns On the Way to Denali National Park*

1) Cantwell
2) Nenana
3) Palmer
4) Talkeetna
5) Trapper Creek
6) Wasilla
7) Willow

### 1) Cantwell-population 166

Cantwell is located on the George Parks Highway at the end of the Denali Highway, 211 miles north of Anchorage and 28 miles south of Denali National Park. The Cantwell River was the former name of the Nenana River. Cantwell began as a stop on the Alaska Railroad. It is a mixture of non-Natives and Athabascan Indians. Cantwell's economy is based on tourism and transportation. Most residents depend upon hunting, fishing and trapping for subsistence. Cantwell is accessible by road, rail and air. The George Parks Highway connects to Fairbanks and Anchorage, and the Denali Highway links Denali National Park with the Richardson Highway during summer months only. Cantwell Heights Property Owners operate an airstrip for public use. The Alaska Railroad still provides train service.

## 2) Nenana-population 393 *Place Your Bets for the Famous Nenana Ice Classic*

The village of Nenana is 68 miles north of the Denali National Park Entrance, but used to be the park's entrance in the early' 20s. Before the Alaska Railroad was completed, Harry Karstens, the park's first superintendent, drove his dog sleds from this starting point to first survey the park's original boarders.

Today, this village is popular for fishing, hunting, and the Nenana Ice Classic (see below). Translated, Nenana means "a good place to camp between two rivers." It sits at the junction of the Nenana and the Tanana rivers.

Salmon fill the rivers starting at the end of June or in early July with the arrival of the "mighty kings" from the Bering Sea. The Tanana River provides not only transportation and fishing but recreational opportunities all year long. The banks of the river in the summer offer a great place to watch traditional fishwheel salmon fishing. Use of the fishwheels is strictly regulated.

Recreational boating and commercial barge shipping are done on the Tanana, as are kayaks and canoes floating down from Fairbanks.

The population of Nenana is approximately 42% Athabascan. The rich history of Nenana reflects tradition and folklore from generations of Native Alaskans. Dances, handicrafts and traditional use of resources are a present-day reminder of residents' heritage.

Points of interest in Nenana include several historical displays, a cultural center, the old Episcopal Mission, Alaska Railroad Station, the second-largest single span railroad bridge in the world, and the infamous Nenana Ice Classic Tripod.

Nenana is located at the head of one of Alaska's most scenic valleys. Moose, caribou, Dall sheep, black bear, and Toklat grizzlies abound in the game-rich valley. The Nenana Dog Mushers Association sponsors a full schedule of winter races, climaxed by championship races in the early spring. Native potlatches highlight all special holidays and the big race weekends. The Nenana Native Dancers provide colorful entertainment during these festivities. Annual boat and bicycle races are featured during the summer.

### The Nenana Ice Classic

Each spring since 1917, Alaskans have waited for breakup on the Tanana River. This magnificent river sweeps westward through Interior Alaska before joining forces with the mighty Yukon River. The breakup of 1917, while similar to many before and many after, was destined for a place in history. Surveyors working on the Alaska Railroad Bridge at Nenana place bets on when the ice on the Tanana River would move out and let them return to work. They rigged up a system that involved stopping a clock when the ice moved. That spring breakup happened on April 30th at 11:30 am. The pool was $800.

Exactly 80 years later, in 1997, the ice broke up on the same date, April 30th, and also just before noon at 10:28. The pool was $300,000.

In the history of the Ice Classic, the earliest breakup was on April 20th (in 1940) and the latest was May 20th (in 1964).

The total jackpot is divided among all the winning tickets. If no ticket is on the winning minute, the ticket with the closest minute or minutes is selected by the Nenana Ice Classic Board of Directors.

Tickets are available year-round in Nenana and sold by businesses throughout Alaska from the first part of February through the first part of April. The tickets are collected and taken to Nenana.

A tripod is placed into the river ice in late February or early March during Tripod Days Weekend, which features fun activities like outdoor ice bowling and the Nenana Banana Eating Contest. When the ice begins to soften, a wire is strung from the watchtower on shore out to the tripod and a 24-hour watch is started for breakup. Many of the specialized jobs involving the Nenana Ice Classic are filled by the same people for many years and handed down to other family members. The watchmen, who have the most contact with visitors hoping to see breakup, frequently have been filling their roles each spring for decades. And even these seasoned observers of the river have a favorite response when asked when they think breakup will happen: "Could be anytime."

And that is what makes the Nenana Ice Classic so much fun—it really could be anytime—and it could be on your minute!

## Camping

Nenana Valley RV Park and Campground. 4th and C Street. Box 38, Nenana, AK 99760, 907-832-5431. 30-amp electrical hook-ups, large pull-through spaces, tent campers welcome, showers and laundromat, water and dump station, picnic tables, firepits, pet area.

## Shopping

Coghill's General Merchants, Box 178, Nenana, AK 99760, 907-832-5422, has groceries, hardware, propane, clothing, magazines, fresh fruits, vegetables and meats, beer, wine, liquor.

## 3) Palmer–population 2,866

Palmer owes its existence to the hardy pioneers who homesteaded the land when the railroad was built in the early part of this century, and to the more than 200 families who came in 1935 from America's depressed Midwest to establish the Matanuska Colony. The colonists, as they are still called, arrived in May and lived in tent camps in and around Palmer until their homes were ready. They drew lots for their 40-acre tracts. They cleared the land and planted it and, in the face of many obstacles, established the Palmer area as the center of Alaskan agriculture. Palmer is home of the Alaska State Fair (late August), where record-size vegetables, a museum, and simple frontier buildings show the struggle and success of Palmer's history as a farm and mining community.

## Activities

Stretch your legs and take a walking tour of historic Palmer. Visit the nearby reindeer farm. More conventional four legged animals, such as horses or llamas, can take you on trail rides or pack trips into the mountains.

In winter, sled dog rides and races, cross-country skiing, snowmobiling, ice fishing and a variety of social events are popular. Alpine skiing is just an hour's drive from Palmer.

See dinosaurs bones and fossils at the Alaska Museum of Natural History located in Eagle River.

Learn about the early years of the Valley at the Palmer Visitor Center and Colony Museum.

Visit the Musk Ox Farm. Pet and feed the "critters" at the Reindeer Farm.

Enjoy fireworks, sleigh rides and Santa's reindeer at Palmer's annual Colony Christmas held at the end of the second week of December.

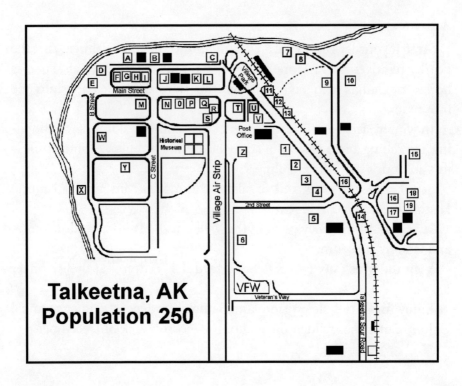

**Talkeetna, AK
Population 250**

## Lodging

| | |
|---|---|
| Backdoor B&B | A |
| Chinook Winds Cabins | 5 |
| Fairview Inn | L |
| Latitude 62 Lodge | 20 |
| Mountain River Cabins | H |
| River Park Campgrounds | E&D |
| Swiss Alaska | 9 |
| Talkeetna Cabins | B |
| Talkeetna Motel | X |
| Talkeetna Roadhouse | N |

## Restaurants

| | |
|---|---|
| Café Michele | 3 |
| West Rib Pub | T |
| McKinley Deli | J |
| Main Street Café & Bike | P |
| Sparky's | U |

## Shops:

| | |
|---|---|
| Nagley's Store | T |
| Willow Wildlife Gallery | Q |
| Kaloin Kuts & Massage | C |
| Denali Dry Goods | O |
| Talkeetna Outdoor Center | G |
| Three Rivers–Gas. | K |
| Talk. Chocolate Corner | F |
| Talkeetna Travel | 4 |
| Village Arts & Crafts | M |
| Talkeetna Landing | 6 |

## Activities

| | |
|---|---|
| Busy Bikes | 14 |
| Museum of Northern Adv. | 13 |
| Mahay's Fishing | 21 |
| Hudson Air Service | 19 |
| Doug Geeting Aviation | 17 |
| Talkeetna Air Taxi | 18 |
| K-2 Aviation | 16 |
| Tri-River Charters | V |
| Talkeetna River Guides | I |
| NPS Ranger Station | W |

## 4) Talkeetna–population 250

Talkeetna means "River of Plenty" in the Dena'ina Indian language. Located at the confluence of Susitna, the Talkeetna and the Chulitna River, Talkeetna offered an abundant harvest for the Dena'ina Indians who hunted and fished this area for centuries. In the late 1890s, a trading station was located along the riverfront to supply trappers and miners. A townsite was established during construction of the Alaska Railroad. Talkeetna became the supply point for the gold fields in the Yentna Mining District and winter home for many of the miners. Today, Talkeetna is the staging area for approximately 1,000 climbers each year who attempt to reach the summit of Denali.

Talkeetna keeps its mining history alive with renovated trapper and miner cabins used as lodging, shops and restaurants. The town's original saloons and roadhouses are still in operation. The frontier flavor of Talkeetna can be experienced on a walking tour of the townsite, taking in the Museum of Northern Adventure or the Talkeetna Historical Society Museum. Laid-back to extreme adventure travel is what Talkeetna is all about. Local flightseeing services specialize in tours to Denali. Guided river rafting and riverboat tours are a Talkeetna specialty, and sport fishing in Talkeetna rivers and lakes is some of the finest in Alaska.

In the summer, the Alaska Railroad provides daily service to Talkeetna from Anchorage. Once here, you're a short distance from the gold mining country near Petersville Road and the outdoor adventure of Denali State Park.

### Talkeetna Moose Dropping Festival

In your quest to sniff out the nittiest, grittiest and downright stinkiest events of the summer, introduce yourself to the poop-centricity of the Annual Moose Dropping Festival. USA TODAY rated this festival on the list of top family festivals in the United States.

It started over 25 years ago, when a couple of local schoolteachers were sitting in Talkeetna's Fairview Inn, knocking back a few brews. They were discussing the controversy over the city's decision to tear down its historic one-room schoolhouse. The Talkeetna Historical Society was formed to save it, but needed money. After many brews, they had the idea of raising cash through a festival focused on local moose droppings.

Gathering moose droppings, drying them out in the sun, and making jewelry of them is a favorite local pastime of the locals in Talkeetna. "The tourists love all the moose dropping stuff we make," explains one local. "They eat it up." (Hopefully not literally.) There's a lot to "doo doo" at the Moose Dropping Festival. (Please note: the author of this book had nothing to do with creating that statement.) There's the Moose Dropping Toss: a four-foot board with a drawing of a moose is sectioned off by body part, each worth a certain number of points. Yet, this is not a strictly moose dung-filled Festival. The Mountain Mother contest is completely feces-free. Mommies only, dressed in hip waders and back-packs holding a baby (doll), must complete a vigorous course, which includes wood-splitting, changing the babies' diapers (okay, it's 90% feces-free), shooting cross-bows at balloons, casting fishing rods through targets and running across logs with two full packages of groceries. And lest we forget more meaningful pursuits, each year, the Festival also has a Main Street Parade of dogs dressed in babies' clothes, and middle-aged women in chicken costumes pecking at the marching band.

## Hiking Around Talkeetna

*Denali Trekking Company*
P.O. Box 93 Talkeetna, Alaska 99676
Phone: 907-733-2566
E-mail: *info@denalitrekking.com*
Website: *www.denalitrekking.com*

Denali Trekking Company is dedicated to providing guests the greatest opportunity for exploring and observing the wonders that surround us in this magnificent grandeur. By utilizing the experiences gained while guiding clients over the past 20 years, we have developed an educational program that is exciting, unforgettable and thoroughly enjoyable. All ages and condition levels are invited to participate; there is adventure for everyone. You can go berserk and cover 50 miles in 5 days or be satisfied with mile long walks from your camp, absorbing your surroundings from the tiniest berry to the largest carnivore.

*Alaska-Denali Guiding, Inc.*
PO Box 566, Talkeetna, AK 99676
Phone: 907-733-2649
Email: *adg@alaska.net*
ADG specializes in Denali-Denali expeditions and other mountaineering, climbing and backpacking trips in the Denali National Park and Preserve. Also in mountains near Talkeetna and statewide, as well.

*Talkeetna Hiking Adventures*
P.O. Box 924-MS, Talkeetna, AK 99676
Phone: 907-733-3478
Email: *sipebrwn@mtaonline.net*
Guided day hikes in the Talkeetna area. Choose from easy three-mile hikes to strenuous 10-mile treks. View wildlife and the Alaska Range. Snacks or lunch provided.

*Talkeetna Outdoor Center*
Talkeetna, AK 99676
Phone: 800-349-0064, 907-733-8352
Email: *journeys@alaska.net*
Website: www.alaskajourneys.com
Guided day hikes in Talkeetna and the surrounding areas.

## 5) Trapper Creek–population 296

Along the Susitna River, gold deposits were reported as early as 1876 by the Alaska Commercial Company. Reports of gold deposits by Indians spurred exploration in the Dutch and Peters Hills.

In 1908, the Cache Creek Mining Company was formed. By 1911, 120 men were mining, and the tiny town of Trapper Creek was born.

Today, Trapper Creek consist of several B&B's, Trapper Creek Inn & General Store, the Spruce Lane Farms Museum, and a variety of other independent businesses and services.

Spruce Lane Farms Museum is an authentic log cabin museum with a view of Denali. Here you can get some background on the area's gold mining history and the homesteader movement. There are local gifts for sale, and you can even pet the ponies before you continue your road safari.

Down the road from Trapper Creek is the Forks Roadhouse. The Forks was built by Mrs. Isabel McDonald and Frank Lee to supply miners and is "a must" to see. The Forks is the oldest operating roadhouse in Alaska today.

### Festival

Hold on to your sanity until it's time for the Cabin Fever Reliever celebration the fourth Saturday of March. Local Citizens compete in events such as Bake Off, Pie Eating, Ski Races, Blind-Folded Snowmachine Race, Dog Race, and Weight Pulling. Its a fun filled day starting with Pancake feed at the Catholic Church, and ending with Spaghetti Feed at the Trapper Creek Trading Post.

## 6) Wasilla–population 5,213

Wasilla, named for a local Dena'ina Indian Chief, was little more than a wide spot along the Carle Trail which ran from the seaport of Knik to the gold mines in Hatcher Pass. It grew into a town practically overnight, during 1917, when the railroad came through from

Anchorage to Fairbanks. A new port was established in Anchorage, effectively turning Knik into a ghost town and establishing Wasilla as the new supply station.

For history buffs, the restored Independence Mine in Hatcher Pass State Park, Dorothy Page Museum and Town Site Park in downtown Wasilla have excellent collections of memorabilia from Natives and early settlers.

Other museums worth seeing are the Museum of Alaska Transportation and Industry located just north of town on the Parks Highway. It houses a vast array of airplanes, trains and antique farm and construction equipment. The Knik Museum and Musher's Hall of Fame on Knik Road honors notable dogs and dog mushers. It houses the history of the Iditarod and local native culture.

Being the home of the Iditarod headquarters, the Iditarod race restart is Wasilla's most notable claim to fame (the ceremonial start is in Anchorage). Every year in March, some seventy mushers converge from around the globe to officially begin the famous thousand-mile trek across Alaska.

### Festivals & Events

Iditarod Days Festival runs late February to early March. Fireworks, ice fishing and softball tournaments, cross-country ski race, trade/craft fair, Ice Golf Classic, and of course, the restart of the Iditarod Race.

Gold Rush Classic Iron Dog Snow Machine Race—the world's longest. Covers 2,274 miles of unforgiving Alaskan terrain from Wasilla to Nome and back. Official start in Wasilla, restart in Big Lake in the third week of February.

### Museums

Dorothy Page Museum. With a log cabin front that was originally the Wasilla Community Hall, built in 1932. In 1967, the building was converted into the Wasilla Museum, renamed for resident Dorothy Page shortly after her death on Nov. 16, 1989. It specializes in Alaskan antiques and artifacts, and in Alaska's past, with a main focus on the history of Wasilla. Some displays consist of equipment used in Alaska in the early 20th century, such as telephones, radios, mail bags, silverware, furniture, and other miscellaneous items. A significant section of the museum is devoted to dog mushing, including a Joe Redington, Sr. memorial. Redington, the Father of the Iditarod, is featured side by side with Dorothy Page, the Mother of the Iditarod, who was also instrumental in founding the museum. The Museum is located at 323 Main Street, Wasilla.

Iditarod Headquarters. Historical displays, dog sled rides and a gift shop are the attractions here. It is open year round. Located Mile 2.2 Knik Road. The Iditarod can't be compare it to any other competitive event in the world. It runs over the roughest, most beautiful terrain Mother Nature has to offer. She throws jagged mountain ranges, frozen rivers, dense forest, desolate tundra and miles of windswept coast at the mushers and their dog teams. Add to that temperatures far below zero, winds that can cause a complete loss of visibility, the hazards of overflow, long hours of darkness, treacherous climbs and side hills, and you have the Iditarod.

From Anchorage, in south central Alaska, to Nome on the western Bering Sea coast, each team of 12 to 16 dogs and their mushers cover over, 1150 miles in nine to 17 days.

## 7) Willow–population 285

Historically, the Dena'ina Indians have occupied this area, living in semi-permanent villages. The community got its start when gold was discovered on Willow Creek in 1897. Supplies and equipment were brought in by boat to Knik. From there, a 26-mile summer trail went northwest, up Cottonwood Creek, and across Bald Mountain to Willow Creek. The winter sled trail went north, crossing the present line of the

Alaska Railroad at Houston, and up the West End of Bald Mountain for 30 miles. This trail, dubbed the "Double Ender Sled Trail," is still being used by skiers, hunters, backpackers and snowmobile enthusiasts. The sleds then followed a trail along Willow Creek in an easterly direction, now Hatcher Pass Road. The Talkeetna Trail also passed through Willow and was used by dog teams and packhorses. Cabins to accommodate freighters and mail carriers were located at Nancy Lake, Willow and other points north. This route was the forerunner of the Parks Highway. During construction of the Alaska Railroad, surveyors, construction crews, homesteaders and other settlers came to Willow. A Railroad station house was constructed in 1920. During World War II, a radar warning station and airfield were built. The Trail's End Lodge was built in 1947; it became a post office in 1948. By 1954, Willow Creek was Alaska's largest gold mining district, with a total production approaching $18 million. Land disposals, homestead subdivisions, and completion of the George Parks Highway (in 1972) fueled growth in the area. In 1976, Alaskans selected Willow as their new state capital. However, funding to enable the capital move was defeated in the November 1982 election.

# Chapter 19

## Men, Women, and Dogs of Denali

**Anderson, Peter**–part of the Sourdough expedition of 1910. He successfully climbed Denali's lower North Peak and planted a 14-foot flagstaff in hopes it could be viewed from Fairbanks by telescope.

**Athabascans**-people who came from Asia about 35,000 years ago across Bering Strait and settled in Alaska and northwest Canada.

**Balto**–the most famous husky. Lead dog in the 1925 team that carried life saving antitoxin from Nenana to Nome. Great kids animated movie.

**Brooks, Alfred**–teamed with D.L. Raeburn to survey the Alaska and Brooks Range in 1902. They were the first white men to set foot on the slopes of Denali.

**Butcher, Susan**–a three time Iditarod champion who teamed with Joe Redington in 1979 to be the first and only successful ascent of Denali by dog sled.

Eielson,

**Cook, Frederick A.**–first explorer to claim he reached Denali's summit. Later, his claims were proven false.

**Crosson, Joe**–the first man to successfully land his plane on an Alaskan glacier. The landing occurred in April of 1932 on Denali's Muldrow Glacier. Today, the makeshift landing strip that unloads mountaineers bears his name.

**Densmore, Frank**-a prospector, wrote such an enthusiastic description of the mountain that Yukon prospectors named it Densmore's Mountain.

**Eldridge, George**–member of the U.S. Geographic Service who surveyed and determined Denali height in 1898 along with Robert Muldrow.

**Foraker, Joseph**-A senator and former governor of Ohio. Lieutenant Herron in 1899 named Mount Foraker, also known as "Denali's Wife" after him.

**Harper, Walter**-part of the 1913 Karstens-Stuck successful summit of Denali.

**Houston, Charles**-was the first to climbed Mt. Foraker on August 6, 1934

**Karstens, Harry**–adventurer extraordinaire. Carried mail by dog sled to Kantishna, and part of the first successful team to ascend Denali in 1913, the first superintendent of Denali National Park.

**Laurence, Sidney**-Laurence was the first professionally trained artist to take up permanent residence in Alaska, and for half a century he has been Alaska's favorite painter.

**Lloyd, Thomas**–part of the Sourdough expedition of 1910.

**Mastiff**–The type of dog Harry Karstens used while he traveled throughout the park as a mail carrier and park ranger.

**McGonogill, Charles**–part of the Sourdough expedition of 1910.

**McKinley, William**–W.A. Dickey in January of 1907 named Denali after this Republican candidate for President of the United States, who later became President. Unfortunately, President McKinley never set foot in Alaska.

**Morino, Maurice**–ran a roadhouse and grew a garden next to the original Denali National Park railroad station. This area is now a campground bearing his name.

**Muldrow, Robert**–member of the U.S. Geographic Service who surveyed and determined Denali height in 1898, along with George Eldridge.

**Murie, Adolph**–studied and wrote several books about the flora and fauna of Denali in the 1920s and 1930s.

**Redington Sr., Joe** Founder of the modern day Iditarod Race. He and Susan Butcher were the first to summit Denali with a dog sled team.

**Sheldon, Charles**-a naturalist and conservationist responsible for having the park established to protect large mammals. Sheldon first traveled to the area in 1906, and returned in 1907 with a guide named Harry Karstens, who was the first to climb Denali's southern side and who became the park's first superintendent. In his trip of 1907 he looked for boundaries he would recommend for the national park. He wanted certain areas established as wildlife refuge. As chairman of the Boone and Crockett Club, Sheldon began his campaign for the national park. He wanted to call the park Denali, but this did not happen until 1980.

**Sheldon, Don**–a bush pilot from Talkeetna who spent 27 years delivering mountaineers to the base of Denali. His high-risk, life-saving rescue missions were legendary throughout the world.

**Stuck, Hudson**–an episcopal archdeacon of the Yukon who led the first successful team to the summit of Denali in 1913.

**Tatum, Robert**–part of the 1913 Karstens-Stuck successful summit of Denali.

**Taylor, William**–part of the Sourdough expedition of 1910, and successfully climbed the North Peak of Denali.

**Washburn, Barbara**–the first woman to climb Denali (1947).

**Washburn, Bradford**–pioneered the West Buttress Route of Denali in 1951. This route is affectionately known as the "Butt." Today, most successful climbs of Denali occur on this route.

**Wickersham, Judge James**–delegate to Congress from Alaska, and made one of the first attempts to climb Denali in 1903. He once stated that only a balloon or a flying machine could reach the summit from the north face.

**Wilson, Woodrow**–president who signed the bill to form Mount McKinley National Park in 1917.

# Chapter 20

## *Alaskan and Denali Terms*

*Alpenglow*-a reddish or pinkish glow seen near sunset or sunrise on the summits of mountains.

*Bulshaia Gora*-the Russian name for Denali. Big Mountain.

*Cache*-an elevated storage cabin used to keep meat and foodstuffs away from prowling animals.

*Cheechako*-a newcomer to the North.

*Densmore's Mountain*-in 1889, Frank Densmore, a prospector, wrote such an enthusiastic description of the Denali that Yukon prospectors named it Densmore's Mountain.

*Dog Salmon*-any poor quality salmon that are dried for dog food.

*Eskimo Ice Cream*-Cisco with local berries.

*Guspuk*-A lightweight, very colorful, cotton summer 'parky' worn as a dress.

*Hootchenoo*-powerful home brew, origin of slang term "Hootch."

*Ice Worm*-a fictional Alaskan critter made up by a gold-rush era newspaperman. The idea was supported for many years by bartenders putting strands of limp spaghetti into drinks, telling tourists they were ice worms. The last laugh is that more recently real ice worms-tiny black creatures- have been discovered.

*LNT*-Leave No Trace. Hiking term. After you leave any park, make sure you leave no trace that you were there.

*Mukluks*-fur boots.

*Muktuk*-an Eskimo delicacy. The outer skin of the whale with a layer of fat attached, eaten raw.

*Mush*-a command dog mushers use. It's an Indian version of the French "marche," but it also can mean a person who has hiked a long way on snowshoes through the bush.

*Outside*-the term Alaskan's use for the lower 48 states. It follows that a person from the "states" is an outsider.

*Parky*-how parka is pronounced in Alaska.

*Permafrost*-permanently frozen ground, beneath the surface water, that thaws in spring.

*Skijor*-a sport that consists of your favorite dog pulling you on cross-country skis.

*Ski-wheel*-a combination wheel and ski that allows bush planes to land on snow, or hard packed surfaces.

*Sookum*-an Indian word for big, strong.

*Sourdough*-an old-timer in Alaska, a name that came from the fermented dough used by prospectors who didn't have yeast.

*Taildragger*-a bush plane with a rear wheel, often with oversized tundra tires.

*Termination Dust*-the first snowfall on the mountains surrounding a summer-only mining operation.

*Taiga*-the scrub evergreen forests of sub-arctic Alaska.

*Toklat*-an interior grizzly bear with a reddish-tan coat. The much larger coastal grizzly is called an Alaskan Brown.

*Trash dog*-any breed of dog in villages that isn't used to pull sleds.

*Tundra*-the swampy, rolling plains that cover much of the Interior.

*Ulu*-native fish knife with half-round blade, with an Alaskan jade grip.

# Chapter 21

## *Calendar of Events Near Denali National Park*

**Willow Winter Carnival**
When: last weekend of January and the first week of February
Community: Willow
Phone: 907-495-6633
Includes dogsled racing, snowmobile racing, cross-country ski event, log chopping event, arts and crafts, trade fair, and talent contest.

**Tesoro Iron Dog 2000 Snowmachine Race**
When: approximately the 3rd Sunday in February.
Community: Wasilla
Phone: 907-563-4414
World's longest snowmachine race. The Pro Race class cover 1,971 miles of unforgiving Alaskan terrain from Wasilla to Big Lake, Nome, and on to Fairbanks.

**Iditarod Days Festival**
When: end of February to early March
Community: Wasilla
Phone: 907-376-1299
Activities include cross-country ski race, softball tournament, ice fishing derby, snowmachine events, and kids events, crafts and trade shows. Ten days of festivities ending with the Iditarod Sled Dog Race Restart on the Sunday following the first Saturday in March.

## Iditarod Sled Dog Race Restart

When: first Saturday in March.
Community: Wasilla
Phone: 907-376-5155
World-class sporting event covered by news media from around the world. Starts in Anchorage on the first Saturday in March, restarts the following day in Wasilla, and concludes in Nome nine-15 days later. The Wasilla area affords a multitude of viewing opportunities at the starting line in the city and along the trail.

## Trapper Creek Cabin Fever Reliever

When: fourth Saturday of March.
Community: Trapper Creek
Phone: 907-733-8001
Includes the northernmost swimsuit competition.

## Annual Coal Miner's Ball

When: late April
Community: Sutton
Phone: 907-745-1006
Annual event celebrating the rich coal-mining heritage of Sutton.

## Palmer Colony Days

When: Early June
Community: Palmer
Phone: 907-745-2880
Festival honoring the people who came in 1935 to start a farming colony. Craft fair, wagon rides, landscaper's market, kid's games, entertainment, annual Bill Mitchell Fun Run, and more.

## Big Lake Regatta Water Festival

When: second and third weekends in June
Community: Big Lake

Phone: 907-892-6884
Boat and street parades, family fun and activities, Solstice celebration, dance, bonfire, water sports, games, and triathlon.

## Moose Dropping Festival
When: second week in July
Community: Talkeetna
Phone: 907-733-2487
Includes Mountain Mother contest, parade, booths, entertainment, the famous moose nugget toss game and moose nugget-dropping contest.

## Farm Market
When: July
Community: Wasilla
Phone: 907-376-5679
Old Wasilla Town site, near library, 4–7 p.m. Wednesdays, all month long.

## Wasilla Water Festival
When: July 4th weekend
Community: Wasilla
Phone: 907-376-1299
Includes Independence Day parade, fireworks, bluegrass festival, canoe/raft races, microbrew tasting, volleyball tournament, power and jetcraft races, 5K road race, businessperson's fantasy grand prix, kids events, and more.

## 7th Annual Blast from the Past
When: early July.
Community: Wasilla
Phone: 907-376-1211

Museum of Alaska Transportation and Industry. A family celebration of Alaska history. Music, food vendors, free homemade ice cream, games, operating exhibits, train rides, antique cars, and hayride.

## Houston Founders Day
When: third Saturday in August.
Community: Houston
Phone: 907-892-6557
Live band, free BBQ, fireworks. Contact Houston Chamber of Commerce.

## Alaska State Fair
When: 11 days ending on Labor Day.
Community: Palmer
Phone: 907-745-4827
Join the celebration at Alaska's premier fair, featuring Alaskan arts and crafts, food, flowers, vegetables, animals, a multitude of vendors, rides, entertainment, and fireworks.

## Talkeetna Bluegrass Festival
When: early August.
Community: Talkeetna
Phone: 907-561-2848, 907-495-6718
$30 fee for event includes camping. Mile 102, Parks Hwy.

## Great Alaska Antique Machinery Show
When: mid August.
Community: Wasilla
Phone: 907-376-1211
At the Museum of Alaska Transportation and Industry. Operating steam, gasoline, and diesel engines, tractor show and hay rides. Visit the owners and re-builders of old time power equipment. Try the

Alaska Live Steamers train ride. Chili and corn bread feed at the Whistle Stop Caboose.

## Colony Christmas Celebration
When: Second Friday and Saturday in December.
Community: Palmer
Phone: 907-745-2880
A Norman Rockwell Christmas celebration! Horse drawn sleigh or wagon rides, reindeer sled rides, parade, community Christmas tree lighting and caroling, arts and crafts fair, entertainment, visits with Santa, contests, fireworks and more.

## Talkeetna Winterfest
Date: December (All month)
Community: Talkeetna
Phone: 907-733-2330
Experience the real Alaskan Christmas. Parade, lighting, Festival of Trees, guest artists, gingerbread contest, treasure hunt, celebrity trees and much more. Month-long celebration.

## Bachelor Society Ball/Wilderness Woman Contest
When: First Saturday of December.
Community: Talkeetna
Phone: 907-733-2330
Internationally recognized event. A day of fun for bachelors, wilderness women and all who enjoy December merrymaking. Women compete in water-hauling, wood-chopping and other wilderness events. Bachelors are auctioned off and a dance culminates the event.

# Bibliography

*Adventuring in Alaska* by Peggy Wayburn, 1994.

*A Naturalist in Alaska*, Adolph Murie, 1964.

*A Tourist Guide to Mount McKinley* by Bradford Washburn, 1971.

*Backcountry Companion* by Jon Nierenberg. 1997.

*Backpacking in Alaska* by Lonely Planet, 1995.

*Denali Climbing Guide* by R.J. Secor, 1998.

*Denali National Park, An Island of Time*, Rick Mcintyre, 1986.

*Denali Road Guide* by Kim Heacox, 1999.

*Eiger Dreams*, Jon Krakauer 1990

*15 Hikes in Denali National Park*, Don Croner, 1989.

*Into the Wild*, Jon Krakauer, 1996

*Mammals of Mount McKinley National Park, Alaska* by Adolph Murie. 1962.

*Sled Dogs of Denali* by Sandy Kogl, 1991.

*The Ascent of Denali*, Hudson Struck,1914.

*The Milepost* by Morris Communition Corp., 1999.

*The Wilderness of Denali*, by Charles Sheldon, 1930.


Periodicals

*Alaska Magazine*, April 1981

*Denali Summer Times*

*The Alpenglow*

*The Denali Dispatch*

*The Talkeetna Good Times*

# Index

0-595-29737-4

1374654

Made in the USA